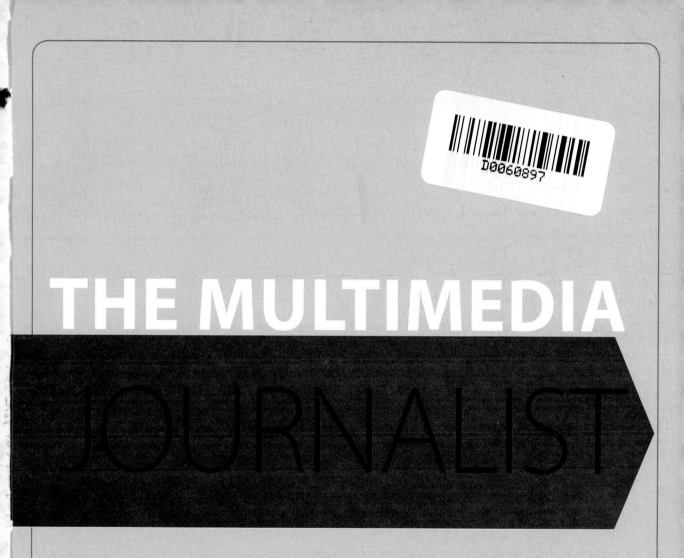

THE MULTIMEDIA JOURNALIST

STORYTELLING FOR TODAY'S MEDIA LANDSCAPE

Jennifer George-Palilonis

BALL STATE UNIVERSITY

NEW YORK OXFORD
OXFORD UNIVERSITY PRESS

Oxford University Press is a department of the University of Oxford. It furthers the University's objective of excellence in research, scholarship, and education by publishing worldwide.

Oxford New York
Auckland Cape Town Dar es Salaam Hong Kong Karachi
Kuala Lumpur Madrid Melbourne Mexico City Nairobi
New Delhi Shanghai Taipei Toronto

With offices in
Argentina Austria Brazil Chile Czech Republic France Greece
Guatemala Hungary Italy Japan Poland Portugal Singapore
South Korea Switzerland Thailand Turkey Ukraine Vietnam

For titles covered by Section 112 of the US Higher Education Opportunity Act, please visit www.oup.com/us/he for the latest information about pricing and alternate formats.

Published by Oxford University Press.
198 Madison Avenue, New York, New York 10016
http://www.oup.com

Library of Congress Cataloging-in-Publication Data

George-Palilonis, Jennifer.
The multimedia journalist Jennifer George-Palilonis.
p. cm.
ISBN 978-0-19-976452-5 (alk. paper)
1. Reporters and reporting. 2. Journalism—Authorship. 3. Online journalism. 4. Broadcast journalism. I. Title.
PN4781.G48 2011
808'.06607—dc23 2011024680

Printing number: 9 8 7 6 5 4 3 2 1

Printed in the United States of America
on acid-free paper

Brief Contents

THE MULTIMEDIA JOURNALIST

CONTENTS

PREFACE

In some ways, the future of journalism has never seemed more uncertain than it does today. Yet, for the most innovative storytellers, there has never been a more exciting time to be a journalist. In the digital age, the number and variety of methods for telling stories abound. Because of this, multimedia journalism is quickly becoming a primary focus for news organizations and journalism and mass communication programs across the U.S. and abroad. *The Multimedia Journalist* was written with this in mind.

Written and produced by a master scholar and teacher, this text provides a comprehensive and dynamic introduction to multimedia storytelling techniques. A mix of theoretical concepts and practical skills instruction, *The Multimedia Journalist* is intended to help tomorrow's media professionals hone their skills and knowledge of a number of different storytelling techniques. From writing to visual storytelling, *The Multimedia Journalist* will help students define an area of personal expertise, as well as teach them to speak a common multimedia language. This book offers a one-of-a-kind approach that equally values all story forms and emphasizes the importance of collaboration, story packaging, and a clear understanding of issues unique to digital journalism. Among the most important concepts provided in this text are:

- Clear context for multimedia in news organizations;
- Emphasis on collaboration among journalists with different areas of expertise;
- Examination of the role of navigation and interactivity in user experience design;

- Discussion of multimedia ethics and legal concerns;
- Individual chapters on writing across platforms, digital photo storytelling, audio and video journalism, and information graphics reporting complete with visual examples;
- Instruction on best practices for bringing rich multimedia content together in a single story package;
- "Professional Perspective" essays featuring insights from industry leaders;
- Engaging exercises that provide direction for students who wish to practice concepts addressed in each chapter.

Likewise, the text is accompanied by a rich multimedia website that further illustrates concepts outlined in the book and provides live multimedia examples and content.

Companion website: www.oup.com/us/palilonis

Writing a traditional book about multimedia journalism is a challenge, for sure. So much of what is discussed in this text is based on digital, multimedia content that can't be displayed on the pages of a printed text. Likewise, the world of digital journalism is evolving at a rapid pace. New platforms, innovations in storytelling, and a changing media landscape are all contributing to this evolution. And one of the most important things a budding multimedia journalist can do is observe the work of others and practice, practice, practice.

In light of this, the print text and an accompanying website are of equal importance as you embark on the road to becoming a multimedia journalist. In addition to a brief synopsis of each chapter, the companion website provides additional content, such as digital examples, interactive exercises, tutorials and an area for users to upload links to their own multimedia work to share with others. The website serves as a living, breathing partner to the print text that will be regularly updated with new tips, case studies, and inspirational multimedia examples.

The website will also support ongoing discussions of industry news and innovations in multimedia storytelling through a forum to which students, professionals and other users can contribute. Finally, the site is designed to serve as a catalogue of useful resources related to multimedia journalism. Together, we can form a community around the book that continues to grow and evolve with the news industry.

ACKNOWLEDGMENTS

Writing a book is a long, arduous process, and I have many people to thank for their encouragement. Above all, I thank my husband Jim Palilonis for his unwavering support and commitment to our family and to my success.

Multimedia storytelling is a constantly changing proposition. And there are a number of professionals who are leading the charge in this rapid evolution. Several of them contributed their insights to this text in the way of "Professional Perspective" essays. Thanks to Miranda Mulligan, Ryan Smith, Laura Ruel, Nora Paul, Juli Metzger, Keith Jenkins, Art Silverman, Suzy Smith and Len DeGroot for lending your expertise to enhance the credibility of this book.

A number of others contributed insight and advice during the development of this book. Perhaps most valuable were the reviews provided by several leaders in multimedia education, including: Daniel von Benthuysen, Hofstra University; Paul Bush, Franklin Pierce University; Eric Chatterjee, Northern Kentucky University; Jeremy Gilbert, Northwestern University; Seth Gitner, Syracuse University; Rich Gordon, Northwestern University; Dennis Herrick, University of New Mexico; Renee Human, Northern Kentucky University; Jenn Mackay, Virginia Tech; Stephen Masiclat, Syracuse University; Bernard Rogers McCoy, University of Nebraska–Lincoln; Linda Menck, Marquette University; Collin Pillow, Arkansas State University; Jessica Retis, California State University–Northridge; Cindy Royal, Texas State University; Laura Ruel, UNC–Chapel Hill; Jacqueline Sauter, University of Maryland. Likewise, my sincerest gratitude to all of my friends at Oxford University Press, including Mark T.

Haynes, Michele Laseau, Marianne Paul, Peter Labella and Caitlin Kaufman, who have been so helpful during this process.

Thanks also to the friends, family, and colleagues who have encouraged and supported me: Gage & Quinn Palilonis, Janet & Jerry George, Christopher & Kari George, Mike & Annette Palilonis, Ryan Sparrow, Pamela Leidig-Farmen, Marilyn Weaver, Dan Waechter, Roger Lavery, Mary Spillman, Ron Reason, Jeremy Gilbert, Brad King, Lori Byers, Ulrika Raue, Michael Price, Deborah Withey, Mario Garcia, Davide Bolchini, Alfredo Marin-Carle, JoAnn Gora, and Terry King.

Finally, none of this work would be possible or relevant without my amazing students, past and present. I am so fortunate to teach in a program that attracts and graduates such fantastic talent. To all of you: Thanks for providing me with the opportunity to do what I love. I can only wish that you are all as fortunate and happy in your careers as I have been.

ABOUT THE AUTHOR

Jennifer George-Palilonis is the George and Frances Ball Distinguished Professor of Multimedia Journalism at Ball State University. There, she is the journalism graphics sequence coordinator and teaches upper-level courses in multimedia storytelling, information graphics reporting, and interactive media design.

She is also a media design consultant and has worked on the redesigns of more than 30 print and online publications, including *The Journal-Gazette, Portland Press-Herald*, and *Crain's Chicago Business.* Prior to joining the faculty at Ball State in 2001, George-Palilonis was the deputy news design editor at the *Chicago Sun-Times* and a news designer and business art director at the *Detroit Free Press.*

Her first book, *A Practical Guide to Graphics Reporting* (Focal Press), was published in 2006. Her research on visual communications, multimedia teaching and learning tools, research-informed design, human-computer interaction, and information graphics in the multimedia age is regularly published in leading scholarly journals. She has spoken at more than 50 professional and academic conferences. She is the education director for the Society for News Design.

She lives in Muncie, Indiana with her husband Jim and twin sons Gage and Quinn.

UNIT 1

MULTIMEDIA JOURNALISM

PERHAPS MORE THAN EVER BEFORE, THE FIELD OF JOURNALISM IS IN TRANSITION. Newspaper readership is shrinking. Television audiences are becoming more fragmented. And the Internet has grown into a veritable sea of information.

Once, trustworthy sources of information were scarce. Journalists served an important role in society by helping mass audiences make sense of the world around them. Now, information is always one click away, and news audiences have become active participants in the open exchange of ideas.

In some ways, the future of journalism has never seemed more uncertain. Yet, for some of the most innovative and brave, it has never been a more exciting time to be a journalist.

Indeed, massive changes in technology and audience reading and viewing trends have led to a great shift in how news is consumed. However, these changes have also brought about great possibilities for storytelling, never before possible. Interactive platforms provide new ways to present content. Digital technology allows us to combine different story forms to create rich media experiences. And journalists are challenged to find ways to engage audiences in new ways. Through all of this emerges the multimedia journalist.

The chapters that comprise this first unit help provide definition for both the role of multimedia in today's evolving landscape, as well as what makes for a good multimedia story. In this sense, Unit One lays the groundwork for broadening a definition of journalistic storytelling that takes into account many big picture concepts, including telling stories for multiple platforms, the importance of healthy, efficient collaboration, and solid story planning. Likewise, we explore navigational structures for complex multimedia stories, how to assess multimedia potential, and how to build storyboards. In essence, this unit lays the groundwork for developing a great multimedia story.

CHAPTER 1

Defining Multimedia

Information Architecture in the Digital World

At first glance, the definition of multimedia seems quite simple. After all, it is built right into the word, isn't it? Multi = many. Media = the primary means for mass communication. And there you have it. The most obvious and common definition is the collective use of many media types—such as text, audio, graphics, animation, video, and photographs—to convey information. Of course, if it were that simple, this book would be unnecessary.

Defining multimedia is really much more complex than the dictionary would have you believe. Missing from the definition above is a sense of the complexities that arise in conceptualizing, producing, and packaging multimedia content. The word "multimedia" has been used in so many fields in recent years that its specific definition also depends on your professional perspective. For example, early definitions referred to any content for digital platforms, such as CD-ROMs, the web, or applications that combine different media into an integrated package. However, when placed in the context of individual fields—such as business, education, or medicine, for example—the term has more specific connotations.

To complicate matters more, working journalists use the term "multimedia storytelling" in a variety of ways. When it comes to job titles, the term "digital journalist"

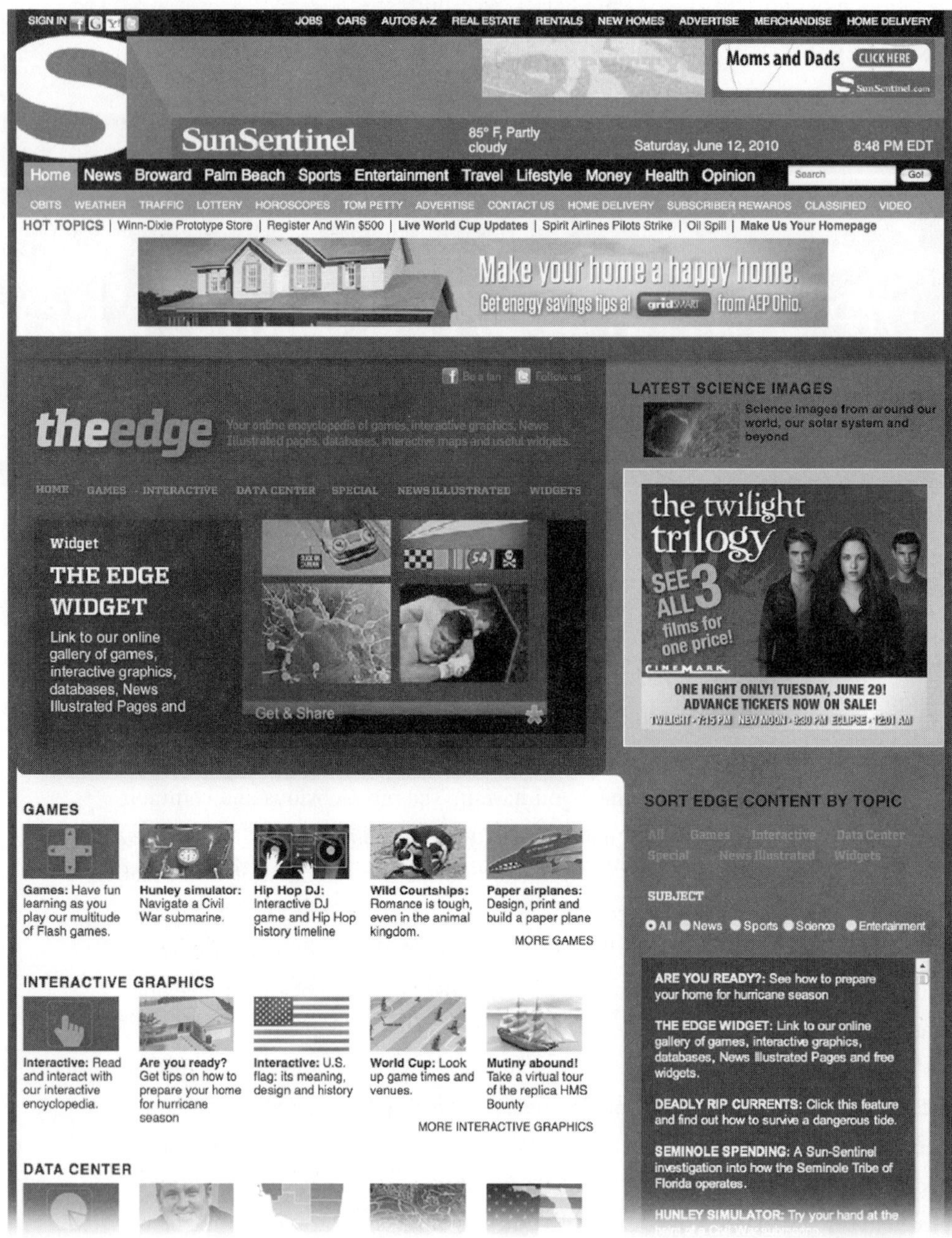

FIGURE 1-1

The Edge is a multimedia gallery featured on the South Florida *Sun-Sentinel*'s website. One of the first of its kind among newspapers, The Edge includes games, interactive news graphics, data visualizations, and photo presentations.

Source: Image courtesy of the South Florida *Sun-Sentinel*.

is a common designation as well among those who think the term "multimedia" is a big too vague. When it comes to content, some types often get more attention than others. For example, videos and photo slideshows are common supplements to text stories among newspaper websites. Likewise, broadcast sites commonly offer lots of video and text, with less emphasis on still images. However, only a few news organizations, such as the South Florida *Sun-Sentinel*, the *New York Times*, and msnbc.com regularly offer interactive graphics and rich data visualizations. Some news websites—such as startribune.com in Minneapolis—include a main link to a section titled "multimedia." Other sites—such as washingtonpost.com—integrate multimedia content with each story package. Likewise, multimedia storytelling in theory and practice is not a fixed concept. Rather, it is a moving target, evolving at a rapid pace.

But regardless of how what we call you or how news sites present multimedia content, media convergence, cross-ownership, and a general migration of journalistic content to the web have all led to increased focus on multimedia storytelling and new digital story forms in contemporary journalism. Thus, "multimedia" refers to job titles, presentation outcomes, and journalistic practices. So this book approaches multimedia as a way to recognize the many tools journalists now have for telling stories and as a form of packaging news and information.

Audience Trends

News content is more accessible today than ever before. As a result, Americans are engaging with news and information more and more. According to a 2010 Pew Research Center report,[1] "digital platforms are playing a larger role in news consumption, and they seem to be more than making up for modest declines in the audience for traditional platforms." Among the key findings of the Pew study: 34 percent of Americans reported they had visited an online news source in the past 24 hours, 34 percent listened to radio news, and 31 percent reported they read a daily newspaper. And 44 percent say they got news through one or more Internet or mobile source yesterday.

These findings are significant for two reasons. First, they illustrate that although people are getting their news from a wider variety of sources, news consumption is a popular activity. And, perhaps even more significant, the average time Americans spend with the news is back to levels not seen since the mid-1990s, when audiences for traditional news sources were larger.

As digital platforms have become more popular, focus on multimedia storytelling has increased, as well. In fact, many journalism educators, researchers, and professionals have suggested the need to reexamine the way we produce online stories to better address users' digital reading habits and expectations. At the same time, contemporary media consumption focuses on visuals more than ever before. Media historian Mitchell Stephens suggested in the late 1990s that we are experiencing a "rise of the image, and fall of the word,"[2] indicating that visual media—such as video, photographs, and information graphics—have become attractive story forms to contemporary audiences. And because the web allows us to effectively bring all of those formats together in one place, multimedia storytelling is often best achieved on the web.

Furthermore, although audiences watch more television than ever, contemporary viewing habits have changed. In the United States, nearly 99 percent of video is still consumed via television. However viewers are also using digital video recorders, streaming video online, or watching digital video on mobile devices and MP3 players. And according to a 2010 Nielsen report, mobile video users grew by 57 percent in 2009 to 17.6 million from 11.2 million people.[3]

Today's media audiences are also much more likely to engage in multitasking where media consumption is concerned. In 2002, a study of more than 7,800 Americans found that more than half engaged with several forms of media at a time.[4] And in 2006, Middletown Media II studies, which produced more than 5,000 hours of

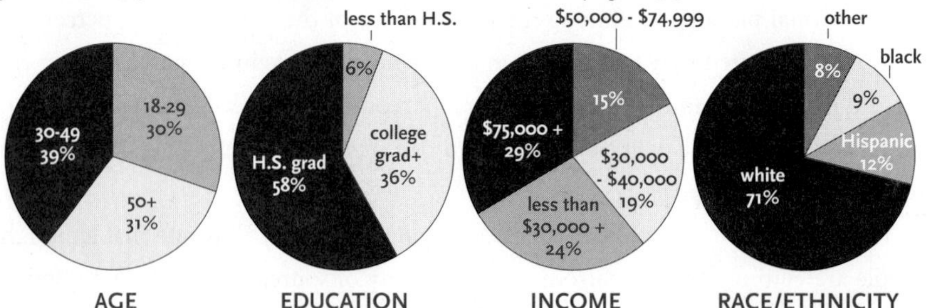

FIGURE 1-2

Source: Pew Research Center Project for Excellence in Journalism and Internet & American Life Project Online News Survey. (Margin of error is +/–2 percentage points.)

media use, reported cross-platform multitasking among a significant number of subjects.[5] In other words, most people are perfectly comfortable watching television or reading magazines and newspapers while also surfing the Internet.

It is also worth noting that generational trends may be an indicator of whether multimedia content will continue to grow in popularity. If so, studies on the Millennial Generation—those born between 1980 and 2000—are particularly significant. In their book, *Millennials Rising,* Neil Howe and William Strauss characterize Millennials as tech-savvy, multitasking digital natives who are heavily engrossed in multimedia consumption and development.[6] Researcher Richard Sweeney writes, "Millennials have spent thousands of hours playing electronic, computer, and video games. They love the constant interactivity, full motion multimedia, colorful graphics, the ability to learn and progress to higher levels, and the ability to collaborate with friends in their learning and competitions."[7] This has prompted some journalists to even consider applying game strategies to journalistic stories in an effort to capture these growing audiences.

There's no doubt that traditional news organizations are struggling to prove their relevance in an increasingly digital media landscape. And the web has turned traditional media business models upside down by providing a free and open exchange of news, information, and ideas. Thus, the concepts of media convergence, cross-platform ownership, backpack journalists, and multimedia content production have all surfaced as ways for future journalists to stake a claim.

The Evolving Media Landscape

The Internet has certainly precipitated dramatic changes in the ways we work, live, and engage with others. It has also become a catalyst for equally dramatic changes in the delivery of news and information. The Internet has accelerated the circulation of ideas, facilitated vast social networks, and altered the economics of media by enabling the distribution of free content. In turn, the web has also provided anyone with access to a computer with the potential to become media providers. Thus, this emerging media landscape is complex, indeed.

Until the early twenty-first century, newspapers enjoyed large profit margins and significant circulation figures in most markets. But by 2000, the number of households that were online had exceeded those subscribing to a newspaper, driving some media analysts to predict that the Internet would dramatically change the way daily

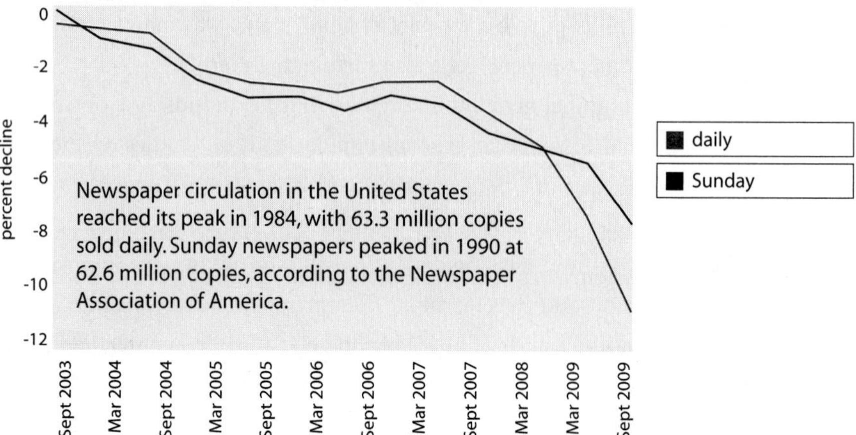

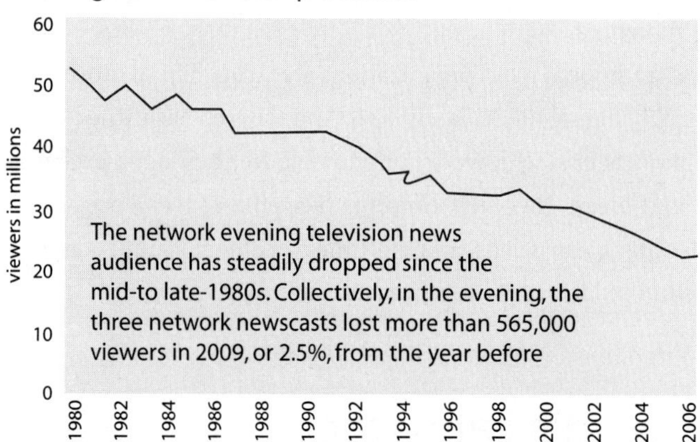

FIGURE 1-3

Source: Deutsche Bank Securities and Audit Bureau of Circulations (first graph).

Source: Nielsen Media Research, used under license. Viewership taken for month of November (second graph).

print journalism is practiced. In a relatively short period of time, newspapers saw rapid declines in readership and advertising revenue, as well as an increase in the cost of doing business. As a result, newsrooms across the country are struggling to stay afloat, and several have already stopped the presses. In 2009 alone, the *Rocky Mountain News, Ann Arbor News,* and *Seattle Post-Intelligencer printed* their final issues. And between 2008 and 2010, at least 166 newspapers in the United States closed down or stopped publishing a print edition. The current state of the news industry is precarious, to say the least.

It is difficult to measure how many journalists at print and broadcast news organizations have online content responsibilities. However, it appears there is a shift in the balance of staffs in favor of merged digital newsrooms. A majority of newly hired print journalists report that their job duties involve the web. Likewise, many news networks have staffs specifically dedicated to their online products. CNN and MSNBC both report as many as 200 employees working on online products.[8] And in late 2010, *USA Today*, the nation's second largest newspaper, announced a dramatic staffing change intended to deemphasize the print edition and ramp up efforts to reach more readers on mobile devices.

Social media also plays an increasingly significant role in the way news and information is distributed and consumed. According to Brad King, a journalism professor and social media researcher, emerging technologies have not changed the fundamental role of the reporter. But they have, in some ways, altered the ways many journalists approach stories. For example, "journalists are using sites such FriendFeed, which can be used to create private, real-time chat networks, to gather topic experts that can help them hone story ideas and parse through data that may be too complicated for a general interest reporter to grasp," King says. "The idea that journalists can create these 'expert networks' can, if done properly, ensure that news organizations tell more accurate and timely stories." King also notes that the general public is also using these tools. "Citizen journalists, have taken to publishing on the web as well, many times using traditional reporting as a jumping off point for conversations. Reporters are increasingly finding it necessary to engage with those publics, to discuss their stories and in many cases, defend their points of view. This entire engagement, from private network to public conversation, creates a real-time feedback loop for journalists, one that couldn't exist before the Internet and emerging world of social media."[9]

News organizations are also augmenting online content in an attempt to create "buzz" around stories. Some have experimented with tipping audiences off about upcoming stories through social media sites. For example, in 2008, the *Chicago Tribune* created online character Colonel Tribune and referred to him as the paper's "web ambassador." His job is to help readers "stay informed and in touch with the latest news." Readers can become fans of the *Chicago Tribune* or the Colonel on Facebook, as well as follow him on Twitter. Those who do, receive regular updates throughout the day with links to breaking stories on chicagotribune.com. *Tribune*

Social Media Strategist Daniel Honigman spearheaded the Colonel Tribune efforts and says the Colonel gives the *Tribune* audience a voice. "Essentially, we wanted to find our audience regardless of the medium. The Colonel acts as a touch point for the *Tribune* and serves as our voice on the web. Thus we needed a front man, which turned into Colonel Tribune, who is kind of a goofy man about town but is an actual person. He would even answer questions that you might have."[10] These and other social media strategies are quickly becoming useful, robust tools for directing audiences to multimedia content. Thus, social media can become yet another tool multimedia journalists can use to do their jobs.

And perhaps the fastest-growing innovation in news delivery is reflected in the rapid emergence of wireless news apps intended for smartphone and tablet devices. In recent years, large and small media outlets alike have scrambled onto the app scene, and by the middle of 2011, there were thousands of news apps in Apple's app store. A 2010 study of 1,600 iPad users showed that print newspaper subscribers who were also heavy iPad users reported they were "very likely" to cancel their print subscriptions.[11] Such trends will surely continue to affect the way news is delivered and the business models that surround mass distribution.

Practicing Multimedia

The concept of the backpack journalist was born in the early days of media convergence. Defined as a single professional that could ultimately save money by creating complete multimedia packages alone, the backpack concept gained a lot of attention at first. However, it quickly fell out of favor because of two fatal flaws. First, many argued that it is unrealistic that a single journalist could excel at so many different storytelling forms. Second, developing a complete multimedia package that includes several different story forms is too time-consuming for a single person working on a tight on deadline.

However, the backpack concept has not been completely abandoned; it has been modified. In the past, students majoring in journalism followed pretty clear paths from school to their careers. Writers, photographers, copy editors, and designers went to newspapers and magazines; and on-air reporters, videographers, and producers joined TV news stations. However, with the emergence of newspaper or broadcast websites and independent news and information sites, those lines have begun to blur. And although most journalists still specialize in a particular craft—that is, writing, photography, design, videography, on-air reporting, and so on—individuals are expected to know more about the other fields than ever before. Now, journalists are taught to speak a common language and understand the complexities of each story form. Many universities are training students to create multimedia content on basic levels, excel at one or two types of storytelling on advanced levels, and collaborate to design, develop, and package multimedia stories. Thus, future communications professionals must understand the power of all of the different tools in their storytelling toolboxes. Likewise, they need to know how and when to use them, what affect they have on the entire story package, and how the reader/viewer/user experience will be affected by multimedia stories. According to Jeremy Gilbert, an assistant professor of multimedia at Northwestern's Medill School of Journalism, "Journalists need to be adaptable. You cannot rely on skill with a single tool or technology. Learn to identify great stories and tell them in the manner most appropriate for the content and the audience. Tools like software, computers and cameras are constantly changing. But having good editorial judgment and being able to explain their judgment is key. The core skills of journalism reporting, analyzing, and communicating stories will be valuable regardless of any other changes in the media landscape or consumption habits."[12]

This is in large part because of the heightened levels of collaboration present in most multimedia settings. Rather than focus on the type of organization you will work for in the future, it may make more sense to focus on how multimedia content is produced, how stories are developed using different story forms, and how a story changes as it crosses platforms. In this sense, the student journalist prepares for a career path that may make stops at several different media outlets.

The Multimedia Journalist

Defining a good journalist has always been complex, and as storytelling has evolved, the definition has, too. On the whole, journalists have always been held to a number of key standards and ethics, including truthfulness, accuracy, objectivity, and fairness. We have always been expected to understand and protect the First Amendment. We have been called public watchdogs and gatekeepers. And as we drill down into the traditional fields of journalism—that is, editor, writer, reporter, photographer, videographer, graphics reporter, designer, producer, and so on—we find that each comes with its own set of skills, standards, and practices. However, regardless of changes in technology or the emergence of new story forms, all journalists must understand how to be good reporters. Conducting thorough background research, asking questions, meeting people, and thinking critically are all just as important as ever.

As new technologies develop that enhance our tools, and as new software surfaces that makes multimedia production easier, the ways we tell stories also change. For example, when pagination systems were introduced to newsrooms in the early 1980s, page design suddenly became a part of the journalistic process instead of the production process. Concepts like information layering and better navigation for newspaper readers arose from that era, and many editors, writers, photographers, and others began to place greater importance on the presentation of stories. More recently, the introduction programs used to easily and quickly create photo/audio slideshows, led to a surge in those types of presentations, as well as increased discussion about how photo stories are best presented online. The Internet alone has provided radio networks such as National Public Radio with an outlet for presenting photos, written pieces, and video content they cannot air on the radio.

Similarly, as news audiences migrate to online sources, we are forced to examine ways the web experience is different from print or traditional broadcast experiences. In the early days of the web and still today, many newspaper and broadcast news organizations have been criticized for a "shovelware" approach to their online products. According a 2007 Pew Research Center study, multimedia potential was one of the six most exploited capabilities of the web by news sites. But most newspaper sites were "still largely dominated by the content that fills newspapers—text and still images"[13] and most broadcast news sites were dominated by text and video. The claim has been that "shovelware"—the practice of running stories from the print newspaper on the website without making any changes—does not take full advantage of the rich multimedia potential of the web. Rather, news websites should offer customized content that appeals to web users whose habits and expectations differ from print or readers television viewers.

So, at this point, you may be thinking, "Cut to the chase! How am I going to get a job?" Well, if we take a look at a few recent job postings, we see that news organizations are taking heed and evolving the nature and definition of the desirable journalist. According to one recent job posting, a Phoenix broadcast station was seeking:

> ...a reporter/photojournalist/video editor who will produce content for multiple platforms as assigned. Successful candidates will have a demonstrated ability to deliver compelling TV and digital media packages, have strong on-camera presentation skills including live presentations, and the time management skills to produce content for multiple platforms on deadline. You'll use the latest technology, including light-

> weight photography and editing gear. A working familiarity with Avid Newscutter and programs such as Final Cut Pro, Photoshop and Flash is a plus.

Around the same time, a Florida newspaper was seeking an interactive graphic artist, citing multimedia skills as:

> ...the most important skills we're looking for...with an understanding of different platforms—including, but not limited to, web, mobile/iPhone and desktop apps...interest in...information architecture, user experience, interactive design, wireframing [and] user experience.

They cited a few other key qualifications:

- Can create, query, map and analyze data;
- Conceptualizes and executes static and interactive graphic features;
- Takes a lead role in finding new ways to represent and communicate data;
- Stays up-to-date with trends in visual communication, especially web design standards and data visualization and analysis;
- Looks ahead not to where technology and storytelling and information distribution are right now, but where they could be in eight months, two years, or even ten.

And a similar ad for an interactive and graphics editor for the Associated Press called for "Expertise with Flash, and at least one of these other areas: Geographical Information Systems, databases, data analysis, and statistics, 3-D rendering."

Their requirements included:

- Knowledge of Final Cut Pro and Soundslides;
- Excellent understanding of web standards, typography, and layout;
- Excellent understanding of information design and standards for different screens and formats, such as print, online, and mobile;
- Should be at ease with basic mathematics, and use of Microsoft Office Excel, Microsoft Access, or similar software;
- Good knowledge of Adobe Illustrator, Adobe Acrobat, and Microsoft Office Suite;
- Highly motivated team player with strong analytical, detailing, and interpersonal skills;
- Must be able to work independently and in a team;
- Ability to conduct research on a variety of subjects, including science, politics, finance, international affairs, and domestic affairs;
- Excellent news judgment;

- Must be able to communicate well verbally and in writing;
- Ability to quickly and accurately grasp complex technical concepts;
- Ability to work in a high-pressure deadline environment;
- Ability to serve as a leader and trainer for other journalists learning about multimedia storytelling.

Intimidated yet? If we take these three descriptions as good examples of how different types of news organizations define the job of a contemporary journalist, we can begin to see another dramatic evolution taking place in the industry. The stakes have been raised as emerging journalists are being challenged to build on the foundations of the craft by adding new media skills to their repertoires. But before you drop the book and go screaming from the room, let's try to synthesize what the preceding job descriptions say about how you can thrive in the ever-changing media landscape.

Granted, these descriptions indicate that today's multimedia journalist may need to know more about all forms of storytelling than yesterday's more siloed broadcast or print journalists. But most still acknowledge that everyone can't be great at everything. So there are a few key skills and concepts relevant to all multimedia journalists.

Develop strong writing skills. Even if you are not a writer in the traditional sense, you will inevitably have to write something for most of your projects. For example, photographers may have to write scripts for audio that will accompany photos in a slideshow. Or graphics reporters may have to write text that accompanies diagrams or narrative animations. So practice your writing regularly, and practice different formats. In addition to standard inverted pyramid news stories or scripts for a teleprompter, practice writing voiceovers, descriptive captions for photo galleries, or explanatory text for information graphics, to name a few.

Understand how stories are best told over multiple platforms. It is not likely that you will work for an organization that publishes or airs in a single format. And, even if you are employed by a newspaper, website, or broadcast station, chances are you will be expected to experiment with new tools and new story forms. So in the very least, you need to consider the user experience for different platforms and understand how that affects storytelling. You should understand the technical considerations, such as standard video compression for a mobile device. And you should consider usability issues, such as how to shoot and edit video packages for TV screens, smaller computer screens, and even smaller mobile devices.

Develop proficiency with as many multimedia tools and software programs as possible. Software and other tools will continue to evolve, upgrade, change, and improve. It is up to you to stay on top of the latest programs. But remember that software, cameras, and other storytelling devices are merely tools for reaching your journalistic goals. So each time you dive into a story, assess which tools are most appropriate. The story's focus, your deadlines, resources, available skill sets, and the functional goals of your presentation will all factor into your decision.

Be flexible, confident, adaptable, and versatile. At a moment's notice, a writer may be on camera; a graphics reporter may be taking photographs; a photographer may be voicing an audio script. Ideally, you will collaborate and work with others whose expertise compliments yours. But realistically, that may not always be possible. So a good multimedia journalist can tell the story in the most effective form and produce the package alone and on deadline if necessary.

Be able to mine for and understand complex data sets. The ability to spot trends in data and direct information to appropriate people for action will ensure that you quickly rise to the top. Every multimedia journalist could benefit from good statistics course. Likewise, understand that social media tools such as Facebook and Twitter provide journalists with new opportunities for directing website traffic, mining data, and taking the pulse of audiences.

Understand the role of digital asset management. Digital assets must be easy to access, quick to download, effectively categorized, and easily searchable. Thus, there is a rich protocol for managing digital assets that multimedia journalists must understand and implement. Digital asset management will be discussed in greater detail later in this book.

And last, but not least, and probably most important:

Be able to assess the multimedia potential for a single story and determine which story forms are most appropriate. Good, compelling writing is still relevant because people still read. They are just doing more reading online than in print. Video is still capable of telling visual stories with intensity and realism. But because users are encountering video on more than one type of platform—television, online, and mobile devices to name a few—broadcast reporters and videographers must consider platform when conceptualizing stories. Likewise, photo galleries, slideshows with or without audio, and the potential for interactivity and animation have significantly added to the tools in the visual journalist's toolbox.

Many photographers and graphics reporters have even taken the early lead as multimedia innovators. In short, the more you know about story forms outside your area of expertise, the more successful you will be.

A Context for Multimedia

Of course the traditional foundations of journalism—truthfulness, accuracy, objectivity, and fairness—are as important as ever. Likewise, the most traditional journalistic forms—writing, editing, design, graphics reporting, photography, video, and audio—are important and powerful as ever. Thus, the remainder of this unit explores the conceptual aspects of multimedia storytelling, including navigation, interactivity, functionality, and usability. Emphasis is placed on the importance of collaboration in multimedia storytelling. And we will explore the importance of being able to create many different story forms on a basic level, excel at one or two types, and understand the complexities and processes associated with all story forms. Finally, this unit explains how to spot multimedia potential in a story, multimedia planning techniques, and information layering.

Unit Two focuses on specific story forms, offering basic tips on how to develop strong stories in various formats. Chapters 6 through 10 address the basics of writing across platforms, photojournalism, audio storytelling, video stories and production, and information graphics reporting. Each chapter touches on technical considerations for each story form and directly refers readers to corresponding web modules that offer examples, exercises, and tips related to each topic. Likewise, each chapter focuses on dos and don'ts and best practices for reporting, production, and presentation. Finally, each skills chapter includes a "Professional Perspective" essay written by a seasoned multimedia journalist. These essays offer support for each chapter by putting the topics in a real-world context. They are intended to illuminate what is discussed in the book through practical analysis of processes, expert opinions, and case studies, as well as experts' views on where multimedia storytelling is heading in the future.

Finally, Unit Three ties it all together by exploring the actual design and presentation of multimedia packages, content management for multimedia stories, and the future of news. Chapters specifically address design considerations for packaging and presenting multimedia content across various platforms and how trends in user habits affect how multimedia content should be arranged and organized across platforms. We explore how story packages must degrade gracefully into individual, freestanding pieces and how the nonlinear narrative is both the whole and the sum of its parts. And the final chapter offers a discussion on the future of news in general terms and focuses on the need for journalists to be more entrepreneurial, innovative, and technically savvy.

In all, this text intends introduce you to a wide range of multimedia topics. Again, you will most likely specialize in one or two of these areas. Thus, none of the chapters offered here will provide an exhaustive look at your individual interests. However, as you embark on the path to becoming a multimedia journalist, this text will hopefully help expand your knowledge of many multimedia skills and concepts; explore how they can be combined in rich, dynamic ways; and go beyond the individual tools to provide you with a well-rounded skill set.

Exercises

1. Later in this book, we will take a look at content management systems that allow multimedia journalists to easily manage website and digital content. Throughout this book, however, you'll be challenged by a number of exercises at the end of each chapter. Many of them require you to develop your own multimedia content. One way to manage that content is to develop your own multimedia website powered by an easy-to-use content management system, such as WordPress. So before you dive into any of these exercises, set up your own WordPress site. Then, when you complete an exercise, you can post it there.

   To do this, visit http://www.wordpress.com and click on the "get started here" button on the homepage. Follow the subsequent steps (it will only take a few minutes), and you'll soon be able to manage and share your work with others.
2. A number of pioneers are paving the way for multimedia journalism. And in this business, finding mentors and learning from others is essential to your development. First, spend some time browsing the web for great multimedia story packages. Then, choose one that you believe is a solid example of great storytelling. Find out who created the package. It might be one person or it may be a team of journalists. Once you know, try making contact with them for a brief interview. In particular, ask them to share with you how the multimedia story came together, what the collaborative process entailed, and what the major challenges of the piece were. Finally, write a three- to five-page case study that

includes a detailed description of the story package, as well as insights from the creator(s). This should be an analysis of the piece itself—that is, strengths and weaknesses—and insights regarding how it came to be. Consider how you should articulate the ways you and other aspiring multimedia journalists can learn from this particular case study.

Post your case study to your WordPress site. If your interview generates particularly insightful advice or information, consider submitting it for publication on www.oup.com/us/palilonis. You can do so via e-mail at themultimediajournalist@yahoo.com.

3. One of the best ways to improve your own creative skills is to first analyze the work of others and then articulate why it was or wasn't effective. This process can also be a great way to find inspiration and learn what NOT to do. Find a multimedia story package online and spend some time with it. After you have thoroughly explored the piece, answer the following questions:
    1. What is the focus of the story?
    2. What story forms were used to tell the story?
    3. What was the focus of each story form and how did each contribute to the overall goals of the piece?
    4. Was the presentation effective? Why or why not?
    5. Was the design and navigational structure easy to follow? Confusing?
    6. Was the package engaging? Why or why not?
    7. What were the strengths of the package?
    8. What were the weaknesses of the package?
    9. Did the piece leave you satisfied? Confused? Wanting more?
    10. What is one significant concept you learned from this package?

Prepare a three- to five-page brief that addresses these questions. Post your brief to your WordPress site.

Notes

1. Pew Research Center (2010). "Americans spending more time following the news."
2. Mitchell Stephens, *Rise of the Image, Fall of the Word* (New York: Oxford University Press, 1998).
3. Nielsen Company, The, "Television, Internet and Mobile Usage in the U.S," 2009.
4. Joseph J. Pilotta, et. al. "Simultaneous Media Usage: A Critical Consumer Orientation to Media Planning," *Journal of Consumer Behavior* (2004).

5. Papper, et. al. "Middletown Media Studies," *International Digital Media and Arts Association Journal 1* (2006).
6. Neil Howe and William Strauss, *Millennials Rising: The Next Great Generation*. (New York: Random House, 2000).
7. Richard Sweeney, "Millennial Behaviors and Demographics," December 2006.
8. Jim Benning, "Inside the Online Newsroom: MSNBC.com," *Online Journalism Review*, July 1, 2002.
9. Interview with Brad King, June 6, 2010.
10. Stuart Foster, "Colonel Tribune: Chicago's Unlikely Social Media Pioneer," Mashable.com, June 2009.
11. Moses, Lucia. (2010). "Are iPad Apps Killing Newspapers?" *AdWeek*, Dec. 9, 2010.
12. Interview with Jeremy Gilbert, June 5, 2010.
13. Pew Research Center, "The State of the News Media 2007: An Annual Report on American Journalism."

CHAPTER 2

Collaboration & Specialization

Reporting and Editing in Interdisciplinary Teams

The communication industry is embracing and resisting new trends at breakneck speeds. Media convergence, multimedia storytelling, citizen journalism, wireless apps, and social media are all hot topics. And along with each of these one consistent theme continues to emerge in print, online, and broadcast journalism: collaboration among individuals from different disciplines.

Of course, journalists with different skill sets have always collaborated within organizations. In newspaper newsrooms, reporters, photographers, information graphics artists, and page designers collaborate daily to cover stories. Broadcast news organizations frequently send reporters and videographers on assignments together. And stories that effectively combine words and visuals are often more powerful than those presented in a single story form.

However, it wasn't until the 1990s that collaboration across print, broadcast, and online organizations began to occur regularly. This phenomenon was quickly dubbed "media convergence." And the early part of the twenty-first century was consumed with assessing how newspaper and broadcast organizations could coordinate efforts to achieve cross-platform news coverage.

More recently, efforts at multimedia storytelling have focused on how newspapers and broadcast stations can better harness the power of the web by presenting stories in multiple forms. The practice has been most transformative for newspapers and broadcast stations where careful consideration is given to both traditional and online products. Reporters write stories for print and online, as well as scripts for audio voiceovers. Photographers make and edit pictures for print packages as well as for interactive slideshows and galleries. In addition, many photographers and reporters have become videographers who collect footage for the web. Add to that graphics reporters who develop maps, charts, and diagrams, for print and online, and you have a much more complex, rich news organization.

This chapter explores the role of collaboration in multimedia storytelling both within and among news organizations. Here, we look at different levels of collaboration, how media convergence has evolved, collaborative processes, and how you can prepare yourself to work with partners from different disciplines.

Media Convergence

One of the most significant concepts tugging at traditional media outlets for the past decade is media convergence. However, the phrase has been pretty loosely defined. Depending on whom you ask, convergence can mean anything from a local newspaper and television news broadcast regularly teasing each other's stories, to formal partnerships that include joint story development.

Some partnerships exist between organizations owned by different media conglomerates. For example in Miami, "news partners" WFOR-TV, a CBS-owned-station, and *The Miami Herald*, a McClatchy-owned newspaper, frequently share content and link to one another's sites within stories. Yet, other partnerships exist among different media types under the same corporate ownership. One of the most well-known and studied converged operations is Media General's Tampa partnership that includes *The Tampa Tribune*, tbo.com, and WFLA-TV, Florida's number-one rated station. In March 2000, Media General opened the Tampa News Center, bringing the newspaper, television station, and website together under one roof. On a daily basis, WFLA-TV reporters appear on camera and then write stories for the newspaper. *Tribune* reporters write their stories and then appear on TV. And both develop online packages for tbo.com. The news building was even designed with convergence in mind and includes a universal news desk with editors and producers from all three entities working together. According to J. Stewart Bryan III, Media General's chair-

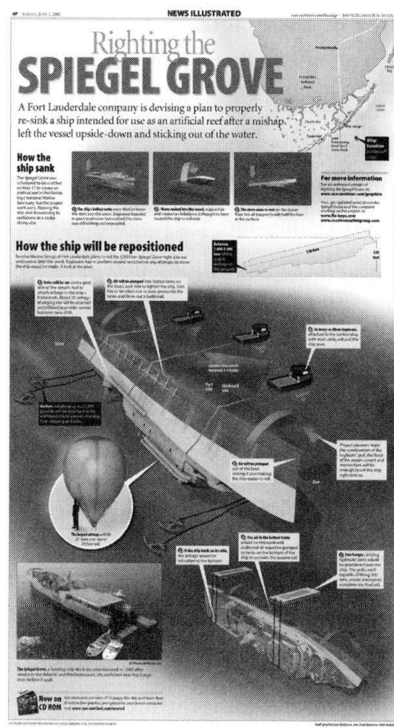
NEWS ILLUSTRATED

Righting the SPIEGEL GROVE

A Fort Lauderdale company is devising a plan to properly re-sink a ship intended for use as an artificial reef after a mishap left the vessel upside-down and sticking out of the water.

How the ship sank

For more information

How the ship will be repositioned

Now on CD ROM

FIGURE 2-1

The *Sun-Sentinel* in Fort Lauderdale frequently partners with other local media. In print, they regularly run full-page print graphics, titled "News Illustrated," on topics that range from science and technology to the War on Terror. In 2002, the *Spiegel Grove*, a retired Navy ship, was left upside down and sticking out of the water after a mishap occurred when officials were trying to sink it for use as an artificial reef. To explain how a Fort Lauderdale company planned to resink the ship, *Sun-Sentinel* graphics reporters created a full-page "News Illustrated" graphic that explained the debacle and how it would be corrected.

FIGURE 2-2

They also developed an animated graphic for the news broadcast on CBS Channel 4, as well as an interactive graphic for the *Sun-Sentinel* website. The animated broadcast graphic included audio voiceover and was combined with video clips of workers preparing the ship for the operation.

Source: Images courtesy of the South Florida *Sun-Sentinel*

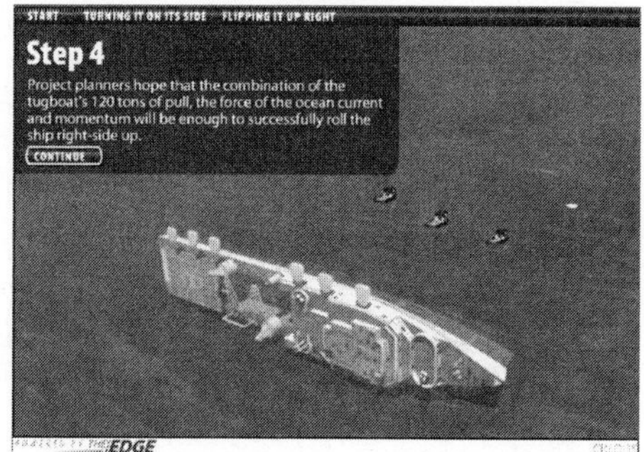

FIGURE 2-3

The interactive graphic presented on the *Sun-Sentinel*'s website allowed users to click through the steps of the resinking process. And each package referred to the others to optimize the number of people who engaged all three.

Source: Images courtesy of the South Florida *Sun-Sentinel*

man and CEO from 1990 to 2005, "the best way to ensure the production and delivery of strong local news is to allow companies like ours to practice good journalism across various media platforms. Convergence brings together the depth of newspaper coverage, the immediacy of television, and the interactivity of the web."[1]

Perhaps one of the most referenced definitions of media convergence was introduced in 2003, when researchers Larry Dailey, Lori Demo, and Mary Spillman proposed the Convergence Continuum, a heuristic model for studying practices in the newsroom.[2] They argue that a single model for convergence does not exist. Rather, convergence occurs at five stages: cross-promotion, cloning, coopetition, content sharing, and full convergence. The continuum has since been used as the foundation for several research projects that have addressed the degree to which media convergence is practiced across news organizations.

One reason that media convergence has come to mean different things to different people is because perception of it largely depends on whether the focus is on the institutional aspects of convergence or the convergence of content. The original intent of media convergence was not necessarily to improve journalistic storytelling. In fact, convergence was first conceived as a way to improve the bottom line.

In the early days of convergence, many predicted that the "backpack journalist" was the key to the future. After all, if we have one person who can write stories, take pictures, and shoot video on location for a single story, we can roll three jobs into one. But, as noted in Chapter 1, that concept didn't exactly thrive or become widely adopted. However, there are individuals out there who excel at more than one form of storytelling and those who specialize in one area of storytelling.

Regardless, multimedia story production requires that we all understand how story forms outside our areas of expertise are created. If you are a brilliant photographer, for example, you do not necessarily have to be the best writer. But you do need to be proficient and know how different kinds of written pieces are constructed. You need to understand the mechanics of good writing and grammar. And perhaps most important, you need to be able to collaborate with writers who will help develop multimedia stories. The most specialized of the aforementioned professions such as videography, photography, design, and graphics reporting require both heightened technical and visual abilities. Of course, writers don't need to know how to illustrate and animate an interactive graphic. However, in the very least, writers (and others) must know what types of information graphics are available, when they are best used, how they fit into a multimedia package, and what types of information must be gathered to make them viable.

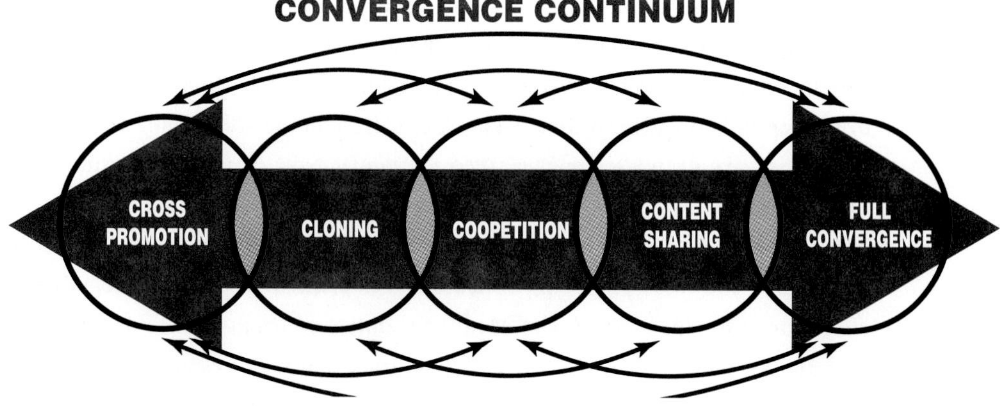

FIGURE 2-4

Cross-promotion includes the least amount of cooperation and interaction among members of different news organizations. At this level, media outlets promote the content of their partners through the use of words or visual elements.

Cloning is the practice of one partner republishing the other partner's product with little editing (e.g., content from a newspaper is displayed on a TV partner's website). At this level, outlets do not discuss their news gathering plans and share content only after a story has been completed.

Coopetition is the stage at which news outlets both cooperate and compete. Staff members of separate media outlets promote and share information about some stories. One entity also might produce some content for its partner.

Content sharing occurs when a media outlet regularly (but not always) shares information gathered by its cross-media partner and publishes it after it has been repackaged. Partners also might share news budgets or attend the partner's planning sessions. Collaboration on a special, investigative, or enterprise piece is possible.

Full convergence is the stage at which partners cooperate in both gathering and disseminating the news. Their common goal is to use the strengths of the different media to tell the story in the most effective way. Under full convergence, hybrid teams of journalists from partnering organizations work together to plan, report, and produce a story, deciding along the way which parts of the story are told most effectively in print, broadcast, and digital forms.

Knowing Your Craft and Collaborating with Others

Historically, journalism and communications programs at universities have focused on training writers, designers, photographers, on-air reporters, and videographers separately. Of course, most programs trained everyone to respect the roles of others in a general sense. However, in the past, students were encouraged to focus specifically on one area of communications/journalism and pursue jobs accordingly. For example, individuals who gravitated toward writing were encouraged to become reporters for newspapers or magazines. Videographers or individuals interested in reporting on air were encouraged to go into broadcast journalism and eventually landed at television or radio stations. And visual journalists, like designers, photographers, and graphics reporters, often gravitated toward print.

However, with the rise of media convergence and the attention most news organizations now give to their web products, a number of notable journalism programs have dramatically revamped curricula. Now, many communications majors focus on all areas of study—from writing and reporting to photojournalism and graphic design. They also emphasize the importance of multimedia storytelling and cross-platform publication (i.e., print, broadcast, online, mobile, etc.). For example, in 2007, the Medill School of Journalism at Northwestern University—widely considered to be one of the premiere programs of its kind—launched the "Medill 2020" curriculum. According to Medill dean John Lavine, "Most important for Medill students who will enter the media and marketing worlds between now and 2020—those who will get the best jobs–not only will know how to find and tell a high-impact story but also how to do it in new forms and on new platforms that better engage their audiences."[3] Similar curriculum revisions have occurred at Ball State University, the University of Florida, the University of Missouri, and the University of North Carolina, to name a few. And a number of new multimedia programs around the world have begun to surface at both liberal arts and technical schools.

This shift in priorities has caught on at some institutions more quickly than others. Of course every school structures its programs and approaches multimedia differently. However, the primary theme is pretty clear: more than ever, communications professionals must be adept at producing content for multiple platforms. Some will do so as backpack journalists. Others will still specialize and collaborate. But it is no longer enough to simply respect what your coworkers from different disciplines do. Rather, you must speak a common language that allows you to fully conceptualize stories with all forms of storytelling in mind. For example, reporters who primarily focus on writing must also be able to think visually, spot graphics potential in stories, and know when video or photos are appropriate.

Likewise, photographers must be able to collect video and still images. Graphics reporters must conduct field research, write text for graphics packages and interactives, and edit photos for galleries and slide shows. And, more than ever, we must all understand how to work together in ways that make the story more meaningful.

Multimedia pioneer Don Wittekind was one of the first working journalists to lead multimedia teams when he was the informational graphics director at the South Florida *Sun-Sentinel*. Under his direction, the *Sun-Sentinel* published its first interactive project in December of 1996 and continued as an industry leader throughout his tenure. But Wittekind says when they first started focusing on multimedia, there was no collaboration at all.

"We would take the photos and other assets and just build what we wanted in graphics, and everyone was happy. We even did our own voiceover work, which was not a good idea," he said. The "big change," came when Wittekind asked the *Sun-Sentinel* radio partner if they could recommend someone to record the narration for a story about Aids in the Caribbean. They agreed and suggested a part-time employee from Jamaica as the voice.

"The difference was HUGE," Wittekind said. "Suddenly we had not just a professional voice, but one from the area we were covering. It was perfect. That was the day I really understood just how I was limiting our work by keeping it all in graphics and I was a believer in collaboration. After that, I stole resources (I mean collaborated) from every other department and news partner as often as they were willing."[4]

From that point on, multimedia teams at the *Sun-Sentinel* have been based on the individual stories at hand. For each project, a reporter, photographer, story editor, and a couple of graphics reporters are normally staples on each team. And depending on the subject, the team might also have a videographer and radio writer to work on the script and voiceover. This team collectively brainstorms, reports, and builds the project, with each team member working within his or her area of expertise. Once the story is published, the group is disbanded and a new team built for the next story.

Of course, talking and writing about the importance of collaboration are easy because few would argue that collaboration isn't important...in theory. Teaching collaboration, however, is a bit trickier. Different people have different ways of communicating ideas. So, there is no guarantee that the communication styles of individuals will mesh. You can bring two equally talented and hard-working individuals together in a team. Yet, if one is more aggressive and talkative, while the other is shy and reserved, the team dynamic can quickly be threatened. Although neither personality trait is wrong, the individuals in this collaborative environment may have trouble effectively navigating group and interpersonal communication.

Part of being a good collaborator has more to do with diplomacy than anything else. Getting along with others often has less to do with how nice or accommodating you are and more to do with your ability to adapt. Good communicators often work hard to assess someone else's personality and then adapt communication styles accordingly. For example, I am pretty cheerful, energetic and open to others' ideas. But I also tend to be pretty straightforward, no-nonsense, thick-skinned, and maybe even a little too blunt for my own good. I don't think I am hard to get along with. In fact, most of my collaborative efforts have been pretty successful. But, I think that is at least partially the result of a lot of effort on my part to read the personality traits and work habits of my cocollaborators. Sometimes, your partners will need and want you to cut the bull and get to the point. Other times, your interactions may require more delicacy because your partners may be shier, quieter, or more reserved in demeanor. However, when a teammate has a dramatically different personality or way of working, a common response is to dismiss or criticize him for his differences. But remember that most of the time, an individual's personality has little to do with his or her potential to do good work. We may not want to hang out and have a beer with everyone we collaborate with. But for the sake of the story, we do need to respect them and find common ground. A good leader and teammate tries to effectively communicate with her partners and navigate differing personalities and viewpoints in ways that encourage everyone to do their best work.

Best Practices in Collaboration

Saying that you understand what makes for good collaboration and actually playing well with others are two different concepts. In fact, if we polled 100 people randomly and asked them to provide tips for effective collaboration, the resulting list would probably look much like the one provided in the next section. But, when push comes to shove (and hopefully it wouldn't really come to that!) it is probably also safe to say that not all of those 100 individuals would collaborate well. In fact, if forced to be honest, you might have to admit that sometimes, you let your pride get the better of you or don't always work well with others in collaborative situations. So, although this section may seem like common sense, it is never a bad idea to revisit three fundamental rules for effective collaboration.

Rule No. 1. Remember that disagreeing with someone about the way a story should come together does not have to be contentious. In fact, a healthy dose of disagreement can be good for your growth as a journalist and for the growth of the story. Disagreement, is different from disrespect. So, try to value all opinions, even if you do not agree with them. Also remember that just because someone disagrees with

QUICK TIPS

Follow these steps for healthy, efficient collaboration.

1. Identify team members and their skill sets. Make sure everyone knows what everyone else is good at.
2. Appoint a project manager.
3. Conduct a brainstorming meeting that includes everyone on the team.
4. Clearly define the story.
5. Use a story planning form that helps the group stay on task and assess multimedia potential.
6. Clearly define the responsibilities of each team member. Make sure that everyone knows what everyone else is doing.
7. Establish intermediate and final deadlines for content.
8. Establish a clear workflow. How will communication occur? How and where will files be named and stored?
9. Check in with the project manager and teammates frequently during reporting.
10. Keep an eye out for information that might help your teammates. Even if information isn't relevant to your piece of the story, it may be relevant to one of the others.

you doesn't mean he can't understand you. Avoid talking down to your partners, patronizing them, or implying they are stupid for disagreeing with you. Right or wrong, you won't get very far in collaborative environments by being disrespectful.

Rule No. 2. Make sure that everyone has an opportunity to express opinions. Believe it or not, this is not necessarily about making everyone feel good. In fact, if we are all doing this for the right reasons, our feelings are irrelevant. This rule is about making sure the story is the best that it can be. Part of the benefit of bringing more than one brain to the table is the value added by a diversity of thoughts, ideas, and perspectives. Likewise, different team members will have different areas of expertise. Thus, it is important that each teammate explain his or her views on how the story should be represented through their respective medium. Photographers need to weigh in on the best way to tell the story through photos. Graphics reporters need to assess the story's graphics potential. And writers and videographers should weigh in on the story's narrative arc and the best way to capture it in words or video. So make sure all those views are laid on the table at the start of a project and revisit those views from time to time as the project progresses.

Rule No. 3. Understand that not everyone is going to be happy all the time. Or as our moms often tell us, choose your battles wisely. Yes, we need to make sure all ideas are represented, but when opinions differ, there will have to be compromise so the project can move forward. Sometimes your ideas will survive, and other times, they won't make it past the brainstorming phase. You have to be okay with this. Of course, fight for what you think is right and always do so with the best interests of the story in mind. But, know when to back down and be supportive of the concepts that do survive. A team player puts his best foot forward, even when he does not agree with the majority opinion.

And beyond these to basic guidelines, there exist a few other rules of the road that will help ensure a smooth workflow:

Clearly define the story. There is a huge difference between a topic and a story. And, for any given topic, there are probably hundreds of possible stories within. For example, "breast cancer" is a topic. Saying you want to do a story about breast cancer is like saying you want to snack on a 16-ounce steak. There are an infinite number of stories you can do about breast cancer. Some are attached to a timely event, such as the Susan G. Komen Race for the Cure. Others could focus on informing women about risks, symptoms, and treatment. Some stories may illuminate one person's fight with the disease. Others may chronicle medical milestones in the fight against breast cancer. But, one thing is for certain: if you do not clearly define your story before diving into the collaborative process, you could end up with a mess on your hands. Add multiple team members, story forms, deadlines, and ideas about focus, and you could have a recipe for disaster. A true story will never have a chance to surface because you never found a clear, concise focus. Thus, every person on the team must have a clear understanding and shared vision for the project.

Appoint a project manager. When I think about some of the more challenging collaborative teams I have been a part of, two phrases instantly come to mind: "too many cooks in the kitchen"; and "too many generals, not enough soldiers." That is not to say one team member's role is more important than the others. But when dealing with several collaborators—all with different skills and areas of expertise—as well as several types of content, one person should be in charge of keeping track of it all. This project manager's most important jobs are to facilitate communication among team members and try to keep track of where everything stands during the process. The project manager should be organized and in regular contact with team members, chart progress, trouble shoot, and maintain the project timeline.

Engage in an initial planning meeting. Team members should come together early in the story planning process to define the story and brainstorm a multimedia presentation. Try to isolate all of the different story forms and asses the multimedia potential for a story in an organized methodical fashion.

Clearly define responsibilities. Once a project manager has been appointed, the story's focus established, and multimedia potential assessed, make sure that each team member is clear on his or her responsibilities. If the team makes these decisions collectively, individuals are more likely to be satisfied with their roles and feel obligated to cooperate.

Establish intermediate and final deadlines, and frequently revisit them. Whenever possible, set deadlines as a team. Make sure team members know that everyone will depend on them to meet deadlines. Likewise, set deadlines together so that everyone can be held accountable. At the same time, understand that deadlines and focus may need to be adjusted as the reporting process evolves. If a piece you are responsible for needs to be modified, make sure your teammates are aware of changes so they can adjust accordingly.

Agree on a common workflow. Determine who will be responsible for editing and reviewing content to ensure accuracy and consistency.

Develop a file management system. Make sure everyone is clear on the necessary file sizes and other technical requirements. Determine where files will be saved and what the naming convention will be. Taking a few minutes to do this early in the process could save hours of confusion later.

Communicate your progress with teammates throughout the reporting process. Aside from the times you meet to discuss the big picture plan, you will spend most of your time working independently. Because of this, it becomes easy to forget your responsibilities to the team. But if you want the process to go smoothly and the final product to be close to what you initially discussed, you have to keep lines of communication open. Make sure your teammates know how your end of the story is progressing, when you encounter roadblocks, and if it becomes necessary to make changes to your approach. Keep an eye out for information that is relevant to pieces your teammates are working on. Missed opportunities are often the result of miscommunication. While you are out in the field, reporting and gathering information, you may encounter content that is not relevant to the piece you are working on but that could help one of your teammates. For example, if you are writing a text-based story and you encounter a scene that would make for great photos or an information graphic, share that information with the photographer, videographer, or graphics reporter. Always be respectful of your teammates and their opinions. You do not have to agree with everyone all the time. And you certainly don't have to sit back and let someone have his way when you don't agree with his approach. But remember that you can't have it your way all the time. Also, try to avoid turf wars. In other words, make sure that every time you find yourself in conflict with a teammate that you are arguing a point for the good of the story, not in defense of your craft. The story should always come first, and sometimes, that will mean stepping back and letting someone else take the lead.

Developing a Workflow

Different stories require different methods for teamwork. In some cases, team members need to be physically close to one another during reporting and production. For example, a writer and graphics reporter may choose to work together on an interactive graphic. The reporter can contribute to the research and written pieces, whereas the graphics reporter focuses on illustration and animation. However, for this collaboration to be effective, there will be a point at which the two must sit side-by-side in front of a computer. Together, they can effectively put all the pieces together and make sure they both agree on storytelling and functionality. Other times, teams can work remotely and pull things together with limited face time. E-mail is great for sharing information and drafts of your work. Furthermore, many online content management systems allow team members to remotely upload content to a final site. But regardless of your chosen workflow, establishing solid workflow is as important to collaboration as getting along with one another throughout the process. Likewise, establishing that workflow can help you avoid conflicts later.

Once a team has been established, quickly negotiate the processes you will follow through story development. How often will you meet? What steps will you take to collaboratively brainstorm parts of the story? How and when will you provide feedback to one another? How will you store and manage digital files? Is there a need to divide the larger team into smaller groups of collaborators? If so, what will those teams look like? And, perhaps most important: What expectations do you have for yourself and others in your team? Collaboratively answering these questions up front is important for several reasons.

First, it will naturally lead to a workflow plan. In addition to multiple collaborators, your project will include multiple media files and often several file types. Establishing a workflow with everyone onboard is essential to keeping track of the people and the content that will comprise your project. Second, answering these questions up front will also help the team set realistic deadlines that everyone feels obligated to make. The more you clearly communicate your expectations, the more likely each team member will feel obligated to rise to the occasion. Meeting deadlines is important to getting the project done on time and ensuring that the story is coming together the way you all envisioned. Likewise, if you find things are not coming together like you originally planned, meeting intermediate deadlines can give you an opportunity to reassess and change direction if necessary.

When you are good at it, collaboration can be one of the most satisfying parts of our jobs. Of course we all know that collaboration is not always easy. Personality clashes, scheduling conflicts, differing opinions about the direction a story should take, turf wars, and resource limitations are all potential roadblocks to smooth collaboration. And even the best collaborators sometimes find themselves wondering why they didn't just "do it all themselves" to avoid the hassles associated with depending on others. However, take it from someone who has made a career out of leading collaborative projects. There is nothing more gratifying than seeing a piece come together that showcases the work of a team of talented collaborators. When successful, multimedia collaboration often results in well-rounded, rich narratives that capture stories with a level of depth and variety that is unmatched.

Professional Perspective

Miranda Mulligan • *Multimedia Presentation Editor*

The Boston Globe

Miranda Mulligan is the design director for BostonGlobe.com and Boston.com, the websites for The Boston Globe. *She is a multimedia designer and educator with over ten years of professional experience in print design, photography, and information graphics reporting. Her work has received awards from the Online News Association, Virginia Press Association, the National Press Photographers Association, and the Society for News Design.*

Anyone. Anywhere. Tracking Meghan Landowski's Killer
http://hamptonroads.com/2010/03/tracking-meghan-landowskis-killer
Reporter: Janie Bryant
Video reporting: Brian Clark (with court video from Steve Earley)
Video story editing: Brian Clark and Miranda Mulligan
Interactivity: Miranda Mulligan

For months in 2008, investigators gathered every Tuesday in a nondescript conference room to strategize their hunt for 16-year-old Meghan Landowski's killer. Her murder went unsolved for six months while fear grew in a southeast Virginia community. And the police waited until the murderer pleaded guilty and a judge sentenced him to 42 years in prison to talk about the investigation that began with a 911 call on April 10, 2008. Reporter Janie Bryant had been chipping away at every angle of the story since the start, and the portion that would explain the investigation was finally scheduled to run in *The Virginian-Pilot's Sunday Magazine* section in the middle of March 2010.

Two weeks before the run date, video wiz Brian Clark asked me to swing by his desk. Over time and several multimedia projects, he and I had developed good communication about stories we thought might have alternative story form potential. In other words, when I came across a story to which video could add depth, or when he ran into a story that could make for an interesting interactive piece, we tried to team up. So collaboration was not a foreign term in our books.

Clark had just returned from collecting video interviews with both of the key detectives. He and Bryant interviewed each detective for about an hour—a rare opportunity. The detectives preferred to avoid video interviews, but Bryant had

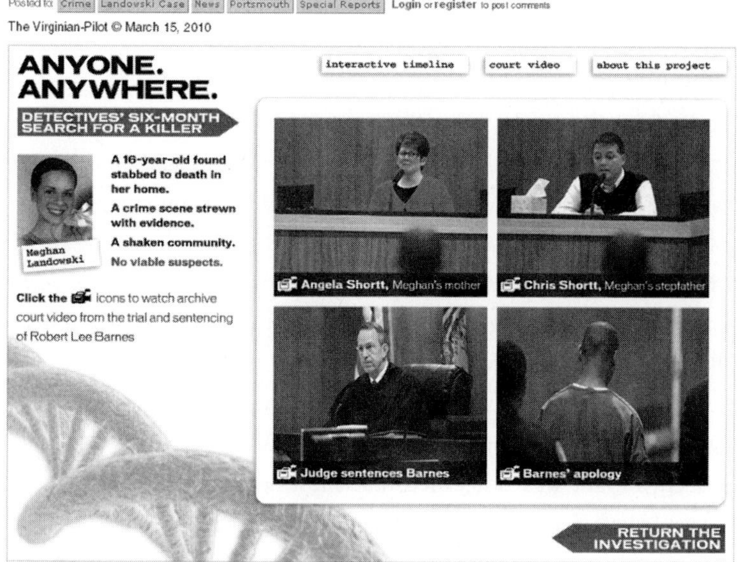
Posted to: Crime | Landowski Case | News | Portsmouth | Special Reports | Login or register to post comments
The Virginian-Pilot © March 15, 2010
ANYONE. ANYWHERE.
DETECTIVES' SIX-MONTH SEARCH FOR A KILLER
interactive timeline
court video
about this project
A 16-year-old found stabbed to death in her home.
A crime scene strewn with evidence.
A shaken community.
No viable suspects.
Meghan Landowski
Click the icons to watch archive court video from the trial and sentencing of Robert Lee Barnes
Angela Shortt, Meghan's mother
Chris Shortt, Meghan's stepfather
Judge sentences Barnes
Barnes' apology
RETURN THE INVESTIGATION
CLICK ON THE INTERACTIVE ABOVE TO WATCH VIDEOS AND LEARN MORE.
A CASE that began with a stepfather's anguished 911 call on April 10, 2008, in Portsmouth ended Feb. 18 when Robert Lee Barnes was sentenced for sexually assaulting and stabbing to death his 16-year-old friend, Meghan Landowski.
READ: Tracking Meghan Landowski's killer - PART 1 | PART 2 | Full archive of the Landowski case

FIGURE 2-6

The simple design structure is maintained throughout the multimedia piece, "Anyone. Anywhere." Top-level navigation is always present, allowing the users to navigate through the package in a nonlinear fashion.

Source: Image courtesy of *The Virginian-Pilot*

pushed, and been patient, and pushed some more. By the time they sat down with the detectives, she could zone in on their stories and what they went through.

"The transcript of the video had already been entered into evidence, and police knew we could FOIA [Freedom of Information Act] the video and the 911 tape," Bryant said. "So they sat down with the family ahead of time and went through what they were giving us. The family wanted it made public. I believe police did, too. Even after Barnes pleaded guilty, there were some who still said it could not have been him. I think they wanted people to see for themselves the story he told them and how he told it."

Both Clark and Bryant are seasoned journalists. But Bryant was motivated by the demands of her print story, and those of the video story burdened Clark. Bryant admitted she had never conducted an interview for a video, and she had never done an interview with a videographer present. These were both aspects of this collaborative process that led to some challenges.

In preparation, Clark asked Bryant to say as little as possible while the camera was recording. Clark preferred to conduct the interview because he had more experience with interviewing for on-camera content. He was anticipating that Bryant would use traditional interview techniques to keep the subjects talking. For example, Bryant might have asked questions that begged shorter more concise answers; she might have used encouraging "yeahs" and "uh-huhs"—reassuring sounds to keep them talking. Or she might have even talked straight through an answer. While these are great techniques for conducting a print interview, they can be disastrous for the overall audio and video quality.

Conversely, Bryant was concerned that allowing someone else to conduct the interview could be a detriment to the story that would run in print. She said, "I had waited so long to get to police and now I was afraid I wouldn't be able to relax and neither would they." Because compromise is an essential ingredient to all collaboration, Clark decided to take a backseat and worry about how to shape the video story during the editing part of the production process. Although in Clark's opinion this wasn't an ideal approach, he decided to accommodate his teammate's concerns.

It is also important to understand that when they were collecting interviews, neither Clark nor Bryant knew yet how the multimedia story would come together from information gathering to publication. And the detectives agreed to give video interviews only one day before the meetings, giving Clark and Bryant only a short time to prepare. In an ideal process, we would have talked about the multimedia story prior to the interviews to, in the very least, develop a rough storyboard and shot list. This helps ensure all assets are collected during the reporting process and prevents the team from wishing we had gotten other material afterward. However, in this case, time constraints meant the team had to work quickly with less preparation on the front end.

After he returned from the police department, I stopped by Clark's desk to chat. He wanted to know if there was potential for an interactive feature instead of the more typical storytelling treatment: a tightly edited video. I couldn't say, "yes!" fast enough.

In general, crime investigations lend themselves to good storytelling. This case of a 16-year-old high school sophomore killed in her family's home in an otherwise quiet neighborhood had tremendous public interest from the beginning. Then, police finally made an arrest and it turned out to be a former classmate—a 16-year-old boy, so talented and studious that half the community could not believe he was the killer.

Over the next two days, Clark and I went through the raw footage to develop a rough storyboard so that I could try to sell the multimedia idea to the editors. As we logged the video, Clark and I didn't always agree. There was a sound bite here or there that I liked, but he didn't, and vice versa. In the end, however, we found a story that could be divided into four basic parts: video interviews, court videos, an interactive timeline and a section about the project. All in all, we would have a nice interactive feature.

Later the same afternoon, the editors, director of photography, Clark, and I talked in depth about whether we should publish the story with so much detail. The story had the potential to be quite explicit, as the crime scene was very bloody, Barnes' video interview footage was eerie, and the victim and then suspect were teenagers. After a much-needed discussion, deliberation, and inevitable disagreement, we decided that the video made for a powerful story and publishing it would be an essential service to our readers.

It took Clark about a week to log and cut back the interview and crime scene footage into a compelling narrative arc. It was a complicated story, and he was disseminating interview footage that had been conducted by a traditional, print-minded reporter. While Clark worked on the video components, I set out to find the remaining assets that I would need for the interactive narrative. I worked with assistant urban team editor Matthew Roy on putting together a condensed timeline of the case. I located the previously published court and sentencing video; and I developed a design for the interactive feature that would eventually house all of the other assets.

Once the video story was in place, Clark and I met with editors one more time. This gave us an opportunity to change the direction of the story if necessary or get a blessing to proceed. Although it is often frustrating to have a change in direction this far along in the process, it does happen. The most important thing is to choose your battles wisely. Although our editors agreed with the general focus of the video narrative, there were a few disagreements about presentation. For example, editor Denis Finley thought it was important to publish the full 13-minute video without breaking it into chunks. I worried about the attention spans of online viewers. In the end, we compromised, and I agreed to present both options to users.

WHAT WE LEARNED

Every new multimedia project comes with different challenges and new ideas. Each time, it's a good idea to sum up the two or three things you learned from the process. Not only will this help you with your next project, but also it will address ways to communicate and collaborate better in the future. This project highlighted three important points:

TIP #1 Think about process when collaborating with others. You can anticipate obstacles and adjust your workflow if necessary.

TIP #2 Talk about multimedia potential in stories early and often! Don't wait until the last minute unless it you can't avoid it.

TIP #3 Don't be afraid to dream big when suggesting presentation ideas. Likewise, don't be afraid to scale back the presentation in accordance with your resources.

Following this meeting, Clark worked through notes, cleaned up transitions and made some adjustments to the audio tracks. He uploaded the individual videos into our video client and I pulled them into the interactive.

Over the next two days, I finished the design elements and produced the Flash interactive. We chose to publish the multimedia at PilotOnline.com on a Monday to take advantage of a peak traffic day. The print version ran in the paper the day before. The end result was so much richer than a traditional text and picture story presentation. We provided the audience with a much deeper story and answered more of their questions through the multimedia piece. We brought them into the interviews. Multimedia allowed readers to see and hear the detectives and Robert Barnes in a way they could not by reading the text alone. One of the registered users commented on the story: "This gave me insight into the hard work these detectives did in solving this heart breaking and brutal murder. I'll be extra sure to hug my kids tonight."

During this process, we all continued to complete our day-to-day tasks. We were not relieved of our routines and daily obligations to the newspaper and online products. We worked around our normal responsibilities, finding pockets of time here and there to finish this project. And, our diligence seems to have paid off.

The interactive feature was very popular compared to other interactive features on PilotOnline.com and HamptonRoads.com. The first-month page views were nearly twice the average for other interactive features. The first-week video play counts for both the chunked video and the 13-minute version were nearly three times the average for similar stories. And the shorter chunked videos were played to completion more often than the 13-minute version of the story.

The only way we have been able to produce interactive narratives like this one is through collaboration. For example, over the past couple of years, Clark and I have developed a mutual trust because we not only respect opposing opinions; we often seek them out to help inform our own decisions. And, we practice compromise for the sake of the story. Because telling the best story with the available resources is at the heart of all of our storytelling decisions, it is easier to work together. We take ownership of each story as a team.

Exercise

Put together a team of three to five of your classmates, each with differing skill sets. Try to make sure your team has at least one writer, one photographer, one videographer, and one graphics reporter or programmer. Identify a potential multimedia story and conduct an initial brainstorming meeting. As outlined in this chapter, make sure to address the following:

1. Clearly define the story.
2. Appoint a project manager. This person should run the meeting and take notes.
3. Develop a storytelling strategy and delegate responsibilities.
4. Set realistic deadlines for all parts of the project.
5. Determine how you will manage files as they are submitted.

After your initial brainstorming meeting, write a three- to five-page project outline that includes a one-paragraph description of the story, a concrete plan for storytelling that includes the types of multimedia pieces that will be produced and who will produce them, a clear deadline summary, and a summary of where files should be saved when they are complete. Post your outline on your WordPress site.

Notes

1. Media General Annual Report, 2002.
2. Larry Dailey, Lori Demo, and Mary Spillman. "Most TV/Newspapers Partner at Cross Promotion Stage," *Newspaper Research Journal* 26, 4 (2005), 36–49.
3. Kristina Cowan. "Medill 2020," posted May 23, 1997, to blogs.payscale.com.
4. Interview with Don Wittekind, June 2, 2010.

CHAPTER 3

Planning Multimedia

Assessing Multimedia Potential for Your Stories

The first step to spotting multimedia potential in a story is determining whether there is enough depth to warrant a layered approach that contains several discreet pieces. In other words, is there an aspect of the story that would make for great video? Is there information graphics potential, that is, maps, charts, or diagrams? If so, how might you approach interactivity? Is there potential for a photo gallery or slide show? Would an audio track strengthen the photo package, or are straight captions more appropriate? These basic questions are often the foundation for a good brainstorming session. And this process can quickly help a multimedia story take shape. In order to answer these questions effectively, however, you must understand the strengths and weaknesses of each story form.

Of course, not every story or piece of information deserves multimedia treatment. In fact, many stories only require a simple, short, one-form presentation. And depending on the circumstances surrounding the story—that is, available staff, deadlines, resources, and so on—it may not always be possible to create multimedia content. Likewise, some media types may not be appropriate or available for the story at hand. In those cases, do what is best for the story using the resources that are available at the time. However, when a multimedia approach is possible, everyone at the planning table must understand how to spot multimedia potential and when different story forms are best used. Chapters 6 through 10 focus on specific story forms in detail, whereas this chapter offers a summary of what to consider when determining how best to tell a multimedia story.

Of course any story can be told in written form and most multimedia stories include some type of writing. Chapter 6 focuses on writing across platforms and addresses different narrative forms for print, online, and broadcast. More and more, writers are encouraged to consider the platforms on which a story will appear and write accordingly. However, other story forms are rising in popularity among journalists and audiences as well. Following is a brief overview of each to help give you an overview of a few considerations for spotting multimedia potential in a story.

Photo galleries present images in nonlinear formats. The gallery structure allows users to control navigation of visual content. Still photography is the most common type of content used in galleries; however, galleries can be used for all manner of visual story forms, including information graphics and video. Galleries also need a fair amount of design work for effective presentation.

Photo slideshows present a series of pictures in linear formats, with images appearing in a predetermined order. Sometimes, the user controls the speed with which images are viewed, and other times, the slideshow simply plays like a movie. Often slideshows are combined with narrative audio or interviews with subjects. Other times, they are only accompanied by captions. Chapter 7 further addresses photojournalism and focuses on the fundamentals of shooting and editing pictures. The chapter covers how photos are used in print and online and discusses the technical and conceptual issues associated with photo slideshows and galleries. We also explore how audio can be combined with photos to create rich, powerful photo stories for digital platforms.

Audio can be a powerful story form. Jonathan Dube, publisher of CyberJournalist.net writes, "There's a reason radio didn't disappear after TV came along; a reason NPR is so popular. Use audio when there are sounds that can't be described in words; when the way a person says something adds meaning that the words alone can't convey. Don't just hotlink text to a sound clip of a quote. Use photos of the speakers to draw users in. And use audio in creative ways, to bring traditional 'man on the street' or 'ask the experts' features to life."[1]

Audio can also be an effective narrative tool for photo presentations, interactive graphics, and animations. Regardless of how it is used, however, remember that good audio keeps the listener's interest with powerful language and vivid descriptions. Avoid unnecessary words and use active voice and clear, concise explanations. Chapter 8 provides more in-depth instruction on audio storytelling.

Video is best used when you want to show action, highlight a location, or hear and see a person central to the story. It is also worth noting that audiences use online video differently than traditional broadcasts and mobile devices. Traditional TV viewing is a 10-foot experience; computer viewing is a two-foot experience; and mobile devices offer an even more intimate, one-foot experience. Thus, both screen size and distance are issues to consider when developing video packages.

Like all forms of media, video can be used as a primary or secondary storytelling tool. However, no matter how video is used, it is most effective when it (1) illustrates the story you are trying to tell; (2) captures the attention of the user/view quickly; (3) is short and to the point; (4) does not repeat the same story told in other formats; (5) tells stories that are best suited for video (it doesn't tell a story with video that is best told with text); and (6) offers a quality on par with traditional broadcast, but presents it in an innovative way. Chapter 9 addresses the basics of video storytelling in greater detail, from definitions of different types of shots to creating a narrative arc. The chapter also covers both conceptual and technical considerations for creating strong video stories. And we address how the size of the platform (i.e., TV, web, or mobile devices), viewing habits, and compression issues affect how videographers shoot and edit video stories.

Information graphics are best used when answers to journalistic questions are visual, when location is a key factor, or when a comparison or visual description of a process is necessary. The best information graphics take you where photos or video cannot. For example, although video and photographs are capable of chronicling a doctor performing laser eye surgery, they cannot provide the depth of visual explanation that an interactive diagram could. The diagram can take you inside the eye and show what happens to it during the procedure. And every multimedia journalist should know that there are a number of different types of information graphics, each of which has distinct characteristics. When, numbers are present in a story, consider charts or data visualizations. When location is a factor, consider locator, diagrammatic, or statistical maps. When it is important to show how something works or how an event unfolded, consider an active or passive diagram. Broadcast and online graphics present animation opportunities not possible in print. And online you can make graphics interactive, presenting a new set of categories from which to choose. Chapter 10 covers print, online, and broadcast graphics in detail and explains how information graphics affect story comprehension.

INTERACTIVE GRAPHIC

Refining Vision Surgery for a Sharper Focus

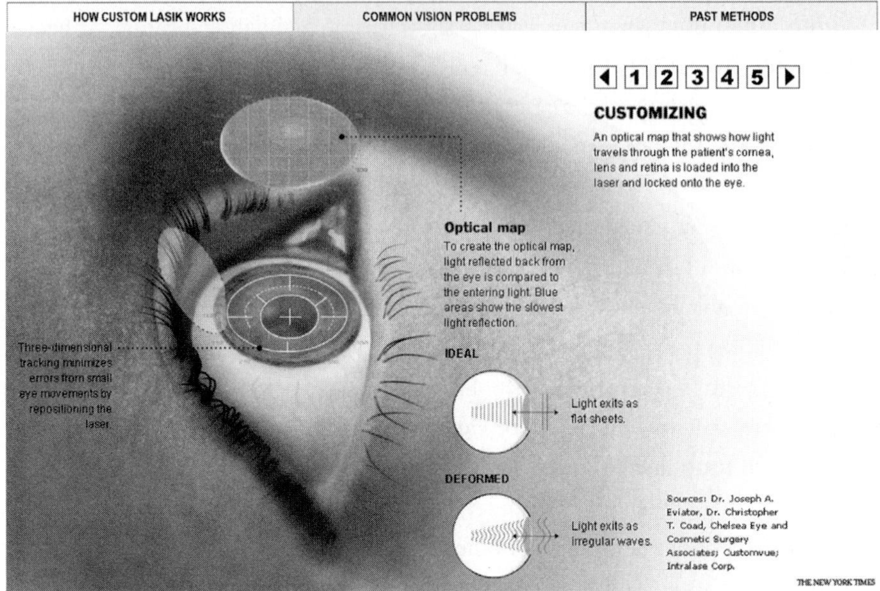

FIGURE 3-1

This *New York Times* interactive combines a rich illustration with animation, interactivity and text to provide a visual description not possible with photos or video alone. Information graphics can be especially effective when a topic lends itself to a step-by-step look at a complex process like Lasik eye surgery.

Source: Image courtesy of *The New York Times.*

Knowing when and how to use different story forms is key to developing a strong multimedia story. Photos capture moments. Videos capture sequences of events and allow subjects to tell their own stories. Interactive graphics provide rich simulations of real-world phenomena and simplify complex data. Text allows you to describe and define parts of the story that don't lend themselves to visual presentations. And, hopefully, these elements together are capable of drilling into the complexities of a story in ways a single medium cannot.

Information Layering

Information layering is a concept used by many different types of news organizations as a method for providing multiple points of entry into a story package. Print media,

QUICK TIPS

Each user may only view parts of a story. In fact, members of your audience will likely pick and choose which elements they will spend time with, depending on what they are most interested in topically and technically. So, when you are developing individual pieces, consider the following tips:

Take advantage of the web's potential for nonlinear presentation. It is one of the most attractive and powerful features of the web. Nonlinear presentations allow the user to make more choices about how to engage with content. This choice is one key to tapping into the power of interactivity.

Create each element to stand alone. In other words, each piece must leave the audience feeling like a complete story was told. You can't guarantee viewers will interact with more than one.

Only include redundancies that are absolutely necessary. If each piece within a multimedia package repeats too much content or information from the others, users can be left feeling like they are just rehashing the same concepts over and over. You have to balance making each piece fresh and reflective of new information and ensuring that each story element contains the most important themes of a story.

Avoid editing your ideas in the early stages of planning. Start by making a list of all possible story forms and a brief description of how each could be used. For example, a multimedia package about the Indianapolis 500 could include interactive graphics, photo galleries and slideshows, video clips, and written pieces. You may not have the time, resources, or desire to develop every possible piece. However, list them all during the planning phase and explore all possibilities before settling on a final plan.

for example, present story packages that include written pieces, photographs, and information graphics. And through the latter part of the twentieth century, many print organizations added alternative story forms that include fact boxes, timelines, tables, and other graphically enhanced quick reads. This method of resenting stories on different visual and textual levels results in organized, reader-friendly pages that provide different types of readers with various points of entry.

Information layering also occurs online. Short, digestible "chunks" of information combined with hyperlinks often provide audiences with interactive, immersive experiences. Dube recommends that multimedia journalists "give [audiences] choices, but limit them. Too few choices, and you're not taking advantage of the strengths of the web. Too many choices and readers may not select any because they might get confused or not want to spend the time deciding. Plus, the more choices you give, the less control you have over how the news is conveyed. Remember, readers are coming to your site in part because they trust your news judgment, so don't be afraid to use it."[2] Dube's assessment is really what lies at the heart of good story planning. So regardless of whether you are planning a story alone or working in a multimedia team, the first few steps to creating a multimedia piece include determining a story's main focus, listing two or three key themes, and then assessing the multimedia potential.

Of course, the more people you have around the table for this discussion, the better. And the more diversity in expertise, the better. The whole team should think about all aspects of a story. But you should also craft a team that is composed of individuals who specialize in video or photo, information graphics, and writing. This variety of expertise will likely make the brainstorming process more fruitful. At the same time, an individual may naturally be more supportive of his personal area of expertise. This fact is often at the foundation of many collaboration roadblocks. The key here is to always ask yourselves and one another one simple question: "How can I/we best serve this story?"

One way to approach early planning meetings is the Maestro Concept, first established for print media in the early 1990s. Adopted in some form in more than a dozen countries, Maestro was proposed by Buck Ryan who was then an assistant professor in the Medill School of Journalism at Northwestern University. This collaborative approach to story planning was based on the notion that newsrooms needed to stop operating like assembly lines where photographers, writers, and graphics reporters develop content for the same stories independent of one another. Ryan argued that a more efficient and beneficial approach includes a planning meeting that involves the key players in a story (i.e., a reporter, photographer, designer, copy editor, and graphics reporter) and the use of a story planning form that helps facilitate the brainstorming process. Although it was initially developed with print media in mind, Maestro is a process that can work for any news organization that presents news and informa-

FIGURE 3-2

This interactive story package is about the cost of milk as an economic indicator. Each segment of the story leads users to submenus that point to content presented in a variety of story forms. The package includes video segments, interactive graphics, photo galleries, and text-based stories.

Source: Kristen Gibson, Tom Demeropolis, Mike Groder, and Sean O'Key, Ball State University.

tion in multiple story forms. Thus, multimedia collaboration is Maestro on steroids. Add a few more skill sets to the table and a few more story forms to your toolbox, and you have all the right ingredients for a solid multimedia Maestro session.

Multimedia Maestro doesn't differ much from Ryan's original process. According to Ryan's original definition, "As a team, those involved in the Maestro session try to identify readers' questions. The goal is to answer those questions in the highest visibility parts of a page: in a photo or artwork, in a headline, in a caption, in a pull-quote, in a graphic or in a box."[3] Thus, multimedia Maestro is just a small twist on Ryan's original plan: answer those same questions using the most appropriate story form—video, interactive graphic, text, photo slideshow or gallery, audio, and so on—through a well-designed digital presentation. Ryan also notes, "The entire package is sketched out, including ideas for possible layouts, headlines, photos, and graphics." Again, multimedia Maestro assumes a greater number of possibilities for media and a more web-focused approach to design. But the most important nugget is still present: Use the Maestro process as a method for brainstorming all of the different approaches you could take with the story. Maestro should occur after you have done preliminary research necessary to define the story's focus, but before individual team members dive into fully reporting and gathering content. A storyboard draft can also help focus the team on what needs to be done. Maestro saves time and frustration because it ensures all members of the team are on the same page and helps establish a clear division of responsibilities.

Questions for Assessing Multimedia Potential

1. Can the story be broken down into several topical "chunks"? Often, multimedia journalists work with stories that are deep and complex. Stories that have multiple parts, involve several people, or focus on a number of topical concepts may make for good multimedia packages. This is particularly true when the many facets of a story can be told effectively in a several different formats.

2. Does the story describe a process? Information graphics, videos, and image galleries can all be great ways to show how a process unfolded or event occurred. Interactive diagrams and narrative animations can take you where photos cannot. Videos can effectively document processes as they occur in a linear form. And photo galleries can offer more segmented and focused approaches by capturing single steps in a process.

3. Is the story laden with figures or statistical information? Data visualizations present complex relationships in multidimensional data. Some of the most common data visualizations are maps that help users establish a qualitative understanding of complicated, location-based data. Visual patterns applied to maps tell stories that can be quickly comprehended at a glance.

4. Is there an emotional narrative to be told? Video shows action and events as they unfold. Likewise, video is often the best medium for taking the user to a location central to the story or introducing a person important to the story.

5. Are there dramatic visual moments that can be captured in photographs? Where videos are best for capturing movement, still photos are best for capturing moments. Still images alone, in a gallery, or combined with audio in a linear slideshow can engage users with dramatic events. Like videos, still images can also introduce the audience to a person who is central to the story.

6. Does the story contain strong historical references? Interactive timelines can add context to a story with historical significance. Timelines can be built with text-based hyperlinks, controlled with graphic buttons, or combined with other media, such as photos, video, illustrations, or audio.

7. Is there potential for animation? Programs such as Adobe Flash have made complex animation relatively easy. More and more, information graphics reporters, photojournalists, and web developers are using animation to show complex processes.

FIGURE 3-3

This *New York Times* interactive timeline allows users to explore Kennedy's life in pictures and text.

Source: Image courtesy of The *New York Times*.

MULTIMEDIA MAESTRO FORM

Use this form to determine the multimedia potential for any story. Fill in the requested information to help brainstorm ideas for your multimedia strategy. Try to make this list as exhaustive as possible so that you have a thorough list of possibilities.

What are the three most important points of this story?

a.

b.

c.

Why should the reader care?

a.

b.

c.

Check the types of story forms that apply to your story, and give a short, one-sentence description of how:

Text:

Audio:

Video:

Photo slide show:

Photo gallery:

Simple chart:

Map:

Interactive timeline:

Interactive diagram:

Data visualization:

Simulation graphic:

Serious game:

Narrative animation:

8. Could a game advance storytelling by engaging users in a simulation or educational experience? The discussion of the educational potential for games spans more than 30 years. Serious games offer highly immersive, interactive experiences and apply traditional gaming strategies to serious storytelling. The idea is that the more you can immerse users in the graphic, the more they will learn and stay engaged. Journalistic games must be both journalistically accurate and appropriately serious in tone, illustration, and content. At the same time, they must be fun, engaging, and worth playing.

Developing Storyboards

Graphic designers are encouraged to sketch pages that include significant levels of information layering. Web designers often develop site maps before diving into site production. And multimedia journalists should create storyboards to better organize content and establish the pace for larger, more detailed presentations. A storyboard is a great way for members of a collaborative team to identify resources, facilitate brainstorming, and get on the same page.

In 2009, three journalists from the New Orleans *Times-Picayune* were named finalists for the Pulitzer Prize for local reporting for their multimedia presentation titled, "Homicide 37: Seeking Justice for Lance." For the multimedia team—staff writer Brendan McCarthy, photographer Michael DeMocker, and graphic artist Ryan Smith—planning and storyboarding was a key part of the storytelling process and essential to developing this award-winning piece. Smith notes that the importance of the storyboard is magnified when a project is started without one.

"I've been guilty of starting a project without a storyboard a few times, either because time was short, I thought I had a good idea of what it would look like in my head, or I was just lazy," he said. "Then, about halfway through the project, I would scrap some of my work because some things went an entirely different direction—a direction that would have been anticipated had there been storyboarding involved."[4]

Developing a storyboard can be broken down into a basic three-step process: (1) divide the story into its main categories; (2) consider which story forms are best for each main chunk; and (3) create sketches that illustrate the how the story will be packaged. By way of example, let's look at the "Homicide 37" presentation to reverse engineer a storyboard using this three-step process.

Step One. Divide the story into its various parts. "Homicide 37" is the story of the murder of 17-year-old Lance Zarders and the police investigation that followed. The story package was built using interviews with the victim's family and the investigators responsible for the case. Based on these interviews, the story was divided into eight main chapters:

Chapter 1: A Deadly Silence
Chapter 2: Who and Why?
Chapter 3: Promise to a Father
Chapter 4: The Witness
Chapter 5: Rest in Peace, Lance
Chapter 6: Eyes on the Accused
Chapter 7: An Abandoned Boy
Chapter 8: Waiting for Justice

Step Two. Divide the contents of the story among media. The main navigation for the story was offered in five categories: the story, the people, the videos, the photos, downloads—each with a number of subsections. This way, users could explore the "Homicide 37" story through several types of media, from written pieces to video. Here's how they broke down:

The Story: This section offers written pieces for each of the eight main chapters listed above. Each chapter includes a link to related photos. Photos were presented in nonlinear photo galleries.

The People: This section is divided into five segments: the victim, the parents, the detective, the partner, and the accused. Each segment provides a brief written bio along with a number of related video clips. Most of the videos are interviews with individuals and are less than a minute in length.

The Videos: This section is comprised of five video clips: "Grieving" is a video interview with the victim's parents; "Burden and Answers" are interviews with the homicide detectives; "R.I.P." is a photo/audio presentation from the funeral services; and "Justice" is a video that provides the detectives' reaction to the grand jury's decision not to indict the suspect.

The Photos: This section takes users directly to the photo galleries referred to in the first section (The Stories). The menu of galleries is divided into eight chapters and each offers a link to the corresponding written pieces.

Downloads: This section provides links to the police report, funeral flyer, and reward flyer.

Step Three. Create sketches that illustrate the structure and design of how the story will be packaged. Storyboard sketches provide a roadmap for your multimedia package by showing where various story elements will appear in a package.

Storyboards also help organize the structure and design of content and navigational elements. Thus, your storyboard should include sketches of what the home page or "splash" page will look like, including the menu or navigation scheme for accessing those sections. Then, consider what subsequent pages will look like and how they

FIGURE 3-4

This sketch represents one of the early storyboards for *The Times-Picayune*'s "Homicide 37." The piece was named a runner-up in the Pulitzer Prize competition for local reporting.

Source: Image courtesy of Ryan Smith.

will be structured. Establish the main element on each page, as well as the other information that should be included there.

Smith says he developed several sets of sketches before landing on the final presentations structure for the "Homicide 37" story. "I sketched and storyboarded a few different ideas that incorporated the story and photo galleries as well," he said. "I knew I wanted to use DeMocker's photos in the main navigation, so I included some sketches that included clickable photo icons used for main navigation. Looking back, a few of the sketches were rather ridiculous. One was of a filing cabinet that readers could click and drag to open. Files with information about the people involved were inside. It wasn't until I sketched this idea out that I realized it made the six people seem like suspects when, in reality, only one was. A subsequent sketch scaled this idea back, and only included folder icons readers could click to open to access more information. In the end, I had made multiple sketches of what the interface would look like, and how the user would navigate."

Of course everyone will develop different approaches to story planning and concept development. So feel free to modify this outline so that you develop a process

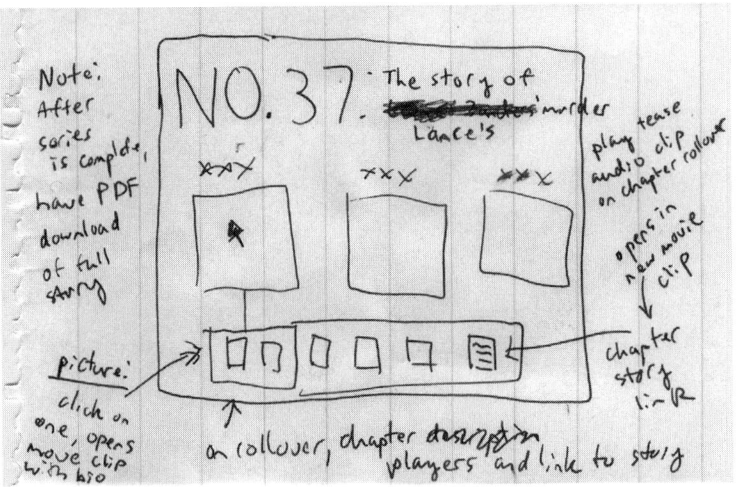

FIGURE 3-5

As the magnitude of the "Homicide 37" story grew, storyboards were adapted to accommodate new approaches to storytelling. This sketch represents one of the last sets of storyboards Smith developed before finalizing the design of the package.

Source: Image courtesy of Ryan Smith.

FIGURES 3-6 & 3-7

The final design of "Homicide 37" was dramatically different from the early storyboards. Smith said it was easy to modify and adapt the overall design because early storyboards helped establish a logical organization of the various parts of the story.

Source: Images courtesy of *The Times-Picayune*.

that works for you and is right for the story at hand. Of course, the tighter your deadlines, the shorter the planning phase will be. Likewise, the larger the story and collaborative team, the more you'll need to consider multiple perspectives. But one thing is certain: Developing a solid multimedia story package without good planning is next to impossible. So never underestimate the importance of developing your story's roadmap before diving into the finer points of reporting, editing and production.

Professional Perspective

Ryan Smith • *Staff Graphic Artist*

New Orleans Times-Picayune

Ryan Smith is an information graphics artist for The Times-Picayune in New Orleans, and has been there since December 2007. His range of work includes maps, charts, diagrams, and interactive presentations. He is a graduate of Ball State University, where he earned his bachelor's degree in Journalism Graphics. In 2008, along with crime reporter Brendan McCarthy and photojournalist Michael DeMocker, he worked on multimedia for a weeklong series about the murder of a 17-year-old male. The series, "Homicide 37," was a Pulitzer Prize runner-up in 2009 and also received two awards from the Louisiana and Mississippi Associated Press Managing Editors. He has been a journalist for 10 years, working as a reporter, designer, information graphics artist, and advertising designer. He is originally from Indianapolis, Indiana.

Homicide 37: Developing a Pulitzer Prize–winning multimedia story
http://www.nola.com/photos/t-p/index.ssf?Homicide37/Homicide37.swf
Reporter: Brendan McCarthy
Videographer: Michael DeMocker
Multimedia developer, designer: Ryan Smith

On July 27, 2008, *The Times-Picayune* began running a series that spanned eight days called "Homicide 37." The series told the story of New Orleans' 37th homicide of the year, which occurred in March. Seventeen-year-old Lance Zarders was murdered near a gutter as he walked down the street. The details of the event were, and are still murky. "Homicide 37" focuses on two police detectives and the harrowing process of tracking down Lance's killer. A suspect was eventually arrested. However, that suspect—a 15-year-old boy—was not indicted and Zarders' killer is still at large.

This series was made possible by terrific reporting and happenstance. When the murder occurred, *Times-Picayne* reporter Brendan McCarthy, happened to be doing an annual ride-along with the New Orleans Police Department (NOPD). McCarthy staid with NOPD Police Detectives Harold Wischan and Anthony Pardo for a few days following the murder as they quickly searched for leads. Videographer Michael DeMocker trailed McCarthy the entire time and was also allowed to collect video footage at Lance's funeral. It was incredibly powerful stuff.

Unfortunately, Lionel and Leatrice Zarders, Lance's parents, were already aware of the heartbreak associated with losing a child. Their eldest son was murdered a few years prior. And as the story unfolded, McCarthy feverishly filled his reporter's notebooks as he shadowed the detectives. The eventual mountain of notebooks would become the foundation for "Homicide 37."

More than a year before the Pulitzer nomination and a few months prior to seeing the first draft of the series, I was finishing my final weeks of college at Ball State University. During that time, a reporter from *The Wall Street Journal* visited campus. He talked about a captivating view of journalism and passionately discussed how stories could better be told in narrative forms that focus on people. It wasn't just about what happened, he said, but about to whom it happened. His enthusiasm was contagious, and this concept clicked with me.

A few months later, I was holding pieces of a story quickly typed out over eight pages that would eventually become a narrative on detective work, a grieving family, and how everyone copes with the sudden loss of a family member or friend. "Homicide 37" wasn't only about New Orleans' 37th homicide. Rather, it was also about the whirlwind of people involved in something that happens nearly every 48 hours in the Crescent City.

In the beginning, the multimedia piece was meant to be supplementary. We planned to package the six main people (Lance, Lionel, Leatrice, Pardo, Wischan, and Fletcher) in the story together in a multimedia component that would include interviews and videos. The user would also be able to view subjects' profiles and video interviews with them. Because the series would run over several days, editors thought this would be an easy way to learn about all of the people involved in the story. And readers who entered the story on days two or three, for example, could get up to speed more quickly. A similar sidebar also ran in the print edition each day.

Early on, the project was not very collaborative. Because we started developing the series long before it would run, most coworkers weren't even aware of it. But, there were a few key collaborators from the start: McCarthy, DeMocker, graphics editor Lynette Johnson, and me. I felt my job would be easy because the visuals were so great. I just had to organize it properly. In the beginning stages of design and development, McCarthy, DeMocker, and Johnson were very hands-off, either only providing me with content, or giving helpful criticism.

However, one important part of the planning process included showing them multiple sketches and storyboards along the way so they had an idea of where I was going with the look, feel, and navigational structure of the piece. In addition to helping conceptualize and visualize ideas, storyboards are also related to efficiency. Putting an idea down on paper, realizing it's not the right way to go, and having to start over takes maybe 15 minutes. By contrast, that same process on a computer can take 45 minutes, or longer. Failing to create storyboards can literally cripple the production process of a multimedia piece, leaving little if any time to correctly develop, program, and conduct usability tests, among other things. In the end, I decided to keep it simple. I let the content carry itself. This allowed time for other things, such as dealing with unforeseen roadblocks.

It wasn't until right before publication that more people become involved when the multimedia piece. And at that point, it suddenly became something entirely different and of larger scope. In fact, two weeks before deadline, an editor suggested we should include the complete story in the online piece. This larger package would include the written pieces, photos, videos, and profiles. The idea was that this presentation method would make it easier for readers to follow the complete series because it would be in all one package. Because early storyboards were developed that organized the original online content effectively, this new approach wasn't a major problem. With early storyboarding, you can be prepared for curveball. Without them, you may be left scrambling.

Old sketches were quickly converted into something that would work for this new approach. Photos from each chapter in the series would provide icons for users to click on to navigate the story. And although the finished product did not look anything like the original sketches, the ideas were all there. And my work was more efficient than it would have been without those original storyboards. I didn't have to stop frequently to figure out how the user would navigate from one page to another, or how each page would be designed because that had been worked out in the beginning.

Although the right amount of planning, storyboarding, and sketching can remove most roadblocks that will arise in a project's future, some unseen issues cannot be prevented. For example, with a deadline looming, more people began to chime in with caption fixes, presentation ideas, and changes to profile information. And in the final two weeks, keeping up with frequent edits was challenging. The edits were necessary, but time-consuming.

The end of the project was a blur. Wrapping up a multimedia piece that changed scope after weeks planning was trying, indeed. However, the entire process was made easier because storyboards helped lay the groundwork for the basic ideas, leaving more time on the backend to deal with the finer nuances of the project.

Always remember that storyboarding is less about sketching out exactly what your presentation will look like and how it will function. Rather, the process is more about removing the silly, incomplete, and unusable ideas from your head. "Homicide 37" would not have gone as smoothly had there not been sketches at the beginning and throughout the process.

Exercises

1. Use the multimedia Maestro form and the information layering questions provided in this chapter to develop multimedia plans for the following stories. If possible, collaborate with two or three others on this exercise. For both stories, augment what is offered here with some research of your own before sitting down to brainstorm multimedia coverage.

   Story No. One: Voyager Enters Solar System's Final Frontier
   Note: Assume you have access to NASA images and file footage, as well as access to Voyager project scientists for interviews.

   NASA's Voyager 1 spacecraft has entered the solar system's final frontier, a vast, turbulent expanse where the Sun's influence ends and the solar wind crashes into the thin gas between stars.

   "Voyager has entered the final lap on its race to the edge of interstellar space, as it begins exploring the solar system's final frontier," said Dr. Edward Stone, Voyager project scientist at the California Institute of Technology in Pasadena. Caltech manages NASA's Jet Propulsion Laboratory in Pasadena, which built and operates Voyager 1 and its twin, Voyager 2.

In November 2003, the Voyager team announced it was seeing events unlike any encountered before in the mission's then 26-year history. The team believed the unusual events indicated Voyager 1 was approaching a strange region of space, likely the beginning of this new frontier called the termination shock region. There was controversy at that time over whether Voyager 1 had it or was just getting close.

"The consensus of the team now is that Voyager 1, at 8.7 billion miles from the Sun, has at last entered the heliosheath, the region beyond the termination shock," said Dr. John Richardson from MIT, Principal Investigator of the Voyager plasma science investigation. The termination shock is where the solar wind, a thin stream of electrically charged gas blowing continuously outward from the Sun, is slowed by pressure from gas between the stars.

Story No. Two: Blackhawks win Stanley Cup for first time in 50 years
Note: Assume you work for a Chicago news agency and have access to playoff file footage and players, coaches, and fans for interviews.

For the first time since 1961, the Chicago Blackhawks have won the Stanley Cup, beating the Philadelphia Flyers in a dramatic overtime. Turning the dream into reality wasn't easy because the Flyers were 9–1 at home and the survivor of four elimination games. "(For) any kid growing up in Canada, this is the dream," Chicago captain Jonathan Toews said.

The Hawks have won four Stanley Cup Championships and fourteen division titles since their founding in 1926. But the Cup had eluded them for nearly 50 years, causing some to wonder whether the team was cursed.

2. After you have developed a multimedia plan for the two stories in exercise one, narrow down your choices and create a final list of story assignments. Then, develop a storyboard for each package. Follow the guidelines provided in this chapter for building effective storyboards. Post your finished Maestro forms and storyboards to your WordPress site.

Notes

1–2. Jonathan Dube. "Online storytelling forms." CyberJournalist.net, July 10, 2000.

3. Buck Ryan, "The Maestro Concept: A New Approach to Writing and Editing for the Newspaper of the Future." A report prepared for the annual convention of the American Society of Newspaper Editors, March 30–April 2, 1993.

4. Interview with Ryan Smith, July 12, 2010.

CHAPTER 4

Navigation & Interactivity

Planning and Testing for the User Experience

For most contemporary audiences, the terms "navigation" and "interactivity" trigger images of computers, digital devices, and the Internet. These terms have, in fact, become common when we talk about interface design, software applications, websites, and other content for digital screens.

But unless you are a designer or programmer, you might be thinking, "What does this have to do with me? I am a content creator (i.e., writer, photographer, videographer, etc.). However, multimedia storytelling makes navigation, interactivity, functionality, and usability everyone's concern. In the digital world, written pieces, photo stories, video packages, and information graphics can all take different forms. And because story structure is so tied to design and presentation, we all have to think about the user experience as we determine how to cover a multimedia story.

Navigational considerations are important on two levels. First, some parts of a story may include interactive features. For example, data visualizations and instructional graphics have strong potential for user interactivity. Likewise, photo galleries often allow users to choose the order in which they will navigate a piece. So, any time a story includes the potential for interactivity, the internal navigation of each interactive piece must be carefully considered.

Second, as the various pieces of a story come together, multimedia developers must pay close attention to the navigational patterns established for the entire story package. In this sense, designing a multimedia story package is much like designing a website. A clear focus must be established, and the story must be logically divided into its nonlinear parts. Only after you have drafted this navigational plan can you begin to decide which parts of the story are best told through video, still photos, audio, informational graphics, or text.

Working Across Platforms

Today, audiences have a number of options regarding the format or device they use to consume content. From print products to mobile devices and from television to desktop computers, the nature of a user's interaction with news and information varies depending on the platform and the format in which a publication is designed.

The web and other digital platforms, such as mobile devices and tablets can bring all storytelling methods—from text to video—together. Add to that immediacy and accessibility that is unmatched by print and television platforms, and you have the makings for ideal multimedia settings. By 2008, the Internet had overtaken most other media as a favored delivery system.[1] In fact from 2004 to 2008, the number of Americans who reported they got "most of their national and international news" online increased 67 percent.[2]

Furthermore, according to Pew's 2011 State of the News Media report, 47 percent of American adults report that they regularly use cell phones and tablets to access local news and information.[3] The report noted, "What they seek out most on mobile platforms is information that is practical and in real time: 42% of mobile device owners report getting weather updates on their phones or tablets; 37% say they get material about restaurants or other local businesses." Likewise, tablet and smartphone apps are rising in popularity at a rapid pace, with 24 percent of mobile news consumers reporting that they regularly use apps to access local news. Although this percentage is relatively low compared to the five in 10 Americans who use mobile devices for local news, evidence suggests this trend will continue. Individuals who consume local news on the go tend to be young, affluent, and highly educated, according to the Pew study. Certainly all of these findings are significant as contemporary news organizations strive to adequately serve these growing audiences.

Of course, user navigational patterns differ widely among desktop computers, smartphones, tablet devices, and print publications such as newspapers and magazines. Smartphones and tablets are mostly characterized by the touch screen experience that allows users to navigate a mobile site, application, or interactive publication using a few simple hand gestures. In fact, a 2011 focus group study found that touch screen tablets have dramatically "changed user expectations and behavior around magazine content."[4] Likewise, the study found that people use digital magazines as "exploration springboards" because they often provide multimedia content that allows them to dig deeper into the topics of interest. Because tablets are intimate, tactile, and personal, they emulate a print reading experience. However, because they are digital and can include hyperlinks, interactivity, and multimedia content, they are similar to an online experience. This merging of print and digital characteristics can make for a rich user experience.

Although tablets and mobile devices are increasing in popularity, most users still access news and information through their desktop browsers. And although print audiences have been steadily declining over the years, newspapers are still in circulation. And as long as they are, it's important to include them in conversations like this one. Thus, some recent research has examined how the print news and online news experiences differ. For example, a 2007 Eyetrack study conducted by the Poynter Institute for Media Studies found that most users read further into stories online than they do in print. Also, online readers generally enter news sites through their home pages that include heavy emphasis on navigational bars, clickable teasers, and menus of up to 60 headlines.[5] It stands to reason that this process encourages scanning. One could argue that print navigation is based on how the eyes scan a page. Conversely, scrolling and clicking dominates online navigation.

In an analysis of the difference between print and web design, web usability guru Jakob Nielsen writes, "Moving around is what the web is all about. When analyzing the 'look-and-feel' of a website, the feel completely dominates the user experience. After all, doing is more memorable and makes a stronger emotional impact than seeing."[6] Additionally, magazine and newspaper readers access content one page at a time, and often encounter whole story packages—complete with photos, graphics, and text—in front of them all at once. However online, individual parts of a story may be accessed through multiple page views. Added together these navigational differences necessitate different approaches to presentation. In fact, Nielsen asserts that anything that considered great print design is likely to be considered poor web

QUICK TIPS

Although this text does not offer a thorough guide on designing for the touch screen experience (that's another book altogether!), there are a few quick tips multimedia designers can keep in mind if faced with the task.

Keep navigation simple. Limit the number of choices you offer users and avoid scroll bars and drop-down menus. Likewise, avoid double click actions and complex gestures to keep users from feeling overwhelmed by a less-than-intuitive navigational scheme.

Design buttons large enough for a finger touch. A finger is larger than a mouse arrow.

Include audio of visual cues so the user knows the touch action was effective. Don't leave users wondering whether the application/publication is adequately responding to their interaction.

Place controls in logical positions. The left-to-right, top-to-bottom navigational patterns common for print publication often carry over into mobile devices like tablets. Thus, buttons and other controls should guide the user through a page or sequence of operations.

Integrate multimedia content with text to create a rich, nonlinear experience. Most early tablet publications have done a great job of combining print and digital navigation concepts in their smartphone and tablet issues. Tablet magazines, for example, are often designed to look very similar to their print counterparts. However, in a digital format, users can simply tap a photo to engage a video presentation without ever leaving the page. Photo slideshows, interactive graphics, and interactive ads can be integrated in the same way, providing users with a digital experience that is heavily influenced by traditional print presentation strategies.

design. He writes, "Print design is based on letting the eyes walk over the information, selectively looking at information objects and using spatial juxtaposition to make page elements enhance and explain each other. Web design functions by letting the hands move the information (by scrolling or clicking); information relationships are expressed temporally as part of an interaction and user movement." The online user experience is almost entirely motivated by feel, while print navigation is largely motivated by look. Because hypertext navigation is such a major component of web design, decisions about the appearance of links, explaining where each link will lead, indication of the user's current location and information architecture are of the utmost importance.

Levels of Interactivity

Degree of interactivity varies depending on the story. Linear photo slideshows, narrative animations, and videos, for example, tend to be relatively passive viewing experiences. Most of the time, interactivity for these types of pieces is limited to the ability to play, pause, rewind, fast-forward, and stop. Photo galleries, instructive graphics, data visualizations, and simulations tend to include more interactivity. They allow users to click through a process, navigate animations and graphics in a nonlinear fashion, and even receive feedback based on their unique input. Likewise, depending on the way it they are presented, traditional text-based pieces can also include interactivity. Text could be structured linearly. Or it could be divided into topical chunks that the user can browse in any order.

How much you allow the user to interact with a story not only affects his or her experience, but it also affects the pacing of the story. The most linear pieces obviously have less interactivity. In fact, the more linear a piece is, the more you should ask yourself if you are really taking full advantage of the digital medium. By making the story nonlinear, you introduce greater levels interactivity. Interactive graphics and galleries, for example, offer users choice and greater control over pace and order. Add discussion boards, online forums, chats, simulations, and games, to name a few, and you take interactivity to the hilt. Although interactivity is not always appropriate or necessary, when it is, it can make a profound difference for the user experience.

Some studies have suggested that a user's age may affect his or her preference for linear or nonlinear presentations. A 2007 study of multimedia storytelling in the digital age found that younger audiences are often more interested in nonlinear packages. The study's author Julie Jones writes, "These users, born into a digital world, look for interactive media and, at least in this study, soundly rejected old-fashioned linear media."[7] This finding is likely a result of the fact that those generations that have grown up in the digital age are more accustomed to engaging with nonlinear content, such as video games, websites, and other hypermedia. If so, stands to reason that as younger audiences get older, this dynamic will become more of a norm among all audiences.

Linear and Nonlinear Story Structures

Multimedia stories are layered and multidimensional. Of course, some stories simply may not lend themselves to a multimedia approach. Other stories, however, have multimedia potential because they are composed of concepts and narrative elements that can be separated into different formats. The most important task is choosing the most compelling and informative story form for a particular segment. Once you have already established that a story has multimedia potential, one of the very next steps is to determine how the story's narrative structure should evolve.

Of course, different rules apply to each story form. For example, individual videos tend to be linear, passive viewing experiences. By contrast, most interactive graphics are often nonlinear and offer multiple modes of entry, as well as choices regarding the navigational path. At the same time, the way these individual pieces are packaged to form a single multimedia story is governed by the story itself.

More often than not, stories that make good use of multimedia presentation strategies are nonlinear. Of course, some of the individual pieces of a nonlinear story are composed in the "beginning-middle-end" narrative structure. However, the larger package of stories should be structured with "this part" and "that part" in mind. By structuring a story in segments that can all be selected at any time during the user experience, you allow users to choose how they will navigate the story.

Giving users this level of control over her experience has both benefits and drawbacks. On the positive side, providing scanning readers with lots of scannable content is obviously a good way to cater to their reading habits. Likewise, providing users with choice is often a good way to keep them engaged. On the negative side, when multimedia packages have many chunks, categories, and layers, it can become easy for users to get lost. In fact, even well designed, carefully planned multimedia packages can be daunting if they get too big. When this disorientation occurs, users often miss key information, lose sense of what they have and haven't seen, and are tempted to move on rather than try to figure it out. So careful thought must be given to creating an intuitive, easy-to-follow navigational structure.

When creating a nonlinear package, you must also consider how the issue of redundancy will be handled. For example, in a linear print story, it is common to refer to individuals by their last names on second reference. Once you have identified a subject by his or her full name, it is no longer necessary to use the first name in subsequent references. However, if you allow your users to navigate the parts of a story in any order, you suddenly make some redundancy—like first names—necessary.

Developing a Navigational Plan

Developing a strategy for how users will navigate your multimedia story package is an important part of the planning process. You may be building a brand new website or micro site, working within an existing site structure, or building a Flash presentation that will be embedded into a site. Regardless, the navigational patterns you establish lay the foundation for how users will engage with the story, how long they will stick with it, and whether they come away feeling satisfied. As noted in the previous chapter, storyboards are important on two levels. They help organize the site and serve as a roadmap for how the site will be designed and structured. Developing a flow chart that represents where each link in your navigation leads can also be helpful. If you are developing a brand new website or micro site for your multimedia package, the home page will serve as the entry into the rest of the story. From the home page, you may have several links or "sub-pages" that will lead the user to various parts of the story. These links could go directly to a page that contains a video piece or interactive graphic, or the links could take you to pages that have a combination of story elements. Your flow chart should look like a hierarchical tree that begins with either a home page for the site or a "splash" page for the multimedia story. Then, each subpage is drawn as a branch from the home page, with subsequent links connecting to those subpages.

The User Experience and Usability Research

Usability refers to how easy interfaces are to use, as well as methods for improving ease-of use during the design process. Usability testing is an essential part of the development of any unique digital interface for a couple key reasons. First,

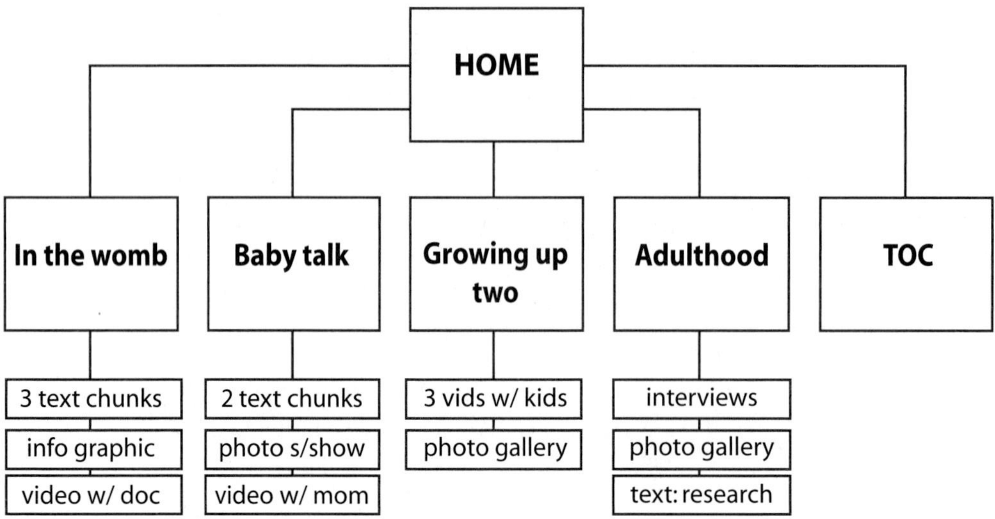

FIGURE 4-1

A flow chart like the one shown here helps organize information developed for a single multimedia package.

usability tests provide developers with important feedback about how effective a site is. And studies have shown that a simple five person usability test is capable of revealing about 80 percent of the problems with a website or multimedia package. By the time your usability test includes 15 subjects, that statistic reaches nearly 100 percent. Thus, usability tests can yield a large payoff for a relatively small investment of time and resources. Second, there generally exists a fairly large gap between developers and users regarding the issue of ease of use. Your choices certainly won't be right all of the time. Thus, usability tests are an important way to determine where you have fallen short of users' expectations or whether your multimedia package is at all confusing or difficult to navigate.

Nielsen elaborates, "If a website is difficult to use, people leave. If the homepage fails to clearly state what a company offers and what users can do on the site, people leave. If users get lost on a website, they leave. If a website's information is hard to read or doesn't answer users' key questions, they leave. Note a pattern here? There's no such thing as a user reading a website manual or otherwise spending much time trying to figure out an interface. There are plenty of other websites available; leaving is the first line of defense when users encounter a difficulty."[8] Of course, this

TIPS FOR BUILDING AND DESIGNING NAVIGATION STRUCTURES

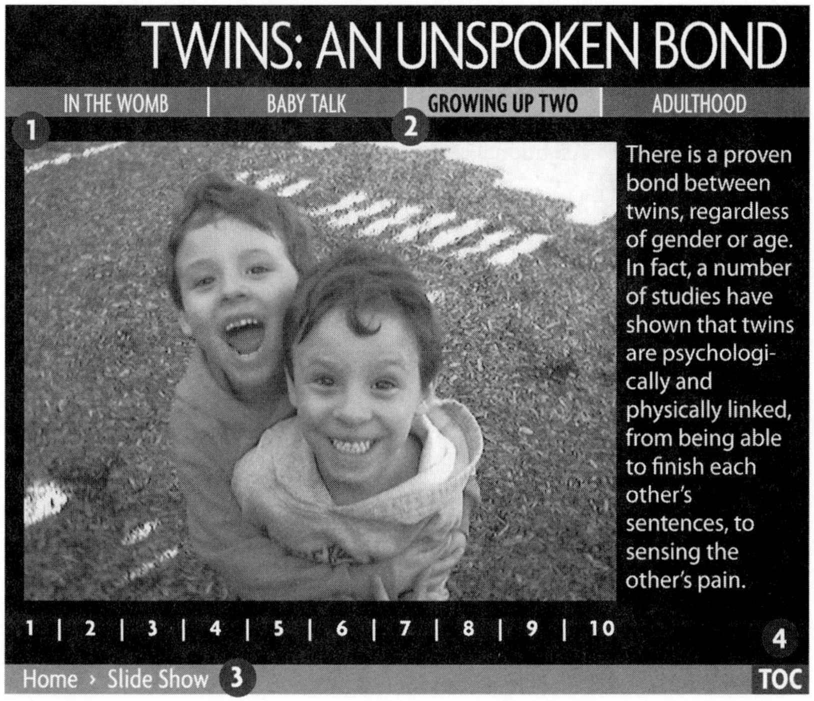

FIGURE 4-2

Regardless of the visual style you establish for your story package, there are a few key techniques for ensuring your story is easy to navigate and intuitive.

1. Use clean, easy-to-read type for navigational elements. Resist the urge to go the "artsy" route with navigation.
2. Build indicators that help users quickly understand where they are in a story.
3. Use breadcrumb navigation trails when your multimedia package has more than two levels of navigation. Navigational trails will help users easily reorient themselves if they get confused or lost within a complex package.
4. Consider including a table of contents link or simple index that shows users at a glance all parts of a story.

continued

TIPS FOR BUILDING AND DESIGNING NAVIGATION STRUCTURES *continued*

Test your navigational structure with a few potential users who have no prior experience with the piece you're creating. If possible, do this more than once during an iterative design process.

Don't remove main navigational buttons that were available before. Changing the navigational options from page to page or leading users to dead-end pages will cause confusion and disorientation.

Don't change the position of links from page to page. Doing so can disorient users and make moving around the site more cumbersome.

Try not to offer more than seven options for primary navigation. Exceeding seven can overwhelm the user.

Avoid the "Easter egg hunt." Make sure that labels and descriptions are clear so that users don't have to guess where a button or link will take them.

Promote easy reading and easy viewing with clean, simple design.

same concept can easily be applied to multimedia packages online. If your story is There are, of course, a number of ways to study usability. The method you choose largely depends on the type of website, multimedia package, or company for which you are testing. Usability tests for journalistic multimedia stories are often limited by a couple of key constraints: (1) tight deadlines; (2) limited resources; and (3) quick access to representative users. So to get the biggest bang for your buck, use basic observational testing that involves five to ten representative users. Observe what they do, where they succeed, and where they run into trouble with the interface. Let them tell you what they think. Test users individually and let them struggle through any areas of the site that seem to give them trouble. By sitting back and watching, you can get a more realistic idea of what the user experience would be like if the package were actually published. Then, if there is time you can revise the design and fix usability flaws before repeating the usability test once more before publication.

From Planning to Production

Too often, journalists dive into a project without first laying the groundwork for healthy, efficient collaboration and solid story planning. However, if these areas of project development are cultivated in the early stages, the story will be stronger and the process will be smoother. Now that we have discovered what makes for a good multimedia story and established the habits that will put us in a position to be strong collaborators and story planners, we can dive into the more practical aspects of multimedia journalism. Unit Two will provide a more thorough look at the most common types of multimedia story forms. Likewise, it will prepare you to make a decision about which area(s) of storytelling you will strive to master, while providing you a baseline proficiency in the others.

Professional Perspective

Laura Ruel • *Assistant professor*

University of North Carolina at Chapel Hill

Laura Ruel is an assistant professor in visual communication and multimedia production in the School of Journalism and Mass Communication at the University of North Carolina at Chapel Hill (UNC). Before coming to UNC, Laura was the inaugural executive director of the Edward W. Estlow International Center for Journalism and New Media at the University of Denver. She worked for more than 15 years as a reporter, editor, designer, and manager at a number of newspapers and magazines, including the South Florida Sun-Sentinel, *the* Omaha World-Herald, *and* Rocky Mountain News *in Denver.*

Nora Paul • *Director of the Institute for New Media Studies*

University of Minnesota

Nora Paul has been the director of the Institute for New Media Studies at the University of Minnesota since 2000. She has also worked at the Poynter Institute, holding programs in news research, computer-assisted reporting, and online news leadership. Before that, she ran the editorial research department at the Miami Herald.

A five-step guide to do-it-yourself website usability testing

Revised and reprinted with permission from *The Online Journalism Review.*

You have put months of work into a special multimedia project. The time-consuming processes of creating and editing text, audio, photos, video, and animated graphics have been arduous but rewarding. You have learned more about Flash programming and debugging than you ever intended. And now that there is an end in sight, you are more than ready to get the package online and out of your life.

Enter the spoiler—the person who utters the words "usability test."

"Why bother?" you think. The site works, you know that. You have been showing it to your newsroom colleagues along the way. You have listened to their feedback. You have made changes you thought were necessary. What more could you learn? What more? How about 80 percent of the problems with the package? How about architecture flaws you never considered? How about the differences between a good design and a great one?

As a *New York Times* Technology's Untanglers article reports, "Sometimes there is a huge disconnect between the people who make a product and the people who use it." Usability testing is vital to uncovering the areas where these disconnects happen. Its value and power should not be underestimated in the e-commerce world or in the multimedia journalism storytelling world.

But it has to be done right with a methodology that works and takes into account a journalist's tight deadlines. Don't worry. All you need to do is:

1. Recruit **FIVE** people.
2. Set aside **FIVE** hours (that is total time, start to finish).
3. Follow the **FIVE** steps described below.

Five People

When done correctly, usability testing with five people can uncover 80 percent of your problems. Moreover, usability testing is the difference between good design and great design. As we have said in the print world for years, if the presentation is aesthetically pleasing, but the user can't find the information, then the design is useless. This concept is even more important in the world of web design where clicking to a new site is even easier than finding a new magazine or newspaper.

What exactly will this accomplish? That is up to you. A properly executed usability test of your multimedia package or website can reveal answers to whatever you design the test to ask. However, in most cases it will uncover three key things:

Areas of confusing navigation. There is no doubt that as the project designer, you know how your site navigation functions. You know that the "Part Two" menu option brings the user to a particular story or audio slide show. But does the new user know this? It is important to realize that about an hour into designing your project, you may have lost all perspective on how the interface appears to others. This also holds true for your colleagues who have been looking at the project as you have been creating it. You all have learned your navigation; you have conditioned yourselves to go where you want. But for others it may not be so easy and intuitive. You need to test and see.

Users' intuitive viewing sequences. Again, this is an area that designers tend to have in mind and follow as they work on or show the site to others in the newsroom. A usability test can reveal if others will follow what you intend.

Roadblocks in the flow or delivery of information. Not everyone in your target audience may know that the e-mail for the reporter is at the end of the text or that the panoramic photograph moves when the arrows on either side are clicked. What seems normal and natural to the creator is not always so with the user.

Five Hours

Although it may seem daunting, think about the hours you have already put into the project. If simple changes you make can help the user actually understand the project better or more completely, isn't it worth it?

The testing method outlined here is a combination of suggestions from technology experts, journalists and usability professionals and is created especially for the busy multimedia journalist. It not only focuses on issues specific to the types of site or package designs we do, but it also takes into account newsroom deadlines. So from start to finish it should take one person about five hours to get solid usability data about your package. Here is the breakdown:

- Thirty minutes to meet with project team and determine key questions
- Thirty minutes to add your specifics to the basic pre- and postsurveys provided
- Thirty minutes to recruit test subjects
- Approximately two-and-a-half hours to test five people for 20 minutes to a half hour each
- Thirty minutes to analyze data
- Thirty minutes to summarize the results and create a task list

This testing is leaner and more streamlined than an expensive one designed by a usability firm, but it has been put to the test by my design students on award-winning multimedia news packages as well as journalistic websites for the past three years and has delivered valuable data each and every time.

Five Steps

Step #1 • Determine Tasks for to Test

Call a meeting of the project team and:

Review. Remind everyone of your target audience and site goals.

BEFORE YOU START

Check your ego at the door and separate yourself from your creation. If you don't think you can do this, have someone else on your team handle the testing. No doubt, you have an emotional attachment to this project. That is only natural. But objectivity is necessary to get test results that will make your project even better. Be sure you want the real answers.

Realize the limitations of the information you are gathering. Usability tests can reveal valuable information about a particular project, but the results should not be misconstrued as pertinent to all web presentations. Here is where that number five (in terms of test subjects) is too small and your test design is too specific. The test results are helpful for the project you are testing. When you do another project, you will need to do another test.

Know that it is okay to ask for feedback. As journalists we have been trained to NOT go back to sources and show them stories beforehand. Remember that this is different. We are asking an uninvolved group (not the story sources) to do what they normally would do with a web package. Then we are taking that information and improving the site. It essentially is another step in the information gathering process.

Choose tasks. Determine at least ten (but no more than 15) tasks that you a user should be able to successfully execute to get the most out of the package. Remember, you cannot analyze the entire presentation. Carefully select tasks based on what actual users of the site would do. These could include items such as finding and playing an interactive game you created, watching the audio slide show through completion, or navigating the site in a specific, preferred order.

Step #2 • Develop Your Experimental Design

Although there are multiple ways to design a usability test, we are providing you with a basic design that has been proven to work on multimedia news packages. As you become more experienced in testing you may want to deviate from this outline, but we strongly suggest you follow it exactly your first few times.

Welcome, complete informed consent and preexperiment questions. It is important you do your best to put users at ease by thanking them, offering them a cup of coffee, or just chatting with them for a few minutes. Remind them that it is the multimedia package that is being tested, not them. You then will want users to read and sign an informed consent—where the experiment is explained for the test subjects. This is necessary to ethically complete this inquiry.

Finally, you will want to have them complete the preexperiment questions that you will develop in Step 3. *Time: five minutes*

Free observation time. This is a time when users explore the site with no interaction from the tester. You simply direct the user to the site and step back. The only instruction should be for users to, "Explore the site for as long as they would like." Here is where you can either videotape their behavior or take copious notes. You want to know what users do when just directed to "explore." Allot 10 minutes total, but if the user tells you he or she is done beforehand, move along. If they are not done at the 10-minute mark, make note of that and tell users it is time to move on. *Time: five to 10 minutes*

Assigned tasks. Using the list you created in the previous step, ask users to execute your preferred tasks. Word the tasks so that you are placing users in a natural scenario. For example, rather than stating, "Find the e-mail for the reporter," say something like, "You have unanswered questions after viewing this presentation and would like to contact the reporter. How would you go about doing that?" Have tasks ordered and prioritized, skipping over any that were completed during the free observation time. Depending on the user and the task you may or may not want the user to "think aloud" or describe their thought processes to you while completing the tasks. At this point in your testing, either silent observation or think aloud protocols are fine approaches. Do whatever feels most comfortable to you. *Time: five to 10 minutes*

Post experiment questionnaire and discussion. There are two parts to this stage in the process. First, have users fill out the questionnaire you will develop in Step 3. Once complete, it is time for open-ended questions that are answered in a conversation with you.

Step #3 • Develop Questions

There are four printed forms you will want to have ready for each test participant:

Informed consent. This is necessary for ethical completion of the study.

Preexperiment questions. The purpose here is to give some context to the results and help you understand the web practices of your test subjects. As the sample form suggests, you want to have users quantify their responses and word questions so that the subjects' personal interpretation of the answers is minimal. For example, instead of asking a user to describe their web usage on a scale of one to 10, with one being none and 10 being heavy, it would be better to ask them to quantify the amount of time they spend online and provide choices such as 0–2 hours/day, 3–5 hours/day, and so on. You also may want to ask questions that gauge the participants' interest in the subject of the presentation you are testing, or the website your work for. Make this a written questionnaire.

Postexperiment questions. You will want to administer a written questionnaire once the tasks are completed. This questionnaire should gather subjective data, and should contain quantifiable inquiries, asking users to rank the success of certain aspects of the site.

Interview questions. Finally, plan a few open-format interview questions to ask each participant at the end of the session. These should elicit more overall, qualitative impressions of the website. You also may want to ask participants what they recall about how the site functions. If they clearly recall the structure, you can bask in the glory of your success. If not, you may want to consider where clearer labeling or directions may help. Users should not write these responses. You should allow them to speak freely and take notes.

Step #4 • Gather Data

The order of data gathering is outlined in Step 2 above. Here are items to consider before you begin with the first test subject.

Test sooner rather than later. No multimedia designer wants to make changes to something they believe is in its final form. Schedule your usability test in the beta stage of development—not quite finalized, but final enough so someone can navigate the site.

Do not test your newsroom colleagues. Anyone already familiar with the project does not represent your typical user. In an ideal world, test subjects are recruited through a marketing research firm, but—for the busy newsroom journalist—this probably isn't possible. So go to other departments. See if someone in ad sales, circulation or marketing (who doesn't know about the project) can spare a half hour to be tested. See if a friend or relative of a colleague can come in. Bottom line, try to make your test subjects as close to typical users as possible.

Test everyone on the same computer, in the same location. This will standardize the results and not allow people's bookmarks or other preset browsing options interfere with results.

Know what you are looking for during the free observation period. Carefully observe each session and take notes about the participants' interactions with the site. Which tasks were performed successfully? How long did they take? Did participants make errors? What problems occurred? Did the participants have a conceptual model of the site? Was it correct? It can be helpful to have a checklist for yourself during this time, so you observe the same behaviors with each participant.

Pay close attention to the steps users take to complete tasks. You want to discern the path that is clear and most natural for users when completing tasks. Ideally they all will complete tasks in fairly predicable ways. But if they do not, you can learn something by the "mistakes" they make. How do they recover? What page of the site do they go back to as a "home base" or starting point? Again, you may want to have your own checklist to refer to here.

Try to be as unobtrusive as possible. We know, you feel like an elephant in the room when observing someone viewing a website. But awareness of your body language and your non-verbal reactions to the users' behaviors can make a huge difference in terms of their comfort. It will take them some time to get used to your presence, but once they do, they will become more relaxed and their behaviors will be more realistic and natural.

Step #5 • Analyze Data and Make a List of Potential Improvements

Now the fun starts—seeing what you have learned. Again, take things step-by-step:

Average all quantifiable responses. Break down the number of men versus women, the average age of participants, and so on. Be sure the demographics match your target audience. You also will want to average the answers to all questions that involve rankings. Place all this data on one sheet and make notes of responses that fall to either extreme.

Look at the free observation notes in light of the quantifiable data. If users ranked navigational controls as weak, what behaviors during the free observation period support this? Can you find similar behaviors that would contribute to this ranking? Were there any non-verbal cues that indicated their frustration at during a certain process? Sighing? Trying to click off the site? Gather as much supporting data for each ranking.

Look at the success/failure to complete usability tasks in light of the quantifiable data. Again, go back and see what common behaviors were exhibited by the users when asked to complete certain tasks. Did they become confused at the same points? Did they all sail through certain tasks? You will discover that their site rankings will correlate with their experiences completing tasks.

Make a list of the top three things that should not change and the top three things that should. You are on a deadline, we realize that. So, be sure to make note of what is working and why. Write down the top three things you did well based on this usability test. Then make a list of three manageable changes to make.

Look at the user suggestions for improvement in light of the changes you need to make. Your users are not designers or interface experts, but their gut reactions can help you determine where to put your professional energies. See what they said they want and find a design solution for it. Again, keep things manageable. You are not going to fix everything, but you are going to tackle the top three you listed in the step above. Do everything you can to address the problem areas, and—if possible—check in with the users and show them the solution.

Bottom Line

Usability testing is a skill that—just like design and programming—you improve the more you practice it. Once you have done this a few times you will find you can use it on the fly when you get into those disagreements about interface design issues within your team.

Exercises

1. Visit www.oup.com/us/palilonis and find the resources/exercises tab. Select navigation & interactivity resources from the drop down menu. There you will find a multimedia presentation. Thoroughly examine the presentation and make a sketch the navigational structure. Then write a one- to two-page report that answers the following questions: Can you find any dead ends in the navigation structures? If so, where are they located? How would you fix any flaws you find with the navigational structure developed for this package? Post your finished report to your WordPress site.
2. Visit www.oup.com/us/palilonis and find the resources/exercises tab. Select navigation & interactivity resources from the drop down menu. There you will find a multimedia presentation. Using the techniques outlined by Nora Paul and Laura Ruel in the "Professional Perspective" section of this chapter, conduct a usability test with five users. Then, write up a report that analyzes the data and assesses potential

improvements that can be made to the multimedia presentation. Post your finished report to your WordPress site.

Notes

1. David Cutts, "Bargain Interactivity," *Broadcast Engineering*, 2007.
2. Project for Excellence in Journalism, "The State of the News Media 2008: An Annual Report on American Journalism." Pew Research Center.
3. Project for Excellence in Journalism, "The State of the News Media 2011: An Annual Report on American Journalism." Pew Research Center.
4. "Bonnier Research Reveals Tablets Radically Alter Magazine Expectations and Behaviors," Bonnier News Bytes, March 22, 2011.
5. Pegie Stark Adam, Sara Quinn, and Rick Edmonds, *Eyetracking the News: A Study of Print and Online Reading*. Poynter Institute for Media Studies, 2007.
6. Jakob Nielsen, "Differences between Print Design and Web Design," useit.com, January 24, 1999.
7. Julie Jones, "Video Storytelling in the Digital Age," newslab.org.
8. Jakob Nielsen, "Differences between Print Design and Web Design," useit.com, January 24, 1999.

UNIT 2

SPEAKING THE LANGUAGE

JOURNALISTS FIRST BEGAN THINKING ABOUT HOW TO HARNESS THE RICH multimedia potential of the web in the mid-1990s. At first, news websites generally mirrored what appeared in their print or broadcast counterparts. And there are still a lot of news outlets that merely push the same content from one platform to another. However, the best multimedia organizations go a step further by providing a mix of written pieces, photo presentations, video, audio, and interactive information graphics.

In this sense, the emergence of multimedia journalism has also come with a number of significant changes in the way journalists do their jobs. Although most journalists still specialize in one form of storytelling, a broad understanding of all story forms is both valuable and expected in the multimedia environment.

This new emphasis on the well-rounded multimedia journalist is, perhaps, one of the most exciting facets of contemporary journalism. You will be encouraged to excel at one or two forms of storytelling, but you will not be relegated to a single medium. And the best multimedia journalists will conceptualize and build stories in various formats either single-handedly or through close collaboration with teammates whose skill sets complement one another. As a multimedia journalist, you will be encouraged and empowered to develop powerful stories through innovative, engaging digital presentations.

Thus, Unit Two focuses on each of the most common multimedia story forms—text, photos, audio, video, and information graphics—and offers basic tips that will help multimedia journalists excel. Of course, if you plan to become an ace writer, you'll surely move on from this text to more in-depth and complex writing techniques. Likewise, photographers and graphics reporters will go on to study visual communications in greater detail. In this sense, the chapters that follow do not offer exhaustive instruction related to any single story form.

Rather, this unit provides the multimedia journalist with a foundation for beginning a long journey to honing multiple storytelling skills. Part of this journey includes not only building skills but also understanding a number of related concepts as well. Each chapter will explore technical and journalistic considerations for each form, as well as provide examples both in print and on the website that accompanies this book.

CHAPTER 5

Groundwork

Information Architecture in the Digital World

A journalist is, in many ways, an information architect. Journalists must regularly wade through complex information and find ways to make it easy to understand and accessible to mass audiences. Journalists tell stories that reflect the state of humanity. They help people connect with a story's subjects. And through this work, journalists strive to provide audiences with a greater sense of understanding and awareness of the world around them. These are important and weighty responsibilities.

Living up to these responsibilities has never been easy. The information architect must identify how to best serve today's audiences in a fast-changing media landscape. Technology will change. New devices will emerge. And in a multimedia world, the ways we do our jobs will certainly evolve. However, there are a few concepts that serve as a foundation for good journalism. And although we will continue to refine approaches to journalistic storytelling, these foundations will, for the most part, remain solid.

Regardless of which form of storytelling you gravitate toward—writing, photography, videography, audio, or information graphics—there are a few skills that apply to all journalistic efforts. So, before we dive into individual story forms, this chapter will explore concepts related to all forms of storytelling. We address how solid research and good interviews establish the basis for your narrative. We examine the importance of focusing your story. And we briefly discuss some ethical considerations that are particularly salient in the digital world. In all, these skills will help lay the groundwork for any good story.

Journalistic Research

The world is full of sources, and well-rounded stories make use of more than one. With the Internet at our fingertips, journalists have more access to many different types of resources than ever before. At the same time, there is a wealth of information out there, and not all of it is good. It is the journalist's responsibility to vet all sources for credibility, consult a variety of sources to ensure all sides of a story are told, and avoid sources that distort the truth or provide fraudulent information. Put simply: Your job is to conduct solid research so the audience doesn't have to.

Thus, skilled multimedia journalists regularly consult a variety of sources, including books, legal documents, annual reports, websites, newspapers, magazines, and experts, to name a few. And the more you cover a particular topic, the larger your list of potential sources will become. When starting a new project, it helps to consult a few standard categories for sources to ensure you have exhausted all of your options. Four common categories exist for journalists: *informal* sources, *institutional* sources, *scholarly* sources, and *journalistic* sources.

Informal sources include the observations a journalist makes during the research and reporting process. In other words, pay attention to your surroundings. For example, what are the relevant observations you can make about your subjects or the story's environment? Are there factors related to workplaces, neighborhoods, or other communities that affect your story or lead to story ideas? In both breaking news situations *and* advance project-oriented stories, informal sources and strong news instincts will go a long way toward informing your story.

Institutional sources are represented by social or cultural organizations with particular special interests. For example, institutional sources include political camps, community or government leaders, and professional organizations, to name a few. Obviously there are a number of reasons to consult these types of sources, not the least of which is that news stories are often driven by the actions of institutional sources. For example, in the public sector, sources like the Bureau of Labor Statistics (http://www.bls.gov) provide a plethora of information about the state of the U.S. economy, such as inflation and consumer spending, national wages, earnings and benefits indexes, productivity, safety and health in the workplace, import and export indexes, demographic characteristics of the American labor force, and employment and unemployment figures.

Similarly, the U.S. Geological Survey (http://www.usgs.gov) acts as a federal source for information about natural and living resources, natural hazards, and the environment. Likewise, in the private sector, businesses, industry associations, religious organizations, and others can provide information that is relevant to multimedia stories.

Scholarly sources exist to expand the body of knowledge for certain topics through research. Scholarly institutions like universities or medical and scientific research centers are often credible sources of information about cultural and scientific phenomena, social science research, and advances in the medical field. There are a number of electronic indexes and databases through which journalists can access the findings of such reports, including Academic Search Premier or Lexis-Nexis.

Journalistic sources, such as newspapers, magazines, trade publications, television, and news and information websites, can also be good sources for new stories. Consulting other media outlets as references for your stories is useful for two reasons. First, it helps ensure that you know what's already been covered on a particular topic. Second, if your goal is to expand on previous coverage, it may help you gain a better understanding of the story at hand.

Ultimately, the best journalistic stories often employ multiple sources and a variety of source types. In other words, don't settle for one type of source. A variety of sources and more important, multiple sources, add credibility to your story and help ensure your story is as thorough as it can be.

Of course, it's important to understand what *isn't* a good source for a news story.

Beware of socially constructed sources, like wikis. Although these can often provide a great start for your research, they shouldn't be cited as primary sources. Because anyone can edit them, they often contain errors. It's better to verify what you have learned with official primary sources.

Avoid citing lesser-known blogs. Remember, anyone can register for a Wordpress site and begin rattling off opinions. But a good journalist takes the time to separate the experts from the uninformed to ensure information is accurate and credible.

Avoid convenient sources like friends, neighbors or family. Not only is this lazy, but it can also lead to biased, one-sided stories. Your job is to find the *best* sources for a story, not the *easiest* sources.

Be able to spot pitfalls in potential sources. For example, informal sources can sometimes be tainted by individual opinions or misconceptions. Information from institutional sources can be biased by specific political or cultural agendas, causing them to be one-sided or self-serving. Research reported by scholarly sources may need to be simplified for a general audience. And, while other journalistic sources can help get you started, your job is to add to what's already been done, not replicate it.

Finally, there are also a few things you can consider when attempting to judge the reliability of a source. If your source is a person, consider their job title or relationship to the story. You may also consider whether there are obvious reasons for bias with a particular source. For example, a tobacco executive may have ulterior motives when it comes to a story about someone who died of lung cancer brought on from inhaling second-hand smoke. If possible, try to find multiple sources that can support the same information with evidence and/or authority.

Narrowing It Down

Whether your sources come from print materials, websites, or individual experts, your primary goal is to draw on the most up-to-date, accurate, and credible information. For example, there are no less than four million websites about or that mention breast cancer. And, there are at least just as many books, periodicals, and other publications that address the topic, as well as thousands of experts in the United States alone. So, how do you find the most reliable sources? Although there may be no one good answer to that question, there are some things you can keep in mind when conducting your search.

Print sources. Books, periodicals, published reports, and other types of printed publications are often great sources of information because you can generally rest assured that they were subject to review. The same is true of scholastic journals, encyclopedias, and other journalistic reports. However, just because something is printed, doesn't make it true or accurate. So it's always best to verify your sources before taking them as fact. For example, you can: (1) do a background check on the author(s) to make sure they are reputable sources on the relative topic; (2) scrutinize data and double check it against multiple sources to determine whether there is any bias present; (3) make sure the date of publication is as recent as possible or that an earlier publication date won't affect accuracy.

Electronic sources. Ever wonder how anyone survived without the Internet? With search engines like Google and Yahoo!, you can simply type in the word or topic you are interested in, and, voila, hundreds of potential sources at your fingertips. However, remember to approach web sources with care. After all, just about anyone can purchase the rights to a URL and then publish just about anything he or she wants. Thus, certain types of sites are often safer than others. Sites used by the U.S. government (.gov), nonprofit organizations (.org), and educational institutions (.edu), for example, are generally considered more reputable than sites administered to commercial organizations or individuals (.com). However, while the sponsoring organizations of these sites may carry more clout than the average person, it's still important to remember that even government or education sites may contain biased or self-serving statements. So, when conducting research using the web, make sure you determine the name of the individual, organization or group responsible for the site's publication so you can check up on them and find out if they are reputable. Also make sure the site includes a revision date to determine whether the information is up-to-date. And find multiple sources that corroborate your primary source to ensure the information found there is accurate.

Human sources. Hopefully, you're always looking for strong human sources for your stories. After all, the most engaging stories are often those that connect subjects with audiences. Human sources may include experts, victims (as well as their friends and family), officials, community members, or family members, to name a few. As you begin making a list of potential sources, consider all aspects of a story and try to cover all of those bases with human subjects. For example, a story about a courageous woman who won a hard-fought battle with breast cancer may include doctors, immediate family members, friends, coworkers, and others affected by the disease. Just remember to maintain your primary focus as you consult these sources for input.

Finding Your Focus

Good journalists understand the difference between a topic and a story. To continue the example offered earlier, breast cancer is a topic. And hearing someone pitch a "story about breast cancer" is like nails on a blackboard. Topics are nothing more than general categories, while stories are precisely focused. Thus, your breast cancer survivor may provide fodder for a great story. And even after the angle of a story has been established, it is important to keep coming back to the concept of focus. For example, you cannot show the audience every detail of this woman's life. If you do, you risk losing some of the more poignant aspects of her struggles. At the same time, if you only focus on the parts of her life directly affected by cancer, you risk leaving out information that helps the audience really get to know her. So, the editing process is a very complex balancing act between finding a tight angle and telling a full story.

Interviewing

Interviewing is truly an art form. And each of your subjects will likely have different personalities and different thresholds for opening up to a reporter. Some will open up with little persuasion, eager to tell their stories openly and honestly. But others will not necessarily be good at speaking extemporaneously about a subject, offering all of the most important details without prompting, or able to open up easily when touchy or controversial subjects are on the table. The interviewer should, therefore, assess each interview scenario individually, adapt to each subject's personality, and put interviewees at ease so that they feel comfortable during the process. Following are a few more tips that any reporter should consider for every interview.

Visit the multimedia examples section of www.oup.com/us/palilonis and select audio from the drop down menu to listen to a sample interview.

Be prepared. The best questions are informed questions. Of course, the degree to which you can prepare yourself for an interview depends on a lot of things, not the least of which is how much lead time you have. If you are on the scene of a breaking news story and collecting audio to accompany a photo slideshow, you may only have a few minutes to think about the questions you will ask a random person on the street who has been caught in the story. In that case, do your best to quickly assess your surroundings, how the person fits into the story, and what you want to ask him or her. That is about the best you can do in any on-the-spot coverage situation. However, if you have some time before an interview, engage in prereporting and research your subject and his or her role in the story before you meet. For example, if a subject's alma mater is relevant to a story, rather than ask her what university she attended, find out beforehand. Then, if you want her to talk about that experience, phrase the question like this, "So, I understand you went to Harvard. How well did you know John Doe when you were students there?" This not only shows the subject that you have done your homework, but it saves valuable time by skipping questions you can obtain answers to on your own.

Practice your interview in front of a mirror or with a friend. As silly as this may seem, rehearsing beforehand should help you feel more at ease during the actual interview, especially if you will be on camera. It gives you a chance to refine your questions and hear how they sound as you ask them. In addition to rehearsing what you will say, you can also practice how you will say it. Speak with confidence. Be friendly and calm. And avoid aggressive, accusatory questioning. Opt instead for a sense of curiosity. This will make even the toughest interviews run more smoothly.

Make small talk before the official interview begins. This will help make your subject feel more comfortable. Sometimes, just chatting as you set up your equipment is enough to ease into a more formal interview. And although you might want to share with your subjects your expectations for the interview, don't talk much about the interview topic during this early conversation. This may overwhelm your subject and make her feel like she is repeating herself later on.

Keep it conversational. One quick way to make a subject feel uncomfortable is to conduct the interview more like an inquisition than a conversation. Do not grill her with one difficult question after another. Instead, vary the intensity of questions, ask her to expand on key thoughts, and give her time to process what she wants to say. An interview is really nothing more than a conversation between two people. It is acceptable to react to what your subject is saying with follow up questions or a nod of the head. However, be careful! If the conversation becomes too much like a laid back chat with a friend, you risk ruining the audio with unnecessary interjections and unwanted background noise.

Prepare a basic outline before the interview, but avoid reading questions from a page. It is tough to have a natural conversation when you are paying more attention to the paper on your lap than the person with whom you are talking. It can also be distracting for you and your subject if you juggle papers while you are talking. So, try to limit your notes to a single page comprised of a few words or phrases that will help you remember what you want to cover in the interview.

Listen. Paying attention to your interviewee is important for a number of reasons. First, it is not difficult to tell when someone is not listening to you. If you do not appear to be engaged and interested, your subject will likely feel uncomfortable and even irritated. Second, a good interviewer is constantly thinking on his feet and conceiving follow-up and clarifying questions based on what the subject is saying. You should also pay attention to other details surrounding the interview. If the location of the interview is relevant to the story, survey the room for significant details. Also, always be aware that one interviewee could lead you to additional sources. For example, if your interview takes place in an office complex, ask the interviewee to introduce you to others in the building who may be able to shed light on the story.

Although every interview and interviewee will be different, there are some common scenarios that can throw a wrench into the interview process. So, here are some tips to help you best handle a few sticky situations.

Begin with a few softball questions rather than diving right into the tough questions on a touchy subject. For example, if you are trying to get the interviewee to turn in her boss for unlawful business practices, start by asking basic questions about her job responsibilities, how long she has been working for the company, and so on. This way, you can make her comfortable before asking tougher questions.

If you ask a question that the interviewee is clearly uncomfortable with, back off and try something else. But don't forget to come back to your original question later. The second time you ask, try rephrasing it so that you subject doesn't feel badgered.

If you find your questions are beginning to agitate your subject to the point that he may try to end the interview, quickly find a way to keep the interview going. Backing off and asking easier, less threatening questions can also be used in this situation. If the subject still resists, you might try gently telling him that you will continue to look for answers to these questions regardless of whether he cooperates.

If you get a "no comment response," point out to your subject that this response doesn't mean you won't include their response to that question. In fact, you intend to report that the subject "declined to comment." Thus, when faced with that answer, you could say something like, "I would hate to have to tell the audience that you declined to comment. Readers/viewers/listeners may feel forced to draw their own conclusions as opposed to learning the facts from a reliable source like yourself." If this doesn't work, there may come a time during the interview that you have to stand firm. For example, you might say, "I am going to report this story with or without your input. You can either cooperate and answer my questions or I can report that you had 'no comment,' which will likely result in the audience thinking you have something to hide."

If your subject won't go on the record, be understanding. Most of the time, when sources are reluctant to go on the record, it is because they are fearful of the repercussions. Acknowledging that you understand why they are concerned may help keep the conversation alive. Then you might explain how valuable your subject's input is and assure her that you will continue to seek other sources that will back her up.

QUICK TIPS

Recording Your Interview

Listen carefully. When asking questions, pay attention to details in subjects' answers. Listening may lead you to additional photo opportunities and follow-up questions that will cultivate a richer story. Likewise, observe the sounds of the natural surroundings. These environmental details can add authenticity and depth to the final sound.

Watch closely. Take the camera away from your face from time to time and take in the scene. Observe the visual mannerisms of your subject. Does she talk with her hands? Does he furrow his brow when he talks about his childhood? These mannerisms may help round out your visual narrative.

Conduct preinterviews. If you plan to let your subjects tell their own stories, it might be necessary to talk to them a couple of times off mic before conducting the final interview. Consider this a part of the research process to collect important information and ascertain whether your subject will provide compelling audio. At the start of the interview, avoid diving right in to the hard-hitting or emotional questions. Begin with a few easy questions to get the conversation going. Wait until your subject seems to have forgotten that the recorder is present before you start in with more substantive questions.

When you have no more questions of your subject, ask whether there is anything he or she would like to add. At the end of the interview, be sure to thank your subject for his or her time and ask if you can contact the subject in the future if any additional questions arise.

Developing a Narrative Arc

The narrative arc concept is present in many forms of storytelling, from cinema to literature. It is a dramatic progression that is composed of a beginning, middle, and end. In the beginning, significance and focus are established. Then, as facts unfold and the story comes to light, the audience begins to understand why it should care about the story and its characters. In the end, conflict is resolved or answers are given that help lend closure to the storyline. These techniques are commonly used in fictional storytelling, but are equally valuable to journalistic stories. And regardless of whether your are developing a piece that will stand alone or accompany another story form, all good journalistic stories contain a narrative arc.

You should not, however, force or otherwise fabricate a narrative arc. The journalist's job is to identify the most salient aspects of a story and allow them to naturally unfold. Thus, establishing a narrative arc has as much to do with how you conduct your interviews, whom you talk to, and how well you collect the facts as it does with what you do in the editing room. And the ways in which you develop your narrative arc may vary, depending on the story structure. For example, audio is an intimate exchange between speaker and listener and has a remarkable ability to create a bond between the two. In fact, researchers have found that audio creates a greater sense of connection between journalist and audience than other storytelling forms. Likewise, audio can make good photos, video, or information graphics feel more real and tangible. Thus, a photo/audio slideshow will establish a narrative arc by building momentum through both the spoken word and the images that accompany it. By contrast, an interactive graphic may be more segmented as users navigate different parts of it in a nonlinear fashion. While the graphic may contain a beginning, middle, and end and certain parts may be more significant than others, the narrative arc will likely have a lot to do with how the users chooses to navigate. Thus the multimedia journalist capitalizes on these differences by considering how each piece is different and how format affects storytelling.

QUICK TIPS

Establish a clear beginning, middle and end to your story. Even the most straightforward news stories can lead the audience through fluid narrative. In the beginning, make it clear why the audience should care. Likewise, consider setting the scene to provide a foundation for the story to come. In the middle, thoroughly explain the key issues. Help the audience understand the story's impact. And in the end, come to a resolution by explaining what's next or summarizing the outcome.

Let the audience get to know your subjects. Whether you're developing a written piece, a photo/audio presentation or a video, you have very little time to make your audience feel "connected" to your story. One way to do so is to define your subject(s) early on. If there's a person or place at the center of your story, provide the audience with rich description that is relevant to the story at hand, such as character traits or physical appearances. You may do this through narration. Or if you're developing an audio or video presentation, you may let the subject so the explaining.

Establish a "plot line" for your story. Common in fictional writing, the plot line pulls the audience through a clear, logical path. This technique is useful in journalistic writing as well. It helps organize information and establish a clear beginning, middle and end to your story. Your plot line may be chronological or topical, or it may be driven by a particular event or chain of events. Regardless, it's important that you develop an outline for your story that maintains a clear narrative flow.

Include logical transitions between key facts. Your story must logically flow from one topic to the next. Avoid jumping from one topic to another without illustrating connections. Likewise, avoid incomplete thoughts and unclear associations among people, places and key facts.

Digital Journalism Ethics and Law

Journalism rests on the foundation of a few key principles: obligation to the truth, loyalty to citizens, discipline for verification, and responsibility to present fair and balanced coverage. And perhaps the most important rule for any journalist is never to alter the meaning of information provided by your sources. Unfortunately, digital technology makes it easier for us to mislead audiences and distort the truth. And although the journalistic principles offered here apply to all story forms, their applications are sometimes slightly different, depending on the circumstances for the individual story at hand. Regarding audio storytelling, the Radio Television and Digital News Association (RTDNA) Code of Ethics and Professional Conduct statements assert two key considerations. They write, "Professional electronic journalists should not manipulate images or sounds in any way that is misleading." The Code also states that journalists should not "present images or sounds that are reenacted without informing the public." It is likely safe to assert that organizations such as Online News Association, Society for Professional Journalists, National Press Photographers Association, and the Society for News Design (among others) all hold similar values regarding news in the digital arena. However, as multimedia storytelling has emerged in mainstream media, we have come to recognize that it is, in many ways, very different from traditional methods. Naturally, then, the question of whether new ethical considerations have emerged as a result of the increasing emphasis on multimedia becomes particularly salient. In this context, ethics associated with presenting content online is of particular interest.

From the start, critics have warned that the Internet has the potential to threaten journalistic credibility for established news organizations. Some describe the web as an anonymous global network where everyone is both producer and consumer of content. Thus, it is often difficult to verify the credibility of sources online. A news story can be distributed worldwide in a few seconds, and anyone can post information under the guise of news. Web news has also been characterized as a "hasty" endeavor with rapid-fire deadlines. And some would argue that journalists working online constantly struggle to maintain credibility.

There are a few key ethical and legal concepts that all journalists should understand, from libel, to copyright. And when your work crosses from print to digital platforms, a few new issues arise.

Libel is defined as "a published false statement that is damaging to a person's reputation. Web content is considered published, so anything you or the news organization you work for publishes online is subject to lawsuits claiming libel. Two additional concerns confront online publications where libel is concerned: liability and forum shopping. Specifically, there has been some debate regarding whether an Internet Service Provider (ISP) can be held libel for statements made on its discussion board. Legal precedents established in a few court cases involving this question have established that if an ISP makes no attempt to edit or monitor comments made on their site, they cannot be held responsible for libelous statements made by users. However, sites that openly exercise editorial control over their sites should be held responsible. Most news sites do attempt to monitor statements made on their discussion boards—at least minimally—to weed out content that is deemed inappropriate. And most news sites include a discussion policy that requires users to agree to its terms and conditions before posting. Terms generally include a statement that asserts that the news organization is not responsible for statements made by its users. Of course, a court may still find the news organization responsible for libelous statements. The second issue, forum shopping, is a bit more complex. Because users can access web pages from any country in the world, a news organization in one country could be sued for libel in another. Thus, forum shopping is when potential plaintiffs attempt to sue an organization in a jurisdiction that may be more willing to rule in their favor. And because different countries have different guidelines for how libel is established, plaintiffs may be more successful in courts that place the burden of proof on the publisher.

Copyright protects authors of original artistic or literary work "fixed in a tangible medium," including books, videos, DVDs, CDs, computer files, and, yes, the web. Copyright of such work belongs exclusively to the creator, and anyone who wants to republish it in any form must obtain permission from the author to do so. Those who republish copyrighted works without express permission are subject to lawsuits for copyright infringement. Journalists should, therefore, treat content they encounter on the web just like they would any other published source. Assume it's copyrighted and contact the author if you want to use it.

Linking to other sites with original content is another important consideration for online journalists. You might think that if you want to avoid legal or ethical scrutiny, just link to someone else's site instead of copying the content on your own. However, it may not be that simple. There are a few key types of links that may cause

TECHNICAL-ETHICAL ISSUES

Perhaps the most significant ethical issue is the notion that multimedia journalists rely heavily on technology as a means for gathering, processing, and distributing information. And technology always brings with it new methods for creating content, some acceptable and others unacceptable for journalistic endeavors. Some of the more common technical-ethical issues multimedia journalists face relate to how sound is gathered in the field and edited in the newsroom and the acceptability of adding special effects in video presentations.

Below are some general dos and don'ts associated with digital media:

Dos

It is permissible to edit out "ums," "ers," stutters and long pauses. You can also remove extraneous words, interjections, repetitive statements, and subordinate clauses. If your intent is to make the audio cleaner and easier to understand, it is okay to tighten the clip. However, never change the meaning of your speaker's quotes.

It is permissible to structure audio clip out of the order in which they were spoken. However, when you do, consider whether the new order changes the speaker's intended meaning. If so, you have probably gone too far. But if you are merely rearranging order to match compelling quotes with the topical flow of the story or accompanying media like photos or graphics, you are probably okay.

Don'ts

Never change and re-record questions to substitute for the questions you actually asked during the interview. It is misleading and unethical to make the listener believe that one response relates to a question that was never asked, even if the question you are substituting is similar to the original.

Never use sound effects or ambient sound you did not collect at the actual scene. For example, if you are doing a story about a training program for German shepherd police dogs, the sounds of dogs barking could add depth to the story. But if you are going to use them, make sure the dog sounds come from a training session for the dogs in the story. Although it may seem harmless, using stock barking clips that you find during the editing process is misleading and unethical.

problems: inline links, associative links, frames, deep links, or links to sites that have infringed on copyright.

Inline linking (also known as piggy-backing) occurs when an image is used as a link from one site to another. This is problematic when the inline image is protected by copyright. In this sense, you may be embedding an image you don't have permission to use.

Associative linking (also known as a "see also" link) is when one site links to another to create a relationship between the content displayed on both sites. For example, in a story about the risks associated with smoking, you might include a "see also" link the website for the Centers for Disease Control. In most cases, these types of links are harmless and acceptable. However, in a few cases, operators of the site being linked to have complained that its reputation had been tarnished by the associative link. Thus, "any link that falsely leads the end user to conclude that the web page author is affiliated, approved, or sponsored by the trademark owner could lead to a claim of trademark infringement."[1]

Frames are based on HTML code that allows website operators to subdivide web pages. For example, using framing code, an organization could create a page with three frames. One frame may includes their web logo and another their site navigation. However, in the third frame, they could embed content from another website, essentially wrapping all of their own identifying information around someone else's content. In this case, it would appear that the content originated with the first organization, misleading users about its origin. In this sense, framing is widely viewed as deceptive and an infringement of copyright.

Deep linking occurs when one site links to a page deep inside another website. In this case, operators of the site being linked to may complain that they are losing advertising revenue because you are driving traffic straight to specific content instead of requiring that users access the content from the homepage of that site. Because ad revenue is based on the number of clicks a user makes on a particular site, revenue is minimized when you link directly to a site's original content in one click.

Linking to a site that contains material that infringes on copyright is also problematic. Just because you aren't the one illegally displaying copyrighted content doesn't mean you can't be held responsible if you link to it. As an ethical journalist, you must verify that the content you link to is displayed legally by the site on which it appears.

Transitioning to Specific Skills

Although different organizations may approach the concept of multimedia storytelling from slightly varying perspectives, the qualities of a good story endure. A good story has a clear narrative arc, a powerful human focus that helps audiences connect with issues and individuals, multiple perspectives, vibrant scene setting, and easy-to-understand contextual references. A good story educates its audience, answers logical questions, and leaves the reader/viewer/user with a sense of completeness. A good story transcends the medium used to present it.

Multimedia journalists must be able to create all multimedia content types on at least a basic level. And as the multimedia journalist migrates from one story form and back again, she must understand the differences among them, as well as they ways in which each achieves those foundational approaches to storytelling. In other words, although all stories require a solid storyline, good sources, and balanced reporting, the ways we achieve those goals in practice and presentation are slightly different, depending on the story form.

Five Considerations for All Producers, Regardless of Medium

Remember that video, photographic, and audio moments often occur simultaneously. When planning and reporting a story, decide which medium will be most effective.

Have a plan, but be ready to adapt it quickly. Do not be afraid to change your mind on the fly for the good of the story.

Make sure you have all of your multimedia equipment with you so that you do not find yourself empty handed.

Do not lose focus or the story may be weakened. It is one thing to determine you need to change directions for the good of the story. It is another to become distracted by irrelevant information.

Be a savvy problem-solver. A good multimedia journalist is always on her toes, anticipates the next shot, assesses multimedia potential, determines the best way to tell parts of the story, and visualizes the story package as it comes together.

Thus, the chapters that follow will dive into specific skills sets—from writing to information graphics—in an effort to help you understand the roles of each in the multimedia sphere. However, as you proceed, please keep in mind everything that was outlined in this chapter and allow these concepts to serve as a foundation for all your multimedia work.

Exercises

1. Choose a topic you are interested in, such as the environment or a hot political topic. Then, conduct enough research to better educate yourself and hone your topic into a focused story. Once you have your focus, develop a list of sources you will reference in your story and indicate why each is significant. Your list should include at least one human source that you could realistically gain access to in the near future. Post your finished reference list to your WordPress site.
2. Choose one human source from the list you completed in exercise one and schedule a time to interview that person. Interview your subject on camera. Before and during the interview employ as many techniques outlined in the interviewing section of this chapter as you can.
3. Edit the audio from your interview into a 60-second audio story. You may need to include narrative transitions between interview clips to create a fluid narrative arc. Post your finished video to your WordPress site.

Note

1. BitLaw Legal Resource, http://www.bitlaw.com/internet/linking.html, May 27, 2011.

CHAPTER 6

Writing

Writing Stories Across Platforms

Most early writing instruction inundates students with rules, from grammar and punctuation, to sentence structure and subject-verb agreement. Of course, these are all extremely important concepts and good writers strive for technically sound writing. But it is also important to understand that there are no hard and fast rules that govern the actual *act* of writing. In fact good writers approach the process in many different ways. Ernest Hemingway, one of the most influential authors of the twentieth century, once said, "There is no rule on how to write. Sometimes it comes easily and perfectly: sometimes it's like drilling rock and then blasting it out with charges."

Accuracy, conciseness, and fairness are all at the core of what constitutes good journalistic writing. However, truly good writing is about more than just being correct. It is about connecting with and engaging your audience, providing a voice for your subjects, and illuminating issues and topics in ways that effectively respond to the interests and needs of readers.

At the same time, in the digital age even writers must consider the platforms on which their work will appear. Multimedia writers are increasingly expected to write for a number of media, news outlets, and story types. And although print and

TEN TIPS FOR ALL WRITERS

Regardless of medium or platform, there are a few tips that journalistic writers could all benefit from. With every story you write, scrutinize your work and consider the big picture of your story as carefully as you think about how to write it.

1. **Watch, look, and listen.** The best reporters spend as much time (if not more) observing their surroundings as they do writing stories. This practice helps identify new story ideas, as well as better understand the stories you are already working on.
2. **Understand the difference between a topic and a story.** A topic is a category that may contain millions of possible stories. A story has clear focus, news peg, sources, and audience.
3. **Stick to the facts.** A fact can be verified. It has a clear source and can be checked for accuracy. An opinion, by contrast, is just one person's or group's viewpoint. Avoid unsubstantiated statements made by sources. But also avoid allowing them to creep into your writing as exposition, as well.
4. **Do not underestimate the interview.** Prepare questions in advance, but be on your toes and ask follow-up questions.
5. **Research, research, research.** Too often, inexperienced writers fail to engage in adequate prereporting. Spend time researching your story to make sure all of the important bases are covered.
6. **Use active, vibrant verbs whenever possible.** Active voice keeps sentences concise, flows more smoothly, and is easier to understand than passive voice. Active sentences also exhibit a sense of immediacy.
7. **Only use quotes when the subject has said something better than you could summarize.** Quotes that merely state facts, that are poorly worded, or that are just plain boring can weigh down your story and cause readers to disengage.
8. **Grab your readers with the lead.** Then use subsequent paragraphs to add depth and context.
9. **Make sure your story has a beginning, middle, and end.** Although your story should be tight and concise, be careful not to create a choppy structure that jumps from one topic to another. Before writing, outline your narrative thread to ensure the story flows well.
10. **Carefully read and revise your work.** Be an editor. Eliminate unnecessary words. Scrutinize your writing, and use spell check! Have someone else read your work.

online stories are often similarly structured, writers must be able to think beyond the traditional long-form story. For example, alternative story forms, quick reads, and text-driven graphics such as time lines and tables are just a few of the different story forms all journalists must be able to construct. More than ever, writers must be adept at many different types of writing to be successful in the multimedia world.

Multimedia writers are also often required to cover a single story that will appear on multiple platforms. And although many print publications simply republish stories from their print edition on their websites, in some cases stories are reformatted to better suit online reading styles. Similarly, story packages that include video, photo/audio slideshows, and interactive graphics may require a number of different written components. A multimedia writer may be asked to contribute to video and audio scripts, captions, narrations for animations, or explainers for information graphics. However, regardless of the platform, format, or story structure, good writing is at the core of good journalism.

This chapter will prepare you for a number of situations in which you will be required to write. And regardless of whether you intend to focus on writing as your primary craft or want to be a photographer, videographer, graphics reporter, designer, or radio reporter, you should be able to write well. We will explore tips for writing longer stories for any platform, as well as address writing for alternative story forms, quick reads, and scripts. However, before we dive into your job as a writer, let's spend some time thinking about how different media affect the actual reading experience.

Reading Trends

A number of studies have identified three types of readers: comprehensive readers, samplers and scanners.[1] Comprehensive readers almost always read a publication from cover to cover or a particular story from beginning to end. Samplers consume stories they are interested in, and often only read portions of stories before stopping and moving on. Finally, scanners rarely read the stories in a publication. Instead, they read headlines and labels, captions and text blocks associated with graphic elements, and fact boxes and other quick reads. A steady increase in the number of scanners and samplers has prompted many print publications to shorten traditional stories and include more quick reads, graphic elements, and typographic layers. Of course, long-form stories are still popular and valuable. Magazine stories, newspaper feature stories, and in-depth news analysis pieces, to name a few, are some examples where long-form writing is commonly valued. So today's media writers must consider all types of readers and plan accordingly.

Online, similar reading patterns have been observed. On the web, people read about 25 percent slower, and they tend to scan pages to find areas of interest, zero in on headlines and hypertext to find stories they are interested in, skim copy for key words and phrases, and click to interact and navigate a site. Online, text draws most readers' attention before graphics and pictures. Unlike print publications, readers often do not look at the images on a web page until the second or third visit. And "online participants read an average of 77 percent of story text they chose to read. This is substantially higher than the amount of story text participants read in broadsheets and tabloids. Broadsheet participants read an average of 62 percent of stories they selected. Tabloid participants read an average of 57 percent."[2]

Above all, online readers want sites that are easy to navigate. According to web usability expert Jakob Nielsen, "On the web, users are engaged and want to go places and get things done. The web is an active medium."[3] Thus, unlike linear print media in which "people expect you to construct their experience for them," readers are less likely to follow an author's lead online. Rather, web users "want to construct their own experience[s] by piecing together content from multiple sources, emphasizing their desires in the current moment. People arrive at a website with a goal in mind, and they are ruthless in pursuing their own interest and in rejecting whatever the site is trying to push."

Thus, writing for the web requires informative, concise headlines, summaries and hyperlinks to longer versions of a story. Likewise, use of bold text to highlight important words and phrases provides the scanning reader with focal points within a block of text. Add to that short, easily digested paragraphs—much like those written for newspaper stories—that each focus on a single idea or concept, and you have all the ingredients for a well-structured online story.

Mobile devices provide an even different reading experience. According to a 2010 *New York Times* article, "although almost 90 percent of households in the United States now have a cell phone, the growth in voice minutes used by consumers has stagnated, according to government and industry data."[4] People are increasingly using their phones to text, Tweet, post to Facebook, surf the web, and consume news.

In fact, most people are spending less time actually making calls on their phones than they are all of these other data-focused activities. At the same time cell phone reading has been largely characterized as an exercise in "information snacking," as readers tend to engage with content during the "in between moments" of their lives. In other words, people read on their phones between classes, during lunch breaks, while waiting for buses or trains, or while sitting at stoplights. Mobile reading is "on-the-go."

Finally, many media analysts have predicted that devices like Apple's well-sold iPad will be "game changers" where media consumption is concerned. Famed media consultant and newspaper design pioneer Mario Garcia shared his thoughts about the potential for tablets like the iPad at a 2010 conference at the Poynter Institute: "I knew just that instant that this would be a device to revolutionize the media as we knew it up to that point," he said. "I also immediately sensed, without touching it or putting it on my lap, that the iPad had relaxation written on its screen.... I have no doubt that the majority of media consumers five years from now will be using a tablet to get their information."[5] Interestingly, early tablets bring together the interactive potential of the web and the leisurely, "sit back" reading experience of print.

So, what does all this mean to writers? Few would argue that reading patterns differ among different platforms. Holding a newspaper in your hand is different from sitting at a computer and clicking through a website. And reading on a computer is different from reading on a cell phone or tablet. At the same time, rewriting a story for every platform on which it might appear is not realistic for deadline-oriented news organizations, nor is it necessary most of the time. However, in the very least, writers should consider the fact that readers will encounter their stories in many different ways on several different platforms. And as the industry continues to evolve, so too will the ways we approach storytelling for different platforms.

Avoid settling into a cookie cutter approach to writing in which every story you write has a similar form. Instead, treat every story individually by first assessing the focus, angle, tone, and intended audience. Understand that in addition to listening to radio, watching television, and reading print publications and websites, audiences are also spending increasing amounts of time engaging with news on mobile devices like cell phones and tablets. Web reading and print reading may be different for different people. And the same person may engage in different reading patterns, depending on the platform, story, or moment she happens to be reading.

Crafting News Stories

Whether you're writing for print or the web, the first step to mastering journalistic writing is to understand how to craft a basic news story. In other words, basic writing instruction does not necessarily change in the multimedia age. Again, we have added to our toolsets and responsibilities, but basic newswriting is still the foundation for journalistic storytelling. So regardless of what platform you are writing for, there are a number of tried and true structures that will serve you well.

Traditionally, news stories are written so they can be edited from the bottom up. The standard: get the most important information in the first paragraph, and then write additional paragraphs with information descending in order of importance. This way, if stories need to be trimmed quickly and on deadline, editors can simply chop the least important paragraphs that fall at the end of a story. Also, get to the point. Because your scanning readers may only spend a few minutes with your story, front load your paragraphs so that the conclusion or results comprise the first sentence. In other words, use that first paragraph to tell the reader what happened and use subsequent paragraphs to explain why it matters. If the most important questions are who and what, for example, make sure the answers are in the lead. Explain when, where, why, and how later. Write short, easily digested paragraphs. Each paragraph should focus on a single idea or concept in one or two sentences.

Interestingly, this inverted pyramid style was originally less about space constraints and more about time constraints. According to some historians, during the American Civil War, correspondents who feared that telegraph lines would break down before they could finish transmitting dispatches, used what later became known as the inverted pyramid to ensure the most important information got through first. The concept continued through the letterpress era when makeup editors eliminated paragraphs of stories from the bottom up until they fit into the frame that held the columns of type. And of course, the practice endures today when under space constraints or time pressure, editors chop the ends of stories to make them fit an allotted space.

HOW WEB AND PRINT HEADLINES DIFFER

One of the biggest mistakes a multimedia journalist can make where headlines are concerned is to treat them all the same regardless of whether they appear in print or online. Although both are intended to entice the reader to engage with the related story, they do so in very different ways.

In print, headlines have both a textual and visual presence. They vary in size and weight to enhance a sense of hierarchy among unrelated stories. Likewise, print headlines are almost always part of a "package" of information presented together. For example, it is common for a headline to be supported by a descriptive subhead and photograph. Thus, main headlines can often include fewer words, such as "Deadly Crash" because other elements in the story package will support and explain in greater detail.

Online, however, headlines must be more descriptive and written to stand alone. Most of the time, web headlines are set in small type, and there is little if any visual differentiation among lists of headlines. Likewise, web headlines often do not appear with related content. For example, headlines appear in multiple areas of a site, as well as in search results by themselves. In these instances, it is important that the substance of a headline is enticing, informative, and clear. Thus, instead of "Deadly Crash," a web headline that reads, "126 killed in British airlines crash" has greater potential to urge people to click.

For the most part, writing stories for the web follows similar patterns, with a few minor differences. Perhaps one of the most important things to master where writing for the web is concerned is crafting informative, concise headlines, summaries, and hyperlinks to longer versions of a story. Likewise, use of bold text to highlight important words and phrases provides the scanning reader with focal points within a block of text.

Of course, stories take many forms, and good writers understand how to craft pieces that are truly reflective of individual topics and subjects, each with a different focus and angle. However, in general, journalistic stories can be divided into two basic categories—hard news and soft news (or features). Hard news stories generally

WEB STORY DIAGRAM

Front-loaded summary lead gets to the point (or the new information) fast.

Bolded or underlined words link to popups or open pages that provide more information about key topics.

Subheads help break up text and move the eye through a story.

Related links drive readers to other sources.

Fact boxes layer stories and provide additional resources.

BP set to test if new cap stops oil

By Colleen Long & Harry R. Weber | Associated Press Writers

Even if BP's new tight-fitting cap secured on top of the **leaking well** in the Gulf of Mexico works, the blown-out well must still be plugged. That may not happen until mid-August.

After securing the new cap, **BP** prepared Tuesday to begin tests to see if it will hold and stop fresh oil from polluting the waters for the first time in nearly three months.

And a permanent fix will have to wait until one of two **relief wells** being drilled reaches the broken well, which will then be plugged up with drilling mud and cement.

No promises

BP and the government's point man on the crisis—the biggest offshore oil spill in U.S. history and one of the nation's worst environmental disasters—stressed there were no guarantees, and they urged patience from Gulf residents.

"They ought to be interested and concerned, but if they hold their breath, they'll run out of oxygen," retired Coast Guard Adm. Thad Allen told The Associated Press.

RELATED LINKS

Spill Panel to Press Obama Team on Drilling Ban

Oil Spill's Impact on Gulf Seafood Remains Uncertain

Environmental Devastation Spreads

RESOURCES

To report oiled wildlife, call 1-866-557-1401

To report oiled shoreline or request volunteer info., call 1-866-448-5816

recount significant events, such as disasters, breaking news, political developments, death, or major crises. Soft news (or features), on the other hand, tends to focus on topics that are lighter. Feature stories may also cover serious topics from more analytic perspectives, offering more context, depth, and texture.

Although good writing is rarely formulaic, both hard and soft news stories have certain characteristics that set them apart. And for beginners, it is often a good idea to practice writing leads that commonly fall under the hard and soft news categories.

Writing Basic Leads

The lead, a story's first sentence or two, is the most important structural element of a news story. Good leads get to the point. They answer core news questions: who, what, when, where, why, or how. And they help readers understand a story's significance, all in just a brief sentence or two. Of course, as you become a more experienced writer, you can experiment with different story structures and leads. However, beginning multimedia journalists can benefit from following these basic guidelines for basic lead writing.

Hard News Leads

Summary leads are the most common hard news leads. They address all of the core news questions—who, what, when, where, why, and how—in the first sentence or two. Thus, a strong summary lead is succinct and active. To effectively write a summary lead, first spend some time clearly identifying the answers to those six core questions. For example, a simple summary lead might look something like this:

> One American and 64 others were killed late Sunday in Uganda when an explosion ripped through a crowd watching the World Cup final. Ugandan authorities suspect Somalia's most feared terrorist group; al-Shabab is responsible for the attack.

Notice how clearly the who, what, when, where, why, and how of the story emerge:

Who: *One American and 64 others*
What: *Killed*
When: *Sunday*
Where: *Uganda*
Why: *Terrorism*
How: *Bombing*

Although you may elaborate on these topics later in the story, the summary lead immediately provides a focused, yet deep entrée into the story. And although these hard leads are very tight and relatively formulaic, there are variations of this concept. In the very least, understand that a hard news lead should begin with the information that is most important to the story. So, although the bombing lead offered here focuses on and consequently begins with the who of the story, another hard news lead might focus on one of the other core questions. For example, the same lead could be worded like this:

An explosion ripped through a crowd watching the World Cup final in Uganda on Sunday, killing 65 people. Ugandan authorities suspect Somalia's most feared terrorist group, al-Shabab, is responsible.

In this case, what and how take center stage. Determining which of the questions to focus on in a summary lead is really a matter of news judgment. But rest assured, regardless of the order in which you answer the questions, the summary lead provides a straight forward, concise method for getting to the point of a story quickly. Of course, good writers do not stop with the highly formulaic summary lead. Rather, they assess the nuances of individual stories and let the written piece take shape accordingly. Thus, there are a number of alternatives to the summary lead frequently used for hard news.

Blind leads help keep the hard news lead tight and focused when identifying the "who" of a story makes for a cumbersome, wordy entrée. Blind leads exclude the name of the person that the story is centered on, offering it in the second paragraph instead.

Example: An Indianapolis man was shot Monday by the owner of a home he broke into, Marion County police said.

Identification of impact and factual leads work well when it is important to let the reader know why he should care about a story. When readers have a personal stake in a story—when their lives are directly affected by it—they will be more likely to engage. Thus, identifying impact right away in these types of stories can be an effective way to capture readers' attention.

Example: Property tax caps should boost Indiana's economy over the next few years by increasing a homeowner's disposable income and lowering costs for businesses, according to a recent Ball State University study.

Umbrella leads bring together two or three topics in a single lead to show relationships between them. Umbrella leads are great for quickly providing context for readers when more than one event or issue is important to a single story.

Example: The Allen County school board voted Friday to eliminate 32 teaching positions across 16 schools in spite of the fact that enrollments will increase by nearly 4 percent county wide this year.

Soft News or Feature Leads

Soft leads tend to be much less formulaic and open to creativity. Again, a feature story often stretches beyond being informative and offers depth and breadth of coverage of a particular topic. Feature stories provide context, analyze an event or issues, and offer stronger human connections. Thus, feature leads offer substantially more variety than their hard news counterparts. And although summary leads are still prevalent in feature stories, they are often longer and more fluid than summary leads in news. Instead of packing answers to the six core questions into one or two sentences, you can give a couple sentences to each of the six. Start with the most interesting or relevant and order them accordingly after that. There are several other options for features as well.

Anecdotal leads are, perhaps, the most popular types of soft news leads and make use of a short vignette or anecdote that is a reflection of the larger story. If done well, anecdotal leads can help writers connect with readers on a more personal level.

Example: Terry Sanchez lumbers onto the football field, his six-foot, five-inch frame casting an enormous shadow on the early-morning ground. Up at 4 a.m. six days a week for early-morning workouts, Sanchez is no stranger to hard work.

Descriptive leads paint a picture by setting a scene or offering vivid detail to draw the reader in. Descriptive leads are capable of making the reader feel she is in the story, experiencing and seeing it.

Example: Just walking through the front door of Jennie Martin's apartment is a challenge. Boxes of everything from dishes to tennis shoes cover the floor of her small living room.

The hall closet door stands wide open, stuffed so full of clutter that it will no longer close completely.

"Just step over it," Jennie says. "Or step on it if you have to."

Such is the life of a hoarder.

Quotation leads can shed light on an event or issue or serve as narrative devices. For the quotation lead to truly work, however, the quote must be engaging. In fact, quotation leads are often discouraged because quotes are rarely strong enough to carry the start of a story. For example, the following quote is not only a mere statement of fact, but it is also just plain boring:

Example: "The 16 passengers and three crew onboard American Airlines flight 7623 survived after the plane crash landed in an open field, Friday," said Joe Roberts, a spokesperson for the airline.

In this case, quote isn't necessary. These details can be paraphrased or offered as statements of fact. On the other hand, when a quote is particularly compelling, it can effectively drop the reader directly into a story through the subject's own voice.

Example: "As the plane began to fall out of the sky, all I could think about was my children and what they would be told about how I died."

The lead examples here do not offer a complete picture of all of the possible avenues your stories may take. However, this is a solid foundation for getting your writing off the ground. Of course, the story doesn't stop with the lead. So, here are a few other tips for planning and organizing your stories:

Establish your angle. One of the journalist's primary jobs through reporting is to determine why a story is important and establish a clear focus. Thus, most stories can be structured around a particular angle or "slant." Of course, journalists must also remain objective. So, determining the focus for a story often requires a great deal of research, reporting, and interviewing.

Stay on point. Once you have determined the appropriate focus for a story, stick to it. If you are focusing on a story about the shortage of teachers in your community school system, don't wander into less relevant territory, such as standardized test scores. Unless a topic is directly relevant to your story's focus, leave out.

Provide context. Do not mistake writing tightly to eliminating the answer to the most significant question: Why should your readers care? Just because your writing should be tight doesn't mean that your story should lack depth. News stories should focus on how people are affected, and your job is to clearly and carefully explain those effects.

Write brief paragraphs of two to three sentences each. This is not an essay, it is a news story. So instead of separating paragraphs by topics, think of the paragraph as an independent unit of thought.

Organize paragraphs in order of importance. List all of the main ideas that need to be addressed in your story and then address those ideas with a clear concise narrative. Begin a new paragraph for each quote, when focus changes, or with each discreet statement of fact.

Establish a fluid narrative. Although news stories are often tightly focused and concise, they should not be choppy and erratic. Make sure you do not abruptly jump from one concept to another without fully explaining significance. Likewise, help readers understand connections between concepts by using clean transitions.

Use quotes wisely. Avoid quotes that merely provide facts. Likewise, avoid paraphrase quotes that aren't compelling or interesting. Instead, use quotes that provide insight, express emotion, or illustrate statements that could not be expressed better any other way.

Avoid unsubstantiated statements. Everything you write must be verifiable. So, do not make statements that cannot be attributed, and leave your own opinions out of your story.

Serve scanning readers. For longer stories, break up paragraphs with subheads when appropriate, and consider adding bulleted lists, fact boxes, or other quick reads that help scanners find information quickly.

But let's not forget that we started this chapter by saying that there are no hard and fast rules for the act of writing. Rather, there are tips and guidelines to help you get started. Like everything else, the more you practice writing, the better you will get. And the better you get, the more you will be able to move away from the guidelines offered here and experiment with more unique writing styles. However, when you are first getting your feet wet, use these lead styles and tips to ensure your stories are structurally sound. And note that all of the guidelines offered here are relevant to web and print writing, newspapers and magazines.

NEWS STORY DIAGRAM

Summary lead answers core news questions: who, what, when, where, why and how.

Story angle and significance are established early in the story.

Quotes are compelling and engaging and offer statements that could not be said better through paraphrase.

Additional context helps readers understand what is next.

No promises as BP set to test if new cap stops oil

By Colleen Long and Harry R. Weber

Associated Press Writers

NEW ORLEANS (AP)—After securing a new, tight-fitting cap on top of the leaking well in the Gulf of Mexico, BP prepared Tuesday to begin tests to see if it will hold and stop fresh oil from polluting the waters for the first time in nearly three months.

The oil giant expects to know within 48 hours if the new cap, which was affixed Monday after almost three days of painstaking, around-the-clock work a mile below the Gulf's surface, can stanch the flow. The solution is only temporary, but it offers the best hope yet for cutting off the gush of billowing brown oil.

The cap's installation was good news to weary Gulf Coast residents who have warily waited for BP to make good on its promise to clean up the mess. Still, they warned that even if the oil is stopped, the consequences are far from over.

"I think we're going to see oil out in the Gulf of Mexico, roaming around, taking shots at us, for the next year, maybe two," Billy Nungesser, president of Louisiana's oil-stained Plaquemines Parish, said Monday. "If you told me today no more oil was coming ashore, we've still got a massive cleanup ahead."

Starting Tuesday, the cap will be tested and monitored to see if it can withstand pressure from the gushing oil and gas. The tests could last anywhere between six to 48 hours, according to National Incident Commander Thad Allen.

Kent Wells, a senior vice president at the oil giant, made no promises in a Tuesday morning news briefing about whether the cap will work.

"We need to wait and see what the test actually tells us," Wells said. "It's not simple stuff. What we don't want to do is speculate around it."

The cap will be tested by closing off three separate valves that fit together snugly, choking off the oil from entering the Gulf. BP expects no oil will be released into the ocean during the tests, but remained cautious about the success of the system.

Pipes can be hooked to the cap to funnel oil to collection ships if BP decides the cap can't take the pressure of the gusher, or if low-pressure readings indicate oil is leaking from elsewhere in the well.

"The sealing cap system never before has been deployed at these depths or under these conditions, and its efficiency and ability to contain the oil and gas cannot be assured," the company said in a statement.

Paragraphs are short and new ones are started for quotes and new concepts.

BP will be watching pressure readings. High pressure is good, because it would mean the leak has been contained inside the wellhead machinery. But if readings are lower than expected, that could mean there is another leak elsewhere in the well.

Not a permanent fix

Subheads help break up large chunks of text and serve the scanning reader by providing a simple navigational aid.

Even if the cap works, the blown-out well must still be plugged. A permanent fix will have to wait until one of two relief wells being drilled reaches the broken well, which will then be plugged up with drilling mud and cement. That may not happen until mid-August.

Even if the flow of oil is choked off while BP works on a permanent fix, the spill has already damaged everything from tourism to the fishing industry.

Tony Wood, director of the National Spill Control School at Texas A&M-Corpus Christi said the sloppiest of the oil—mousse-like brown stuff that has not yet broken down—will keep washing ashore for several months, with the volume slowly decreasing over time.

He added that hardened tar balls could keep hitting beaches and marshes each time a major storm rolls through for a year or more. Those tar balls are likely trapped for now in the surf zone, gathering behind sand bars just like sea shells.

"It will still be getting on people's feet on the beaches probably a year or two from now," Wood said.

But on Monday, the region absorbed a rare piece of good news in the placement of the 150,000-pound cap on top of the gushing leak.

Clean transitions make for a fluid narrative and provide an opportunity to change direction.

Around 6:30 P.M. CDT, live video streams trained on the wellhead showed the cap being slowly lowered into place. BP officials said the device was attached around 7 P.M.

"I'm very hopeful that this cap works and we wake up in the morning and they're catching all the oil. I would be the happiest person around here," said Mitch Jurisich, a third generation oysterman from Empire, La., who has been out of work for weeks.

The deeper you go into the story, the less important or timely the information becomes. More important facts are at the beginning.

Residents are skeptical BP can deliver on its promise to control the spill greeted the news cautiously.

QUICK TIPS

Do not make assumptions or statements that the data cannot support. Let the data speak for itself.

Avoid making predictions beyond what the data and your research supports.

Use complete data If numbers are missing or you do not have access to complete visual reference material, rethink your graphic. Leaving out key information will likely leave the audience with questions.

Avoid jargon, vague, or misleading language. Use language that is easy to understand.

Do not overwrite. Allow the chart or illustration to represent key information.

Be concise and get to the point. Avoid unnecessary words and sentences.

Avoid redundancy. Summarize important information, and evaluate the data in the context of the news event.

Write in present tense, active voice. Present tense carries a quality of urgency and timeliness. Likewise, sentences that make use of active verbs are generally more concise and interesting to read. Of course, there are some instances where passive voice is acceptable: shifts of time or sentences where the person who performs the action is unknown or unimportant.

Write in third person. Avoid "I," "we," "us," and other personal pronouns.

Use terminology correctly. Graphics often show breakdowns, comparisons, trends, cutaways, perspectives, angles of view, amounts, numbers, and locations. Make sure that you use these terms correctly to describe what your graphic really shows.

Scrutinize your writing and edit your work. Eliminate unnecessary words. Run spell check and review all data and illustrations for accuracy.

It is also worth noting again that traditional long-form pieces will not be the only types of stories you will write in a multimedia world. As previously noted, information layering is increasingly important on all platforms, including print and online. And nearly every other story form, from information graphics to video and audio presentations, include written components. So moving forward, it is important that we address concepts unique to each of those story forms.

Writing for Information Graphics

Different types of graphics call for different writing styles. However, regardless of type or platform, all of the written components for an information graphic should be tight, direct, active, and easy to understand. There are a number of reasons for this. In newspapers and magazines, space is limited. Similarly, animated graphics are often to time limits, so voiceovers should be succinct and direct. And even online, where space and time are unlimited for the content provider, they are not unlimited for the user. Thus, keeping your audience's attention is paramount, as is making sure your graphics are easy to navigate and visually accurate and engaging. The job of an information graphic is to simplify complicated information and effective graphics get to the point using clear, simple language.

Chapter 9 addresses information graphics in greater detail, so here, we will just focus on the written components. However, for the sake of context, it is worth listing the types of information graphics for which you may write. Maps, charts, and diagrams are the basic information graphics categories.

- **Text-based graphics** like time lines and tables present text in a graphical structure that promotes an at-a-glance approach to reading.
- **Locator maps** generally include a simple headline and basic labels for referential locations and points of interest.
- **Detailed maps and diagrams** that explain complex events may include introductory text and other explainers when necessary, as well as additional labels to give more explanation and context for the graphic.
- **Charts and graphs** generally contain a headline and introductory text, also known as "chatter," composed of one to two sentences.

When writing chatter, callouts, and explainers, remember that although they are short chunks, together they represent a narrative with a beginning, middle, and end. Headlines, explainers, copy blocks, and callouts should help establish a proper flow, and readers should recognize that order. Likewise, you cannot adequately explain something that you do not understand. So, you should always make sure you clearly understand the data and related information before attempting to pass that understanding on to the audience. Once you have a clear understanding of the content, try to boil it down to a concise, simplified explanation.

Anatomy of an Information Graphic

Headline: Most graphics should include a headline, title, or label. The headline should summarize the focus of the graphic in a few concise, descriptive words.

Chatter: The introduction summarizes the graphic and provides context. The last sentence can also serve as a transition to the graphic. Chatter is usually two to four sentences.

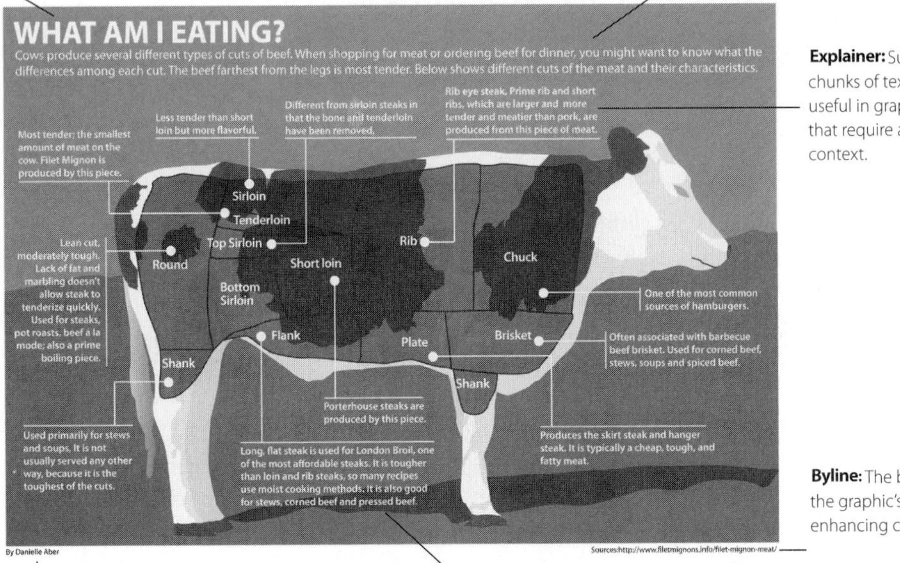

Explainer: Supplemental chunks of text are often useful in graphics packages that require additional context.

Byline: The byline identifies the graphic's creator, enhancing credibility.

Source line: A source line should accompany all credible graphics packages to let the reader know where the information originated.

Callouts: When labels need more explanation or definition, they can be accompanied by callouts. Generally a sentence fragment, callouts briefly provide more information about the visual portion of the graphic.

FIGURE 6-1

Writing Captions/Cutlines

Strong captions (or "cutlines," as they are called in most newspaper newsrooms) contain more than just a subject's name or description of the scene. In fact, one of the worst ways to approach caption writing is to merely describe what is going on in the photo. The well-written caption adds value to the image instead of describing its contents. So consider including information that goes beyond what the viewer can already see by looking at the photo. If it is an event photo, provide context. Who are the key players beyond the person featured in the photo? What was the purpose of the event? When was the event held? Where was the event held? Why should the viewer care? If it is a portrait, tell me more about the person than what the photos shows. If it is a detail shot, help the viewer understand why it is significant to the story. And

FIGURE 6-2

GOOD CAP

Sampson, the zoo's most beloved attraction, will undergo surgery Friday to remove a benign tumor in his leg.

BAD CAP

Sampson the lion lays on a rock and sunbathes at the zoo Thursday.

always remember that when you are presenting a collection of images, the captions must pull you through the story the same way the images do. Thus, the pacing of the copy must be carefully considered in concert with the pacing of the images.

Writing Scripts

Concision has been the theme throughout this chapter, and writing scripts that will serve as the foundation for audio voiceover is no exception. In fact, one could argue that precision, short words, active voice, and pointed writing is most important for pieces that will not be read, but rather, heard. Remember, your audience will not have the benefit of being able to reread a sentence to clarify its meaning. Once the words of your script are spoken, they evaporate into thin air. Of course, online, the user may be able to rewind. However, that process is much more cumbersome for users than just scanning back a few words. So do not count on them to do it. Convey ideas in short, concise segments so that listeners can easily follow the path of the narrative. Most good scriptwriters advise that you keep sentences to 25 words or less so that listeners do not get lost in compound sentences and multiple thoughts.

The fact that there is a voice behind the narrative of an audio script creates an instant, and perhaps more personal, connection between writer and audience. Again, you are writing for the ear, not the eye, so the style should be more conversational and the writing should sound fluid and natural. Likewise, pay attention to the rhythm of the words as they are spoken. Avoid linking together too many sentences that are similar in length. Variety in cadence and sentence length will better hold the audience's attention. In the same vein, avoid words that sound alike (or homonyms and homophones) whenever possible. For example, because the audience cannot read the words *they're*, *there*, and *their*, the intended version may be difficult to discern and ultimately confuse listeners. When you can, remove them altogether.

Additionally, never underestimate the power of silence in an audio piece. Well-timed pauses give the audience time to absorb what has been said. Pauses also make it easier to edit recordings later, leaving clean breaks between sentences and ideas. Planning for moments of silence within a script can help establish a clear tone, engaging rhythm, and dramatic voice when appropriate. One of the best ways to ensure you are achieving all of these goals is to read your copy aloud as you write, refine, and edit.

Professional Perspective

Juli Metzger • *Journalism Instructor*

Ball State University

About the time that the Commodore 64 was introduced, Juli Metzger walked into her hometown newspaper and asked for a job. She was immediately intoxicated by the smell and the hum of massive presses running continuously in the bowels of the building to the clamor of manual typewriters in the newsroom. She spent the next 30 years in newspapers evolving with the business with executive rolls in the newsroom to running community newspapers as publisher, including her hometown paper where she got her first job in the business. Most recently, Juli was the executive editor, digital and custom publications for The Indianapolis Star. Juli has a Bachelor's degree journalism from Ball State University and a master's degree in Information and Communication Sciences also from Ball State University. She's worked at eight newspapers and is now an instructor of journalism at Ball State.

These days you may be wondering whether there is a place for you in journalism. The industry is in the midst of a transformation unlike any in its history and the seismic shift isn't over yet. There will be aftershocks for some time to come.

In the last five years, journalism—especially but not only print media—has undergone profound right-sizing and the result has meant changes in what we cover and how many resources we devote to a subject.

Your outlook largely depends on whether you're a glass-half-full kind of person. What's different today is we have far more choices and far more tools than ever before and those choices sometimes clutter the media landscape and clog the information pipeline. As journalists, we have the ability more than ever to control our medium and maximize our message.

When I was considering a direction for my career 30 years ago, some journalists in the business warned me of a similar impending catastrophe. They argued we were on the verge of a journalistic collapse and that I would be better off finding another discipline. Find another way to make a living, they said. As I was in the midst of my college career, *USA Today* was founded and "real journalists" once again began a drum beat of doom and gloom for journalism. The stories were too short and graphics were too pretty to be taken seriously.

In my first newsroom, I used a manual typewriter and fed thick, continuous rolls of yellow paper through it. Corrections were made by backing up and striking through a word or letter. Copy editors used proofreading marks to signal changes to the compositor. The women smoked cigarettes and the men smoked cigars in the newsroom. We drank with sources after work and sometimes during work. It wasn't uncommon to open a desk drawer and find a bottle of Jim Beam.

You get the idea.

Today, we print on recycled newsprint. Ink is made with soybeans. Our buildings are smoke-free zones and drinking at lunchtime could get you fired.

The world of journalism is more complicated and more layered than ever before yet at its core it is the reporting and writing that matters. Today is a much more exciting, more robust environment in which to work, in which to hone our craft and to be more precise with our words and our message. It also is an increasingly intimidating environment—perhaps more for those of us who have been in it than those who are entering it for the first time.

Multiple platforms, social media, not to mention the Internet has changed the process of journalism but not its objective. Reporting has changed most in the act of information gathering—even at the conversation level. Today, this phase of reporting might very well start on social networking sites such as Twitter or Facebook. It is at this stage that journalism—the profession—can either distinguish itself or embarrass itself.

Journalism still means verifying facts before throwing them out under the auspices of free-flowing information. The public, by the way, wants verification. They don't want us to simply empty our notebooks onto newsprint or digital tape recorders onto the web; they don't want endless Twitter feeds or the vast abyss of a blog. They want to know what's true and what isn't and they want us to figure that out for them.

One major change is the process of journalism has become remarkably transparent.

The consumer will often see the news in stages, from the beginnings, almost in note form on Twitter or Facebook to a quasi-explanatory level by bloggers who may have gathered the information themselves from various sources, then the story may move onto new levels of verifiability—usually an online news source or in print or versions of both. As consumers, we gather our news incrementally—almost in fits and starts. It's largely a result of a time-crunched public meets fast-advancing technology.

Because of this technology we have the ability now to quickly measure interest levels and to take that knowledge and use it to target coverage accordingly, if we choose to.

But readers expect journalists to provide more than just more of what they like; they expect editorial judgment, too. Knowing what drives online traffic doesn't necessarily equate to what journalists should be covering. There is room for editorial judgment and that is a skill that readers value.

Nothing will EVER replace the written word. Nothing ever has, no matter the massive number of communication innovations and technological advancements. Somehow, those of us in the "word" business manage to turn all those things to our advantage—using them to enhance our stories, not supplant them.

My own mentor puts it this way: "When telling young newspaper journalists how important it is to embrace the technology, add it to their skills sets and let it add new dimensions to their storytelling, I am always careful to point out to them that all the prize-winning photos and videos in the world will not mask poor writing and reporting skills. *The story is the entreé*—all the rest is appetizer, accompaniment and dessert."

Become a master storyteller and don't ever stop honing your reporting skills. The best newspaper journalists have been doing this for hundreds and hundreds of years, and we can thank our lucky stars they have. They are why newspapers are still such a dominant and important part of the media landscape in 2010.

Doubts about going into journalism today? Are you kidding me? We've just entered into an exhilarating era. We've never had so many tools and skills at our disposal to help illustrate and enhance our stories.

There has never been a more exciting time to *be* a journalist.

Now, more than ever, journalism matters. Due to computers and mobile devices and, of course, the Internet, more people are getting more information than ever before. That information can either be right, or wrong. It is the job of a journalist to figure that out.

In the end, it doesn't matter if the information is delivered on newsprint, or on a computer or some sort of handheld device. What matters is accuracy. What matters is fairness. What matters is delivering facts in an understandable way. What matters is getting both sides of the story and giving the reader choices. What matters are the words and the effort put into those words.

That's what a journalist does.

Today, a journalist can do so much more than merely write a story. He or she can produce a multimedia package that not only informs, but captures the imagination of readers. Today's writing involves multiple layers of storytelling and as journalists we've become more educated along the way, too. We know that one medium does not fit all. In fact, it is a blend of those mediums that usually works best in storytelling.

But it's the effort, the shoe-leather reporting of digging into records and backgrounds and then having the skill to take that work and connect the dots that really matters.

That's why we need journalism and journalists. Over the years, I have come to admire dozens of journalists. Even now, I am in awe of what they do and downright blown away that I get to do it, too. Practicing journalism is a privilege and it is best not taken for granted. Great damage has been done by arrogant journalists. No, it's best to keep your feet firmly planted so you see the world around you and tell the stories that move societies into action.

SAMPLE AUDIO SCRIPT

Oil Cap	**Story name**
Smith	**Reporter name**
7-19-10	**Date**
:60	**Length of story**

THE GUSHER HAS STOPPED. AFTER NEARLY THREE MONTHS, OIL FROM BRITISH PETROLEUMS UNDERSEA WELL HAS STOPPED GUSHING INTO THE GULF OF MEXICO. EVEN PRESIDENT OBAMA IS CAUTIOUSLY OPTIMISTIC.

IN: I THINK IT'S IMPORTANT...
RUNS: :10
OUT: ...PERMANENT SOLUTION IN PLACE."

A CAP HAS BEEN PLACED ON THE WELL THAT EXPLODED ON APRIL 20th. VIDEO FROM TWO UNDERWATER ROBOTIC CAMERAS SHOW NO OIL LEAKING FROM THE WELL. BP'S SENIOR VICE PRESIDENT KENT WELLS SAYS THE CAP MAY BE HOLDING NOW BUT THE WELL IS FAR FROM FIXED.

IN: I DON'T WANT TO CREATE...
RUNS: :12
OUT: THE RIGHT DECISIONS."

FOR NOW BP OFFICIALS WILL CONTINUE TO MONITOR THE PRESSURE INSIDE THE WELL CAP. WORK WILL ALSO CONTINUE ON TWO RELIEF WELLS THAT ARE CONSIDERED A MORE PERMANENT SOLUTION TO THE PROBLEM. I'M JANE DOE REPORTING.

FIGURE 6-3

The three black paragraphs in script above are intended to be spoken by a reporter. The provide transitions between interview segments. The lines in red represent the first few words ("IN") and last few words ("OUT") of a particular interview clip. "RUNS" refers to the number of seconds the corresponding interview clip will run.

Source: Script contributed by Suzy Smith, Ball State University

SAMPLE VIDEO SCRIPT

ANCHOR ON CAMERA	THE OIL HAS STOPPED GUSHING INTO THE GULF. BRITISH PETROLEUM EXECUTIVES SAY THEY ARE CAUTIOUSLY OPTIMISTIC ABOUT THE CAP THAT HAS BEEN PLACED ON THE RUPTURED UNDERSEA WELL. REPORTER JANE DOE IS IN NEW ORLEANS AND REPORTS THAT THE WELL CAP APPEARS TO BE HOLDING SO FAR.
TAKE SOT 18903 RUNS: 1:34 OC "I'M JANE DOE. [:00 CG: New Orleans	------------------------------------PACKAGE------------------------------------ THIS IS THE SIGHT THAT BRITISH PETROLEUM AND THOSE LIVING ALONG THE GULF COAST HAVE WAITED THREE MONTHS TO SEE. NO OIL. TWO ROBOTIC CAMERAS SHOW THE CAP PLACED ON TOP OF THE WELL IS KEEPING OIL FROM GUSHING FROM B-P'S UNDERWATER WELL. BUT PRESIDENT OBAMA ISN'T READY TO CELEBRATE JUST YET. (SOT) "I think it's important that we don't get ahead of ourselves here. You know, one of the problems with having this camera down there is that when the oil stops gushing, everybody feels like we're done, and we're not." B-P OFFICIALS ARE MONITORING THE PRESSURE INSIDE THE CAP. THE LONGER THE CAP GOES WITHOUT A LEAK, THE BETTER THE CHANCE THE CAP WILL CONTINUE TO WORK. IT'S WELCOME NEWS IN A SAGA THAT BEGAN BACK ON APRIL 20TH. ELEVEN MEN DIED AFTER THIS OIL RIG EXPLODED THEN CAUGHT ON FIRE AND SANK IN THE GULF OF MEXICO. SINCE THEN AS MUCH AS 60-THOUSAND BARRELS OF OIL A DAY HAVE BEEN LEAKING INTO THE GULF...CAUSING THE WORST OIL SPILL IN U.S. HISTORY. PEOPLE LIVING ALONG THE GULF COAST ARE HOPING THINGS CONTINUE TO IMPROVE.
[:50 CG: Jamie Munoz New Orleans	(SOT) "See the smile, that's my reaction. It's cautious optimism. Obviously I'm very happy. It's been our goal for 88 days now. It's been a long run. But hopefully we get it done right and begin the cleaning. That's the most important part. Let's clean up and get our fishermen back to work." BUT THAT MAY TAKE SOME TIME. B-P SENIOR VICE PRESIDENT KEN WELLS SAYS THE CAP IS A TEMPORARY SOLUTION.

FIGURE 6-4

Source: Script contributed by Suzy Smith, Ball State University

SAMPLE VIDEO SCRIPT

[1:15 CG: Ken Wells BP Senior Vice President	(SOT) "We won't be done until we actually know that we killed the well and have a permanent solution in place."
[1:22 CG: Jane Doe New Orleans	(STAND-UP CLOSE) WELLS SAYS DRILLING WORK ON THE TWO RELIEF WELLS RESTARTED FRIDAY. THE COMPANY SAYS THE RELIEF WELLS ARE A MORE PERMANENT WAY TO PLUG AND SEAL THE RUPTURED WELL. B-P SAYS THE RELIEF WELLS ARE EXPECTED TO BE COMPLETED SOMETIME IN AUGUST. REPORTING FROM NEW ORLEANS, I'M JANE DOE.
ANCHOR ON CAMERA	THE OIL HAS STOPPED GUSHING INTO THE GULF. BRITISH PETROLEUM EXECUTIVES SAY THEY ARE CAUTIOUSLY OPTIMISTIC ABOUT THE CAP THAT HAS BEEN PLACED ON THE RUPTURED UNDERSEA WELL. REPORTER JANE DOE IS IN NEW ORLEANS AND REPORTS THAT THE WELL CAP APPEARS TO BE HOLDING SO FAR.
TAKE SOT 18903RUNS: 1:34OC "I'M JANE DOE. [:00 CG: New Orleans	-------------------------------------PACKAGE-------------------------------------
((VO)) (:00-:15 Underwater video showing No signs of leaking from the well cap-Video from today's feed timecode 13:23:44-13:24:40 (best shot in that range)	THIS IS THE SIGHT THAT BRITISH PETROLEUM AND THOSE LIVING ALONG THE GULF COAST HAVE WAITED THREE MONTHS TO SEE. NO OIL. TWO ROBOTIC CAMERAS SHOW THE CAP PLACED ON TOP OF THE WELL IS KEEPING OIL FROM GUSHING FROM B-P'S UNDERWATER WELL. BUT PRESIDENT OBAMA ISN'T READY TO CELEBRATE JUST YET.
((SOT)) (:15-:27 President Obama sot from Friday Presser- timecode: 14:22:34-14:22:46)	(SOT) "I think it's important that we don't get ahead of ourselves here. You know, one of the problems with having this camera down there is that when the oil stops gushing, everybody feels like we're done, and we're not."
((VO)) (:27- :33 Video of B-P officials on ship Monitoring gauges and looking at video being sent back from sea floor—Use today feed timecode: 16:45:00-16:55:00—use variety of shots)	B-P OFFICIALS ARE MONITORING THE PRESSURE INSIDE THE CAP. THE LONGER THE CAP GOES WITHOUT A LEAK, THE BETTER THE CHANCE THE CAP WILL CONTINUE TO WORK.

[:34 CG: April 20 ((VO)) (:34-:40 Video of Oil rig on fire from April 20th…. Shots of firefighting tankers Trying to douse the flames—Use most Spectacular video available)	IT'S WELCOME NEWS IN A SAGA THAT BEGAN BACK ON APRIL 20TH. ELEVEN MEN DIED AFTER THIS OIL RIG EXPLODED THEN CAUGHT ON FIRE AND SANK IN THE GULF OF MEXICO.
((VO) (:40- 45 show underwater video of oil Leaking into the Gulf—any feed) ((VO)) (:45-50 Video of oil on the beaches Use video from any of the feeds)	SINCE THEN AS MUCH AS 60-THOUSANDBARRELS OF OIL A DAY HAVE BEEN LEAKING INTO THE GULF…CAUSING THE WORST OIL SPILL IN U.S. HISTORY. PEOPLE LIVING ALONG THE GULF COAST ARE HOPING THINGS CONTINUE TO IMPROVE.
[:50 CG: Jamie Munoz New Orleans ((SOT)) (:50-1:07 sot from today's feed Timecode 16:30:44-16:31:01)	(SOT) "See the smile, that's my reaction. It's cautious optimism. Obviously I'm very happy. It's been our goal for 88 days now. It's been a long run. But hopefully we get it done right and begin the cleaning. That's the most important part. Let's clean up and get our fishermen back to work."
((VO)) (1:07-1:14 underwater video of the Cap from today's feed)	BUT THAT MAY TAKE SOME TIME. B-P SENIOR VICE PRESIDENT KEN WELLS SAYS THE CAP IS A TEMPORARY SOLUTION.
[1:15 CG: Ken Wells BP Senior Vice President ((SOT)) (1:15-1:21 use from today's feed Timecode 16:35:00-16:35:07)	(SOT) "We won't be done until we actually know that we killed the well and have a permanent solution in place."
[1:22 CG: Jane Doe New Orleans ((SOT)) (1:22-1:34 standup close From today's feed timecode: 16:45:15-16:45:35)	(STAND-UP CLOSE) WELLS SAYS DRILLING WORK ON THE TWO RELIEF WELLS RESTARTED FRIDAY. THE COMPANY SAYS THE RELIEF WELLS ARE A MORE PERMANENT WAY TO PLUG AND SEAL THE RUPTURED WELL. B-P SAYS THE RELIEF WELLS ARE EXPECTED TO BE COMPLETED SOMETIME IN AUGUST. REPORTING FROM NEW ORLEANS, I'M JANE DOE.

FIGURE 6-4

Source: Script contributed by Suzy Smith, Ball State University

There will always be a need for skeptical, no-nonsense, tenacious, thorough, take-no-prisoners reporting. There will always be a need for someone to watch over the public's money and the public's interests. There will always be a need to take on government and big business and politicians and expose them to scrutiny. There will always be a need to tell universal stories of courage and sacrifice and triumph and defeat.

There will always—ALWAYS—be a need for journalism, real journalism, and real journalists. If you're lucky enough to figure that out in time, you'll have a rewarding career and you'll have a chance to make the world a better place.

Exercises

1. Identify a news story in your community or on your campus. Then construct six different summary news leads. Each lead should focus on one of the six core journalistic questions: who, what, when, where, why, and how. Post your finished leads to your WordPress site.
2. Identify a news or feature story in your community or on your campus. Then construct a lead for each of the following types: blind lead, umbrella lead, identification of impact lead, anecdotal lead, descriptive lead, and quotation lead. Post your finished leads to your WordPress site.
3. Choose one of the stories you identified for exercises one and two and write a complete story. Consider how information layering might enhance storytelling and write at least one fact box or time line that might accompany the story. Write two versions of the story, one that is structured for print and one for the web. Post your finished stories to your WordPress site.
4. Identify a topic for a diagrammatic graphic. Conduct all of the research necessary to conceptualize the visual approach. Regardless of your illustration abilities, draw up a quick sketch for how the graphic will be structured and indicate where the textual elements of the graphic will be placed. Then, write a headline, introductory chatter, and all necessary labels, callouts, and explainers. Remember to include a byline and source lines as well. Post your finished graphics text to your WordPress site.
5. Visit npr.org and choose the "listen" tab from the top of the page. There, you will find a few options, including an hourly news summary. First, spend a few moments listening to the summaries that begin playing. Then, choose one to

record, transcribe, and analyze for structure. Pay close attention to how well the piece(s) adhere(s) to the guidelines listed in the writing for audio scripts section of this chapter. Then, write a paragraph or two that describes sentence structure, word choice, rhythm, and placement of silence within the piece. Post your finished report to your WordPress site.

6. Identify a news or feature story in your community or on your campus.

   Then write a script for a radio news report as well as one for a video news report. Post your finished scripts to your WordPress site.

Notes

1. Mario Garcia and Pegie Stark, *Eyes on the News* (Poynter Institute, 1991).
2. Sara Quinn, Pegie Stark, and Rick Edmonds, *Eyetracking the News* (Poynter Institute, 1997).
3. Jakob Nielsen, "How Users Read on the Web." Jakob Nielsen's Alertbox, October 1, 1997. http://www.useit.com/alertbox/9710a.html.
4. Jenna Wortham, "Cellphones Now Used More for Data than for Calls." *New York Times*, May 13, 2010.
5. Mario Garcia, "The Power of the Tablet" seminar, June 14–15, 2010. Live blog transcript.

CHAPTER 7

Photojournalism

Capturing the Moments That Transcend Language

We "read" journalistic photos for the emotions they portray and invoke. We read them to get a sense of scene, environment, or place. In them, we seek reflections of ourselves and portraits of the human condition. Journalistic photos capture moments in time, chronicle events, and convey the details of a scene with visual precision unlike any other form of storytelling. These are all powerful concepts, indeed. Photojournalism provides visual cues that transcend language.

The use of photos to illustrate news stories began in the late 1800s. The first photojournalist, Carol Szathmari, covered the Crimean War, and a few of the images survive today. And in 1880, *The Daily Graphic*, a popular New York newspaper, published the first halftone news photo. Interestingly, at the time, a number of print journalists speculated that the use of photos in conjunction with news was just a "passing fad." They argued that images would never come close to achieving the level of importance of the written word. But the power of the image prevailed as the public craved the realistic depictions of news stories that photos could provide. Likewise, news photos were commonly exhibited in art galleries. Over the years, photojournalism has benefited from better printing technologies, color capabilities, and the emergence of digital cameras.

The multimedia movement has transformed photojournalism perhaps more than any other medium. Space has always been a major limitation for most print publications. So, although photographers might shoot scores of photos for a single story, most of the time, only one or two make it to press. However, when print publications

NHL PLAYOFFS Game 5: Red Wings 4, Coyotes 1 | Red Wings lead series, 3-2

COYOTES LOSE KEY GAME

Detroit victory puts Phoenix on verge of elimination SPORTS, C1

Shopping for foreclosed homes

What to watch out for YOUR HOME, HO1

THE ARIZONA REPUBLIC

azcentral.com

SATURDAY, APRIL 24, 2010

IMMIGRATION BILL BECOMES LAW

CENTER OF THE STORM

As nation watches, Brewer decries immigration 'crisis'

Rights groups vow legal challenge; D.C. weighs action

Gov. Jan Brewer signs Senate Bill 1070 into law on Friday. "I firmly believe it represents what's best for Arizona," she says.

By Craig Harris, Alia Beard Rau and Glen Creno
THE ARIZONA REPUBLIC

Moments after Gov. Jan Brewer signed Arizona's controversial new immigration law Friday, opponents promised legal challenges and economic sanctions against a state still reeling from the housing meltdown.

Brewer, who faces a stiff primary challenge and needs conservatives to keep her in office, said the law represents another tool for the state to "work to solve a crisis we did not create and the federal government has refused to fix — the crisis caused by illegal immigration and Arizona's porous border."

The legislation put Arizona in the national spotlight, with President Barack Obama weighing in on it earlier in the day and cable-news giant CNN showing live broadcasts of Brewer's signing and the Capitol demonstrations.

Before and after Senate Bill 1070

See IMMIGRATION Page A8

Among the more than 1,500 demonstrators outside the state Capitol, many expressed outrage and dismay upon learning of the bill's signing.

Law revives calls for federal action on migrant reform

By Erin Kelly
REPUBLIC WASHINGTON BUREAU

WASHINGTON — Arizona's new law cracking down on illegal immigrants has thrust the dormant issue of immigration reform back into the national spotlight.

Immigrant-rights advocates are showing a renewed urgency to push Congress and President Barack Obama to adopt a federal law combining tough enforcement with a path to citizenship for the estimated 11 million illegal immigrants in the country.

Obama said Friday that he agrees that the federal government must act to avoid "irresponsibility by others." He called Arizona's law "misguided" and instructed the Justice Department to examine whether the bill is a violation of civil rights.

See LAW Page A9

Others outside the Capitol on Friday demonstrate in favor of the bill, including Ernie Getford. A poll has indicated that most voters support the law.

COMPLETE COVERAGE

Highlights: What the new law does
New roles for police, limits on cities, restrictions on day laborers: A breakdown of key points in the new immigration law, among the toughest in the nation. **A9**

Roberts: It didn't have to be this way
Amid our frustration, we now fear both immigration violations and civil-rights violations, stuck in a fight with little middle ground. If only Washington had done more to secure our border, things wouldn't have come to this. **Laurie Roberts, B1**

Photos: Coverage from the protests
See slide shows from Friday's demonstrations for and against the new immigration law, at **news.azcentral.com**.

Coming Sunday: The legal road ahead
What federal laws say about local enforcement of immigration, and what legal challenges are likely.

BUSINESS

LAWMAKERS READY FINANCIAL REFORM
Sweeping proposals to reform the nation's financial system take shape in Congress. An analysis of the key elements shows how Democratic lawmakers' new regulations would bring improved oversight of Wall Street's biggest banks. **D1**

GETTY IMAGES

NATION & WORLD

DOZENS KILLED BY BOMBINGS IN IRAQ
The bloodiest day of the year in Iraq leaves 69 dead in a series of bombings in Shiite areas. The attacks, blamed on Sunni-led insurgents, reinforce fears of a return to sectarian violence seen at the height of the war. **A5**

VALLEY & STATE

Sheriff's Office investigated: Maricopa County officials look into whether the Sheriff's Office misspent money that was intended to pay jail employees. **B1**

SPORTS

Cards draft linebacker: In Day 2 of the NFL draft, the Cardinals again focus on defense, trading up to take Texas Christian inside linebacker Daryl Washington. **C1**

EXPLORE ARIZONA

A perfect blend: In Arizona, when it comes to cocktails, nothing beats a well-mixed margarita. Find out who's serving up the best concoctions around the state. **E1**

WEATHER High 82. Low 56. Lots of sunshine expected across the Valley. ▸ Complete forecast on B8

120 Homes in 60 Days!
60 Additional Homes WILL BE SOLD by April 30th!
See Our Ad Inside This Section
BLANDFORD HOMES
BlandfordHomes.com

Live alerts on your cellphone: Text **aznews** to **44636** to get news updates sent to your phone. For more news and photos on your Web-enabled phone or PDA, go to **m.azcentral.com**

A Gannett Newspaper

FIGURE 7-1

Typical newspaper packages such as the one at left generally include a written story accompanied by one to three photos. The number of photos generally depends on the magnitude and complexity of the event, as well as image quality.

Source: Image courtesy of © *The Arizona Republic*, published April 24, 2010. Used with permission. Permission does not imply endorsement.

began to take full advantage of the web, photojournalists benefited from rich new story structures that go beyond the single image presentation. Before, images were largely seen as supplements to written stories. Now, photo presentations may comprise the whole of a story.

One of the most popular story forms to arise in the digital age is the photo/audio slideshow presentation. In fact, the addition of audio to the photojournalist's repertoire is one of the most significant changes photojournalism has experienced in recent years. Now, photojournalists can combine sound with still images and to create packages that are more cinematic. Likewise, photo gallery formats present multiple images users can navigate in any order. This nonlinear approach increases interactivity and provides a more dynamic presentation. In both the case of the photo slideshow and the gallery, the storytelling potential for still images is dramatically enhanced.

This chapter addresses both the power of the photo as a storytelling device, as well as the different ways photos are presented in print and online formats. Likewise, we will explore some of the more innovative ways news organizations use slideshow and gallery structures. We will also examine how the photojournalist's role has changed in the multimedia landscape and look at the role of audio in multimedia photo stories.

Photos in Print

Print publications have long used photographs to capture the visual moments of a story. Traditionally, print photos are presented in two basic ways: in combination with a written story or as a stand-alone visual story. In the case of the text/photo combination, photos punctuate the written piece by capturing a scene, visually chronicling an event, or putting faces to the names of people mentioned in a story. For example, a story about the outcome of a presidential election may include two main photos, one of each candidate. Most likely, the image of the winner would be larger and more dominant than the other. Together, they tell a story of success and defeat, happiness and disappointment. And since there are obviously a number of other important facts to convey for this story, the text can do the rest.

FIGURE 7-2

Photo stories like the one above often stand alone to tell a complete story visually.

Source: Image courtesy of The Ball State *Daily News.*

PAGE 6 | FEATURES MONDAY, JULY 20, 2009 | THE BALL STATE DAILY NEWS

DN PHOTO/PETER GAUNT

FELLOW RACERS AND SPECTATORS line up along the track at the Delaware County Fairgrounds on Sunday evening to watch the motorcross events. This year's racing events had the most entries of racers in Delaware County Fair history.

Motorcross: Gasoline, Guts and Glory

Photos by Peter Gaunt and Sam Householder

Online Exclusive
Check out an interactive audio slideshow at bsudailynews.com for more in-depth coverage on the Delaware County Fair Motorcross racing.

DN PHOTO/SAM HOUSEHOLDER

A MOTORCROSS RACER goes through the course during a race Sunday at the Delaware County Fairgrounds.

DN PHOTO/PETER GAUNT

ZACH COX, 15, makes sure that the younger racers make it through the course without problem. Cox has been racing for the last 10 years and was competing in the 125C class later in the day.

DN PHOTO/SAM HOUSEHOLDER

A MOTORCROSS RACER looks at the ground while jumping through the air during a race Sunday. The race at the Delaware County Fairgrounds kicks off fair week.

NETS BEAT CELTICS FOR 3-2 SERIES LEAD; YANKEES, RED SOX WIN • SPORTS, C1

WEATHER

FBI: We Might Have Stopped It

Director Acknowledges Agency Might Have Been Able To Detect Terror Attacks

MISSED CLUES

A HIGH ACHIEVEMENT IN MEMORY OF A FRIEND

America Still In The Dark About Sex

Political Agendas Crimp Research Into Behavior

INSIDE

'Al Qaeda Footprints'

The Search For PT109

Scare Closes River

Cannes' Gems

Prosecution Puts On Its Rebuttal

State Calls Skakel's Sister And A Former Elan Student To Testify

GOP ON THE TRAIL OF LOS VOTANTES

Hispanic Vote Grows In Number, Importance

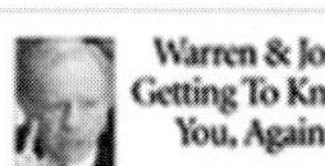

Warren & Joe: Getting To Know You, Again

FIGURE 7-3

Stand-alone photos are often used when a written story is not necessary or when a photo is so compelling that it warrants singular play.

Source: Image courtesy of the *Hartford Courant*.

Sometimes, however, images are presented alone. Single stand-alone images can be used when a particularly visual event doesn't warrant a complete story. In this case, a single image with a longer-than-usual caption can do the trick. For example, on the hottest day of the year, a local newspaper may choose to run a standalone photo of children splashing in a local pool. This topic doesn't necessarily warrant a whole written story but is interesting nonetheless. A single image along with a few sentences that provide context for the photo and its significance is a perfect way to tell the story. Other times, more space may be given to a photo story containing several images, all of which show different aspects of a highly visual story. For example, a newspaper covering the local 4-H fair may choose to run a number of images of different events at the fair. This type of presentation allows the newspaper to focus on people and *show* the story rather than *tell* it—a perfect strategy for a story of this nature.

PRINT FILE SPECS

File sizes: Standard photo file sizes for print vary, depending on the type of publication. As a general rule, most newspaper photos should be 150 to 300 dpi. Most photos in books and magazines should be 300 to 600 dpi. Save images the exact width and height they will run on screen before importing them into your design program. Resizing them once they are in the program may damage photo quality and will not decrease the amount of time the images take to load.

File formats: File formats vary among print publications. The most common are JPG and TIF. The degree of compression for JPG images is adjustable, allowing a selectable tradeoff between storage size and image quality. JPG typically achieves 10:1 compression with little noticeable loss in image quality. TIF files are not compressed and are popular for high color-depth images.

Color: CMYK is a subtractive color model used for print in which values of cyan, magenta, yellow, and black inks are mixed together to create other color values. As inks are mixed together, some wavelengths of light are absorbed (or subtracted) and others are reflected and made visible.

QUICK TIPS

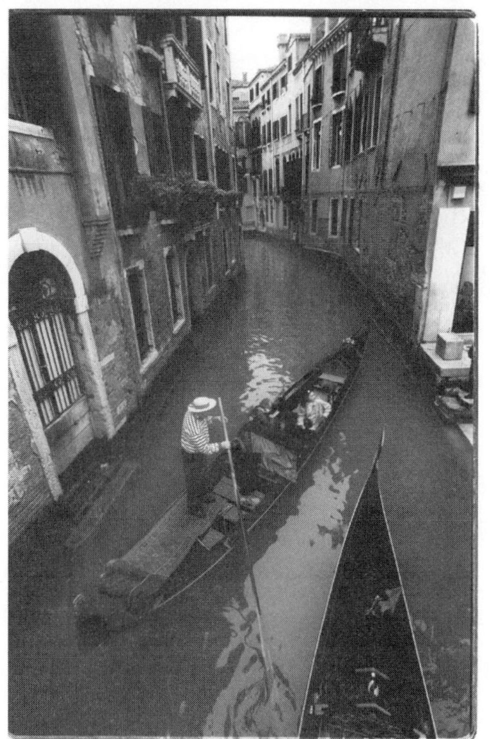

FIGURE 7-4

Source: Image courtesy of Ryan J. Sparrow, Ball State University

Identify key moments, and don't let them pass you by without snapping the shot. Capturing moments is at the heart of telling stories with photographs. Look for people interacting with one another and their environments. Watch faces, eyes, and body language to capture emotion and expression. Stay focused on the action to ensure you capture the most compelling moments.

Change angles and points of view while shooting. Capture long shots to establish location, medium shots to chronicle the action, and close-up shots to focus on details. You will want photos from all three distances in your final edit for variety and thorough storytelling. Likewise, squat down and climb hills or stairs, to change your point of view.

FIGURE 7-5

Source: Image courtesy of Ryan J. Sparrow, Ball State University

Make sure that the subject stands out from the background. Dark figures on dark backgrounds or light figures on light backgrounds will wash together, making for weak images that are difficult to read. Likewise, if your background is not relevant, move to find a new environment.

(*Continued*)

QUICK TIPS (continued)

FIGURE 7-6

Source: Image courtesy of Ryan J. Sparrow, Ball State University

FIGURE 7-7

Source: Image courtesy of Ryan J. Sparrow, Ball State University

Employ the rule of thirds. Avoid placing the subject in the center of the photograph, which creates a static composition.

Look for leading lines in a composition. Leading lines move the eye from one point to another. Anything with a definite line can be a leading line. The horizon, shoreline, fences, bridges, and skylines can move the eye. Leading lines are a great way to establish a dynamic composition.

FIGURE 7-8

Source: Image courtesy of Ryan J. Sparrow, Ball State University

FIGURE 7-9

Source: Image courtesy of Ryan J. Sparrow, Ball State University

QUICK TIPS (continued)

Use depth of field to create dimension in an image. Depth of field is the sharpest portion of an image. A shallow depth of field (shown earlier) occurs when the nearest object in an image is sharp. Sometimes, a large depth of field is appropriate, and other times, you will want to deemphasize the foreground or background.

Make sure there are no distracting elements, such as lampposts that extend from a subject's head. As you establish your point of view, examine the frame and move around accordingly to eliminate these distractions.

Make sure your lighting is appropriate. Avoid flat frontal lighting. Instead, make sure you subjects are lit from the side or back. Sometimes it may be necessary to seek dramatic lighting for a stronger visual effect.

FIVE-FRAME PHOTO STORY

A popular Flickr group, "Tell a Story in 5 Frames" provides a valuable exercise in focusing a photo story. The group includes a shared photo pool in which winners of the "Tell a Story in 5 Frames" contest can share their images. Each story consists of five photos, with no captions or explanatory text. Of course, winners are those who most successfully tell a story "through visual means with only a title to help guide the interpretation." The group's moderators provide the following guidelines for choosing photos:

- The first photo should establish characters and location.
- The second photo should establish the scenario and provide viewers with possible outcomes.
- The third photo should involve the characters in the scenario.
- The fourth photo should build probable outcomes
- The fifth photo should have a logical but surprising end.

Of course, telling a story with five images is hardly easy. But the outline provided here can be a fantastic guide for developing focused, engaging photo stories.

Photos on the Web

Although there are a number of variations on how images are used online, we can break them down into three basic categories: single images that accompany other story forms, photo slideshows with or without audio, and photo galleries. Single image presentations do not need much explanation. In fact, this format is nearly identical to its print counterpart: an image is used to supplement a text-based story or stands alone with a caption. However, slideshows and galleries are more complex, providing photojournalists with different options for image presentation. The main difference between slideshows and galleries is in their navigational structures. A slideshow tends to offer a more linear experience in which the user pushes the play button to watch photos fade in and out, and listen as some form of audio provides narration. Galleries, on the other hand, often display a number of photos and allow the user to decide the order in which they are viewed.

Slideshows

Photos: Take as many photos as you can while on assignment. Look for images that tell a well-rounded story and a wide range of compositions, from tight detail images, to scene setters, to wide-angle shots. Remember that slideshows are linear presentations of multiple images. So, together, your images should tell a cohesive story, with a clear beginning, middle, and end. The photos, however, may not be sequenced according to time when they are edited into a slideshow package. So, it will be important to capture as many images as possible to give yourself enough room to edit later. Any good editor will tell you that it is better to have too much than too little. Once an event is over, you cannot go back to take pictures you did not capture the first time around. Capture sequences of events, as well images shot consecutively in quick frames.

Captions: Captions are important to journalistic photo presentations because they are a means for indentifying individuals and explaining the circumstances of a shot. Good captions aid in a viewer's understanding of the story and should contain more than just a subject's name or description of the scene. Include information that goes beyond what the viewer can already figure out by looking at the image. Help the viewer understand why the image is significant to the story, and write captions that help pull the viewer through the story from beginning to end.

Photo galleries: Galleries are largely driven by how they are designed and presented. As previously noted, galleries are similar to slideshows in that they offer a collection

WEB FILE SPECS

File sizes: The standard file size/resolution for images that will appear on the web is 72 dpi. Online, larger files take longer to load. Slideshows with multiple images can get large quickly if you are not careful about image sizes. Again, save photos and other image files at the exact width and height they will run to preserve image quality.

File formats: File formats vary among digital platforms. The most common are JPG, PNG, and GIF. JPG formats provide better image quality, but are often larger files that may load a bit slower than the other two. PNG and GIF images are more compressed and allow for low-resolution images to maintain good quality. PNG files preserve transparencies in images, while GIF files do not.

Color: Computer monitors and television screens use a method of color reproduction called optical mixing. In this model, red, green, and blue (RGB) pixels are side-by-side. Only the green pixels illuminate, when green is visible to the eye. Both green and blue pixels light up when cyan appears. When white appears, all the pixels illuminate. Because the pixels are so small and close together our eyes blend them together, making different color values visible to the eye.

of photos on a single topic. However, they are generally presented nonlinearly. And although galleries can be used for any story, they are particularly useful for presenting many images, each of which provides a different look at a single subject. For example, the story about the local 4-H fair would make for a great gallery. Each image could show the blue ribbon winner in every category, from best hog to largest pumpkin. Given the right design, the user could view images by category and go straight to the ones she is interested in.

There are a number of ways to structure and design a photo gallery. Galleries may contain captions, audio clips with each image, or both. They may be designed with a numbering system for each image or use thumbnail images that when clicked become larger.

Sound: Connecting sound with photos is a delicate task that often includes going back and forth between audio and photos several times before settling on the final set of images and audio cut. The key to a great photo/audio slideshow is matching the photos with the natural sound and what the narrator is talking about. For example, if the subject of your interview is talking about how much she loves her children, the image that appears in concert with that audio clip could show her hugging or playing with them. Remember, you are telling someone else's story. So the story's angle should largely be determined by the interviewee's anecdotes and answers to questions. Reporter voiceovers may fill in important details left out by interview subjects or transition between key moments in the storyline.

Visit the multimedia examples section of www.oup.com/us/palilonis and select photojournalism from the drop down menu for live examples of linear slideshows and galleries.

Photo Editing

Photo editing for journalistic storytelling is often a very complex process that involves a number of important considerations. The editing process actually starts in the field when a photographer begins taking pictures. And observations and shot choices in the field are all part of the early editing stages. However, a good photographer may take hundreds of photos covering a single story, only to use one or two in print and 21 to 24 in a gallery or slideshow. So, the first step is to cut down the number of images to create a tightly focused visual narrative. If you are trying to edit down to one or two images, look for the image that illustrates the main focus of the story. A story about a surfing competition, for example, may be accompanied by an image of the winner during one of his most challenging waves. A secondary image may depict a crowd of spectators watching incredulously as one of the competitors takes a nasty spill. Of course, can't show every aspect of a story in one or two images. So, when choosing the few that you will use, look for the most engaging, lively, expressive, relevant, interesting, well-executed images in the bunch.

Although space is less of a concern online, it is still very important that photo packages be edited with a tightly focused storyline. You must strike a careful balance between telling a complete story and avoiding redundancy among images. Consider again the story about the courageous woman who won a hard-fought battle with breast cancer. As you start to edit photos for this story, begin by searching for single images that provide a well-rounded look at her life. One image may show her receiving chemotherapy treatments. Another may show her

QUICK TIPS ON SOUND

Test your equipment before going into the field to conduct interviews and again before beginning an interview. Have your subject say a few words and then play back the sound before starting the interview. There is nothing worse than conducting a long interview only to find out later that the sound quality was poor or the equipment was not recording properly.

Conduct your interview in a quiet place. Even the subtlest sounds, such as a buzzing light fixture can wreak havoc on your audio.

Position your subject four to six inches from the microphone. Steady the mic on a hard surface or hold it steady by gripping it in the middle. Do not let the subject hold the mic.

Eliminate unnecessary movement so you don't pick up noises that will distort or drown out parts of the interview.

Wear headphones during the interview. This will allow you to hear the subject the way the audience does.

And avoid interrupting your subject. You might not realize how often you say, "hmmm," or "oh," or "uh-huh" when you are having a conversation with someone. It is common in a casual conversation to interject separate questions or thoughts. But this is not a casual conversation; so don't ruin a great quote by inserting your own voice into the audio clip.

Pick up ambient sound separately at another time. This will allow you to control the audio levels for ambient sound and interviews separately.

Create an audio log. after you have collected interviews and ambient sound. To do this, listen to your interview clips in an audio editing program. As you listen, create a list that includes descriptive phrases or significant quotes along with the time at which they occur in your audio timeline. This log will serve as a helpful guide when it comes time to edit your piece down to a finished slideshow.

COMMON SLIDESHOW MISTAKES

Too few or too many images: Most producers recommend that each image in a slideshow appear for six to 10 seconds. So, select the optimal number of photos to effectively match the length of your audio.

Photos that do not match the audio (or vice versa): The quickest way to lose and/or confuse your audience is to show images that do not match what the speaker is saying. Photos and audio must work together to tell the story.

Rambling or choppy narratives: Avoid audio in which a speaker is rambling, jumping from topic to topic or interjecting new thoughts before finishing others. Do not edit audio so tightly that it becomes a series of sound bites as opposed to a fluid narrative.

Missing captions or identifying audio: Regardless of how you identify subjects, do so consistently. Likewise, if you are using interview footage, identify the speaker visually and by name early in the show.

Loosely edited photos or audio: Editing journalistic content requires scrutiny to ensure the story is focused, the audience is captivated, and the angle is clear. Regardless of how compelling your story or gripping your content, the average viewer is willing to spend a mere one to three minutes with online videos, slideshows, or narrative animations.

Dead air: Avoid long periods of unexplained silence in your narrative. Keep images and audio moving at a comfortable pace that is continuous and cohesive.

Weak or missing transitions: Just as the content of the images should match the context of the audio narrative, the pace of the image must match the pace of the audio. For example, try to match fades in and out with natural pauses in narration. Natural sound can also make for a strong transition. Use it to punctuate the end of a narrative or to set the scene when a new topic is introduced.

Poor audio quality: Low audio levels, imbalance between overlapping tracks, and distracting background noise are a few of the technical problems that can arise.

Eliminate unnecessary noise by interviewing in quiet places when possible. During production, normalize audio by adjusting the volume of all of the different audio files to a standard level.

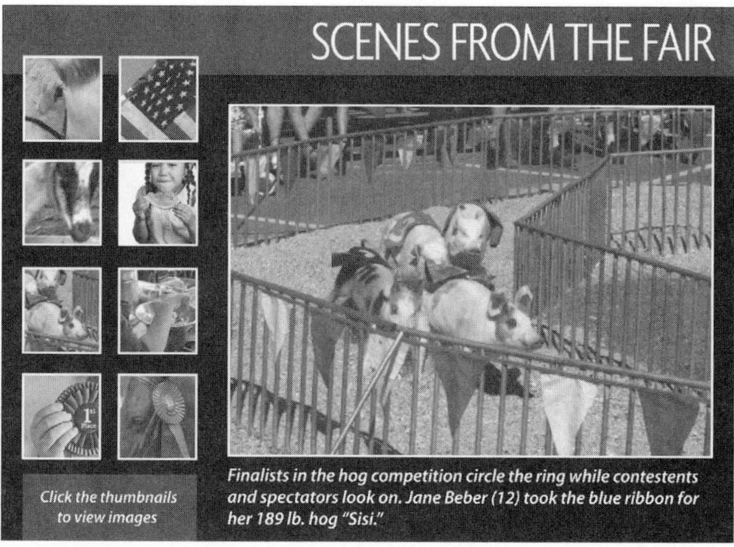

SCENES FROM THE FAIR
Click the thumbnails to view images
Finalists in the hog competition circle the ring while contestents and spectators look on. Jane Beber (12) took the blue ribbon for her 189 lb. hog "Sisi."

FIGURE 7-10

This photo gallery allows the user to view photos in any order. When the user clicks on a thumbnail image on the left, the selected photo is displayed larger in the viewing area to the right. *Source:* iStockphoto.com

attending church. A third may depict her playing with her children on a Saturday afternoon. And yet another may show her participating in a cancer charity event. Together, these images provide a small window into her life and offer insights into how her disease is affecting it. You may have shot 50 great images of her interacting with her family and another 50 of her receiving treatment. Look for the ones that have the strongest composition, clearest emotions, and most engaging narratives. Editing photos is as much about showing restraint in your work as it is finding focus.

Cropping 101

Nothing destroys a great photograph like a bad crop job. And nearly every experienced photojournalist can tell horror stories about photos being mishandled by an inexperienced colleague. Cropping can eliminate unnecessary visual information, zero in on the area of interest, or create a more compelling composition. However, avoid cropping photos simply to make them fit a predetermined space. Rather, pay

QUICK TIPS

FIGURE 7-11

FIGURE 7-12

Do not crop people at key joints, such as the wrists, elbows, ankles, and knees. It creates a jarring composition.

Do not crop too closely. Leave headroom and make sure key points of interest do not seem crammed into the frame.

FIGURE 7-13

Crop out unnecessary information as long as the crop doesn't interfere with other, important parts of the image.

Crop to create a rule of thirds. A good crop can improve the composition of an image.

careful attention to how your crop affects the overall composition, and trim photos only when the crop makes them better. And before you attempt to crop someone else's image, it is a good idea to consult the photographer first.

Innovative Photo Packages Across Platforms

Innovation in digital photojournalism has not stopped with slideshows and galleries. In fact, a number of talented multimedia photographers have begun to experiment with techniques that provide even more texture and depth to visual stories.

For example, in anticipation of the 2008 Rock Hall of Fame inductions, msnbc .com created a photo gallery with images and extended captions for each of the inductees, from the Dave Clark Five to Madonna. However, they didn't stop there. They included two additional features that made the gallery more engaging and ramped up the degree of multimedia storytelling. In addition to images and captions, they also allowed the user to play a musical audio clip from each artist as well as vote on his or her favorite nominee. After voting, they could see how their choice ranked among other users.

Similarly, a photo presentation titled "Last Days, Last Rays: Evenings at Ontario Beach Park" created by photographer Will Yurman of the *Rochester Democrat and Chronicle* (New York) provides an innovative gallery/slideshow hybrid. It starts with a 250-word introduction, a relatively substantial block of text for a slideshow. Upon entering the presentation, the user can choose to watch it straight through—with or without audio—as well as turn captions and sound on and off. But perhaps most innovative is the way the audio was edited. The complete set of images is perfectly timed with a matching audio clip. However, if images are selected one at a time, the audio corresponds perfectly with the selected image. This technique results in a rich experience that allows the user varying degrees of interactivity.

Both of these examples certainly exhibit characteristics of more traditional approaches to slideshows and galleries. But those extra touches such as musical clips, voting features, and hybrid combinations show how sophisticated and interactive digital photo presentations can be. And although there is nothing wrong with using the tried and true approaches offered by the standard photo/audio slideshow or image/caption gallery, going the extra mile can really add value to storytelling. The key is to be thoughtful about your story. Before taking the "easy" way out by going

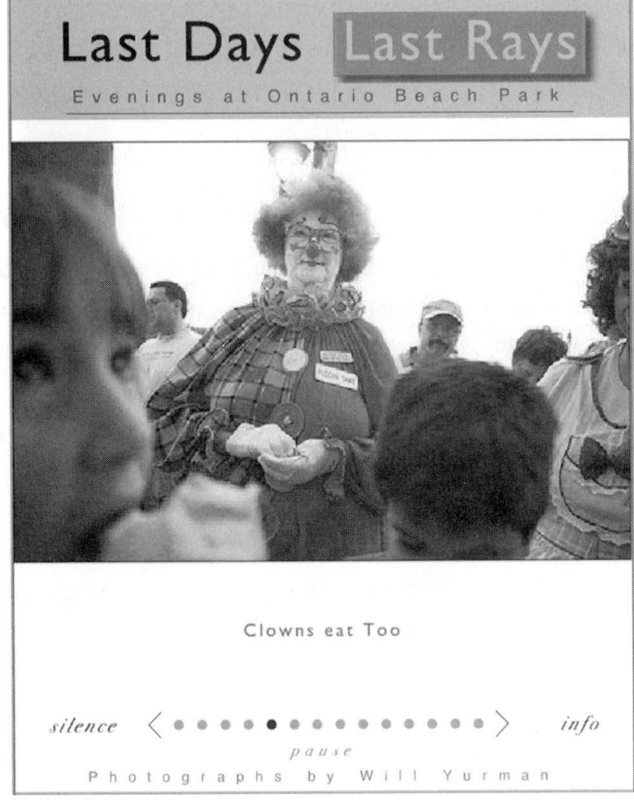

FIGURE 7-14

"Last Days, Last Rays: Evenings at Ontario Beach Park" published by the *Rochester Democrat and Chronicle* is structured so that the user can either watch the slideshow straight through, with or without audio, as well as turn captions and sound on and off. Each image is perfectly timed with a single audio clip that matches its content.

Source: Image courtesy of the *Rochester Democrat and Chronicle.*

with what you know, think about how the content for a specific photo package can drive more innovative approaches to design and presentation. Then, consider the tools and methods available and be creative in how you implement them. Let content drive design.

Visit the multimedia examples section of www.oup.com/us/palilonis and select photojournalism from the drop down menu for live examples of innovative approaches to multimedia photo presentation.

Serving Mobile Users

As we discuss innovation, we must also consider alternative platforms and devices like smartphones and tablet readers. For example, how does screen size affect a

FIGURE 7-15

The Guardian's "Eyewitness" iPad application showcases compelling images printed in color in the center spread of *The Guardian* newspaper each day. The app allows users to share images, save favorites, and view "pro tips."

Source: Image courtesy of *The Guardian.*

photo gallery or slideshow when viewed on a two- to three-inch mobile device? Suddenly, tighter detail shots read better than wider shots in which there is too much going on for the scene to be easily discernable. Likewise, it may be necessary to offer both captions and audio so that users can choose to view the photo package with or without headphones. Of course, it is not always possible to edit a package twice—once for the online version and once for the small-screen device. However, as the desktop Internet experience switches to "on the go" when users leave the house, handheld devices become a viable place for bite-sized story forms like slideshows and galleries.

Early tablet applications have been a great venue for photos because of the formidable screen size and exceptional screen resolution. One early iPad photo application received quite a bit of attention, both for its presentation of compelling images, as well as its distribution model. *The Guardian's* "Eyewitness" app showcases the newspaper's popular Eyewitness images, which are printed in color in the center spread of *The Guardian* newspaper each day. And there's added value with the iPad app. In addition to offering a gallery of beautiful, provocative journalistic photos from around the world, the app also includes the ability to share images with others, save favorites, and view "pro tips." The pro tips feature includes explanations from the *Guardian* photo team regarding the technical and artistic merits of each image. The app is free and sponsored by Canon. This partnership also represents a unique revenue model for editorial content. Similar apps continue to emerge, presenting journalists with even more options regarding how photographs are consumed and used to tell stories.

Professional Perspective

Keith Jenkins • *Supervising Senior Producer for Multimedia*

National Public Radio

Keith Jenkins oversees the multimedia unit of npr.org, responsible for photography and videography. Jenkins and his staff work with NPR shows, reporters, and editors on projects and provide compelling visuals to match the rich audio storytelling of NPR. Jenkins spent 13 years at The Washington Post. *He was a staff photographer and photography director of washingtonpost.com, photography editor of Washington Post Magazine and deputy assistant managing editor for photography. From 1997 to 1999, Jenkins worked as AOL's first director of photography. Jenkins began his photography career working for graphic designer Dietmar R. Winkler and then spent five years as a staff photographer for* The Boston Globe.

The panic over the paradigm shift that is the web, which has gripped the news industry has, curiously, also gripped portions of the world of photography and photojournalism. Personally, I find this very hard to explain. With very few exceptions, photography should be the art (and profession) least concerned about the changes wrought by evolving technology. Photography is, in fact, a product of the world of technology and has benefited from its evolution at almost every turn.

Why is it then, that in the early years following the birth of Internet, we lost our faith in the power of the still image? If this is just part of human nature, to fear the new, then we should get over it soon. Much as our predecessors had to deal with the transition from glass plates to negatives, and from large cameras on tripods to cameras small enough to be cradled in the palm of a hand, we, too, must change. Visual journalism on the web, on cell phones, on set top boxes, and on car navigation screens will still be based on "the image" (moving or not) and the basic building block will always be "the photograph."

Technique Adapts to the Tools

Mathew Brady—best known for his portraits of celebrities and documentation of the American Civil War—created photos that reflected his tools: large camera, delicate glass plates, difficult field processing. And through these tools, he showed us the quiet calm of the dead on the Civil War's battlefield. He told the appropriate story and revealed it with the help of his available tools. The same was true for Weegee's Speed Graphic, Diane Arbus and her Rolleiflex, Henri Cartier-Bresson and his Leica. Although each tool is different from the other, in the hands of their respective owners, all were capable of telling the appropriate, powerful visual story. Why should today's photographers be any worse off?

Neither photography nor photojournalism is destined for the scrap heap. In fact, with the easy availability of cheap, "smart" cameras for the masses, the future of photography has never been more integrated into everyday life. What the profession of photojournalism needs, however, is clarity of purpose and faith in the enduring power the still image.

Photography and Multimedia

Photography is the foundation for today's visual storytelling. Make no mistake, the past and the future of modern visual storytelling lies with the photograph (early cave drawings not withstanding). If anything, the early twenty-first century offers an unprecedented opportunity to use still photographs to tell more stories, more quickly, than ever before. Suddenly, the ability to produce a "*Life* magazine style" photo essay is within the reach of everyone who has a camera and access to the web. Film is no longer a necessary expense. And if you can muster the creativity, your photographic tool can be as simple as your cell phone. As small screens get bigger, and all screens gain higher resolution, what was only possible in the best quality gravure photo book will be available in your pocket.

What makes this evolution in photography all the more exciting is the ability to marry the still image, seamlessly, to some other powerful storytelling tools. First among these is the human voice through sound and audio. Place a compelling W. Eugene Smith–style photo essay along side a National Public Radio "driveway moment" and you can see where this is headed. This does not work for every story, but when it does, magic ensues. If this were a mathematical equation, *pictures + sound* would yield a result greater than the sum of its parts.

And of course, we have to mention the 800-pound gorilla in the room: video. In the late 1990s and early in the current century, many photojournalists (and the organizations they worked for) abandoned the still photo for the moving image, often with disastrous results. Carefully crafted images were replaced with formulaic shots and predictable storytelling. The new pattern: "b-roll, talking head, b-roll with voice-over, talking head, b-roll." The natural flow of the story, which photographer's held dear as "fly on the wall" journalists, gave way to the plastic, TV-like news spot. And often, these were not even as good as TV, because these new video-journalists only had months, not years of experience under their belts.

However, the rise of "digicam video" offers some hope. Now, the photojournalist has the primary storytelling tool he's most familiar with back in his hands: the single-lens reflex camera. Its "extended" technology—the ability to capture cinema quality video (if not audio)—means that visual skills learned over decades can easily be put to use creating something new. Most important, however, the still image remains at the forefront of this new, storytelling device. We don't have to abandon the past in order to visualize the future.

Putting the Multiple Media Pieces Together

"Think less like a factory worker, more like a jazz musician." This modification of a statement made to me at the start of my career applies well today. In other words, don't think of multimedia as a trade—one where you are taught how to *use* tools instead of how to *think* about story structure and narrative. The basics are still at the heart of what we do. Learn how to conduct a good interview. Learn about the rule of thirds. Learn the rhythm of W. Eugene Smith's photo essays or how to frame a shot like Sergio Leone. And if you do these things first, then learning how to use Photoshop or Final Cut Pro will make much more sense.

In this rapidly changing twenty-first century, the tools we use will change every few months. But don't build your education or your career around mastering them. Rather, if you learn how to think about the elements of successful, multi-platform journalism, you'll be equipped for a lifetime of telling good stories and prepared for the media landscape yet to be imagined.

Exercises

1. Visit www.oup.com/us/palilonis and find the resources/exercises drop down menu. Select photo resources. Click the link labeled "Photo Story." There you will find a collection of 30 photos with captions and an Adobe InDesign template for a print photo story. Choose seven images and captions that will comprise your photo story. Then, use the InDesign template to design a photo story. You are free to modify the InDesign template. However, if you are less confident about your design skills, use the layout that is provided. Just make sure you consider the sizing and placement of each image as you decide where they belong in the layout. Post your finished page in the form of a PDF file or JPEF image to your WordPress site.
2. Visit www.oup.com/us/palilonis and find the resources/exercises drop down menu. Select photo resources. Click the link labeled "Cropping." There you will find a collection of 10 photos. Using Adobe Photoshop, crop them as you see fit and save them as JPG files. Post the cropped images on your WordPress site along with the originals.
3. Visit www.oup.com/us/palilonis and find the resources/exercises drop down menu. Select photo resources. Click the link labeled "Linear Slideshow." There you will find a collection of 30 images with captions. First, edit the photos and captions to form a linear slideshow composed of 15 images. Navigation should be executed using simple forward and backward buttons. Also included in this package is a slideshow template built in Adobe Flash titled slideshow.swf. Follow the directions for saving your photos and captions so they automatically load into your slideshow template. Post your finished slideshow to your WordPress site.
4. Visit www.oup.com/us/palilonis and find the resources/exercises drop down menu. Select photo resources. Click the link labeled "Photo/Audio Slideshow." There you will find a collection of 30 images with captions and five minutes of audio clips for each of two stories. For one or both, edit the photos and audio into a 90-second slideshow. Use the slideshow development program of your choice. Post your finished slideshow to your WordPress site.

CHAPTER 8

Audio

Sound Storytelling

Great audio stories engage listeners with rich, personal narratives. Sound can paint pictures of the human condition that reach listeners on deep emotional levels. And although audio storytelling is most commonly associated with radio, audio is a versatile story form that can add depth and dimension to other types of stories as well. In all cases, audio narratives should provide rich descriptions; be comprehensive, compelling, fair, and balanced; and produced with technical and editorial accuracy.

There are a number of different formats for audio stories. News is often read in short segments between blocks of other (generally music) programming on commercial radio stations. For example, brief news segments are often presented for a few minutes at the top of each hour during "drive time." Drive time refers to the morning hours when listeners wake up, get ready, and head to work or school, and the afternoon hours when they are heading home. At the same time, there are a number of commercial radio stations with all-news, talk formats. In 2010, there were 27 stations of this kind in the United States. Commercial news stations, as well as National Public Radio (NPR), often provide in-depth story segments, complete with interviews, ambient sound, and longer narratives. And, of course, let's not forget that

EARLY RADIO NEWS

Early radio news consisted of recorded dramatizations of news events because at the time, live recordings were not technologically possible. In 1928, *NewsCasts*, a series of 10-minute news briefs drawn from the pages of *Time* magazine aired on more than 33 stations across the country. And in 1929, an additional series called *NewsActing* launched. *NewsActing* featured sound effects and professional actors who read current news stories in a dramatic fashion. *NewsActing* was renamed *March of Time* and first aired on CBS in 1931. The show centered on a narrator who led listeners through dramatized events, and real actors actually imitated the voices of the subjects in a story. For example, stories about World War II included an actor voicing Adolf Hitler. According to the Old Time Radio Link Society, "The actors were chosen for these roles based on their ability to closely duplicate the actual person. Sometimes an actor was required to listen from a library of records with 30-second sound bites of the actual personality, or view the March of Time's newsreels and listen to the voice."[1] By 1940, dramatized news programs were phased out in favor of the more modern format in which journalists presented news stories as reporters, not actors. Since then, news talk radio programs on stations such as NPR have made an art form of connecting audiences with salient issues and compelling subjects via sound.

in recent years, podcasts have become a popular way for broadcasts and other audio-driven stories to be downloaded via the web.

Today, audio is capable of serving many different purposes in a multimedia environment. Audio may stand alone on the radio or online, or be used to complement another story form, such as video, photo slideshows, information graphics, and animations. Thus, all journalists must know how to develop audio story ideas, record interviews with subjects, write scripts for narration, and read on air. Likewise, you should have a clear understanding of all of the ways audio appears in news. This chapter will help pave the way for building these skills.

QUICK TIPS

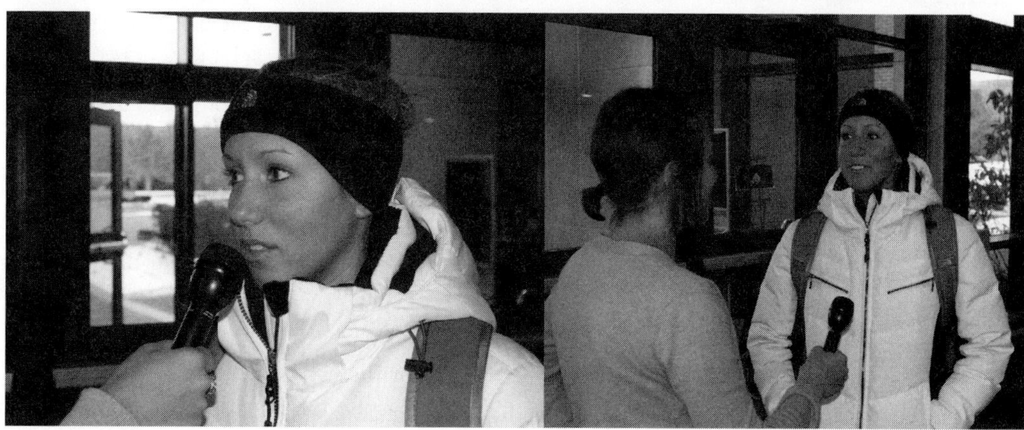

FIGURE 8-1

If a mic is too close to the subject's mouth (left), the sound will be muffled—not to mention the fact that the speaker might be a little annoyed and distracted. By contrast, if the mic is too far from the mouth (right), the speaker's voice may be too low. You may also pick up unwanted background noise.

FIGURE 8-2

The mic should be held about six inches from the subject's mouth for the clearest sound at the optimal levels.

Make sure your subject's mouth is four to six inches from the microphone when collecting audio. If the mic is too far from the speaker's mouth or the distance between mic and mouth varies during the interview, the audio will be weak, hard to hear, and hard to edit.

Always carry spare batteries for your equipment, and check to make sure it is all working properly before going out on assignment. Also, be sure to check your recording before leaving the field.

Never overwrite or erase your original audio file. If you erase it, you cannot get it back. So, better to make a copy and keep it safe in case you need to return to the original file during the editing process.

(Continued)

QUICK TIPS (continued)

Try exporting your final audio story in a few different file formats before deciding which gives you the smallest file size that still sounds good. The proper file size may also depend on how the file is being used. An acceptable data rate for audio is 48 Kbps. The most common types of uncompressed file formats are .wav (Windowns) and .aiff (Mac OS). MP3 is a compressed format that reduces the amount of data required for the audio piece to maintain its reproduction quality for most listeners.

Developing the Audio-Only Story

Knowing when and how to craft each of these types of audio experiences is an important skill for all multimedia journalists. So, let's take a brief look at what makes each type unique.

Audio Briefs

Audio news briefs should be tightly focused, written in active voice, and elaborate a particular story in a mere four to eight sentences. A collection of briefs is often presented together, and the entire collection may only last a few minutes. Although audio briefs may contain additional sound bites from interviews or natural sound, they are often nothing more than a reporter reading directly from a script. By way of example, the following 55-second brief appeared along with a collection of other briefs online on AudioWickinews in August 2010:

After a rare clash between Israeli and Lebanese forces over the cutting down of a tree near the border of the two countries, it appears that all sides are attempting to restore peace.

The skirmish started after an Israeli soldier began cutting down a tree that had the capability to provide cover to Lebanese infiltrators.

Israel stated that they clear the border of underbrush weekly. After the tree was cut down, the Lebanese army started firing.

The Lebanese were allegedly aiming at a base nearby and the resulting skirmish killed a senior Israeli military officer, a Lebanese journalist and two Lebanese army soldiers.

The United Nations peacekeeping force in South Lebanon has stated that Israel was operating in its own territory.

However, Lebanese information minister Tarek Mitri said that the area of land that had the tree was Lebanese territory and also state that though Lebanon respects the border, the country still contests part of it.

Just seven sentences in length, this audio brief is short and to-the-point. At the same time, its author manages to paint a vivid picture for the listener and explains the conflict with sufficient detail.

Audio Story Packages

If you listen to talk news radio like NPR, you are probably familiar with audio story packages. The best audio stories require a lot of research and reporting. A reporter may conduct multiple interviews; gather natural sound from news scenes; and narrate an introduction, transitions, and a conclusion for a typical audio news package. Pulled together, these elements can be offered as a radio segment, online news report, or podcast. Most stand-alone audio packages begin by setting the scene with a few seconds of ambient sound. They then lead with a reporter track or compelling interview clip to introduce the story. Interview laced together with reporter-spoken transitions comprise the bulk of most packages. And when appropriate, ambient sound is added underneath spoken tracks to lend a sense of place to storytelling. Most packages conclude with a reporter track or compelling interview clip that sums up the story.

When starting out, you can follow this basic formula for constructing your audio stories. Of course, as you get better and more experienced, you can develop variations that are more creative and equally effective.

Step One

Begin with a few seconds of ambient sound to set the scene.

AMBIENCE: UNDERWATER ROBOTIC CAMERAS WORKING IN BACKGROUND WITH BUBBLING WATER.

Step Two

Lead with a reporter track or compelling interview clip to introduce the story.

Reporter: *Video from two underwater cameras shows no oil leaking from British Petroleum's undersea well. A cap has been placed on the* *well that exploded nearly three months ago. BP's chief operating officer for exploration and production, Doug Suttles says the cap may be holding now, but there is quite a bit of work still to be done.*

Step Three

Weave in a series of interview clips and reporter-spoken transitions for the body of the story. It's important that these clips are not strung together with no indication of how they relate. Make sure there are sufficient transitions between interview clips to ensure the story is fluid.

Mr. SUTTLES: *All of the indications so far look very encouraging. But clearly, we are far from finished.*

Reporter: *At a morning press briefing, President Obama said the developments are good news but stressed that scientists are still reviewing data to determine whether the temporary cap can stay in place without creating new problems.*

President OBAMA: *I think it's important that we don't get ahead of ourselves here. You know, one of the problems with having this camera down there is that when the oil stops gushing, everybody feels like we're done, and we're not.*

Step Four

Add ambient sound to lend a sense of place to the storytelling.

AMBIENCE: WORKERS ON BOATS SHOUTING ORDERS WITH SOUNDS OF OCEAN IN BACKGROUND.

Step Five

Conclude with a reporter track or compelling interview clip that sums up the story.

Reporter: *For now, BP officials will continue to monitor the pressure inside the well cap. Work will also continue on two relief wells that are considered a more permanent solution to the problem. This is Jane Doe, reporting.*

Of course, the more experienced you become, the less you will need to stick to a formulaic approach to storytelling. However, when you're just getting started, pre-defined structures like this one can help you focus your story and refine your editing stills.

Podcasts

Podcasts are generally released episodically and many different journalistic outlets—from NPR to ESPN.com—regulary make podcasts of their programming available to their audiences. The Community, Journalism & Communication Research group at the University of Texas–Austin assert that an audio podcast must meet four criteria. It must be: "1) a digital audio file that is episodic; 2) downloadable; 3) program-driven, mainly with a host and/or theme; 4) and conveniently accessed, usually via an automated feed with computer software."

If you intend to offer audio-only presentations online, make them available for download as often as possible. Audio by itself online can be somewhat problematic because using a computer is more of a visual, immersive experience. By making audio-only pieces/podcasts available for download, you allow users to listen on the go and avoid tying them to a computer monitor.

Regardless of the form your audio stories take, like all good journalism, your most significant task is to make your story clear and focused. And remember: Great audio narrative is written for the *ear*, not the *eye*. So your descriptions must engage the listener's imagination by painting pictures with words. Likewise, good audio facilitates human connections through rich context and a clear elaboration of the story's significance.

Combining Audio with Other Media

As previously noted, when audio stands alone, the listening experience is generally combined with other activities. And, of course, good audio with video has always been very important. Without it, there exists a disconnect between what the user *sees* and *hears*, and video becomes inherently weak. However, the rich multimedia capabilities of the web and other digital devices have paved the way for journalists to creatively join audio with other story forms as well. Good audio combined with compelling still images or information graphics can provide a different experience altogether.

There are three primary kinds of audio used to enhance photo slideshows: subject interviews, voiceovers or reporter narratives, and ambient sound. A single slideshow may include one or all of these. And although ideally, the photographer will also be

THE AUDIO TOOLBOX

Specific hardware models and software programs change so frequently that by the time this book is published new and better models will have hit store shelves. So, rather than recommend specific models, here are some general guidelines.

Recorder: When shopping for an audio recorder, choose one that has an external mic jack. If you are looking for best quality, use a digital voice recorder or high-end digital video camera that can capture sound by itself. Some mp3 players can even be used as recording devices. For example, you can collect medium quality audio using an iPod or iPhone that has iTalk recording program installed. Some digital recorders have built-in mics as well.

Microphones: Using an external mic can greatly improve the quality of your audio because it allows you to pick up sounds more accurately. External mics can be used with both audio recorders and video cameras that have a jack for connecting them. There are two main types of mics to choose from for audio collection: lapel (or lavaliere) and handheld.

Lapel microphones: are good when you can schedule the interview ahead of time. They can be attached to an interviewee's shirt, and because the mic is so close to the person's mouth, they capture the voice clearly. If you are also capturing video of the interview, lapel mics are nice because they are inconspicuous and willnot be a distraction on camera. interviewee's shirt, and because the mic is so close to the person's mouth, they capture the voice clearly. If you are also capturing video of the interview, lapel mics are nice because they are inconspicuous and will not be a distraction on camera.

Omni-directional handheld mics: These are good for general audio collection and interviews. Handheld mics are also great for collecting nearby sound. You get both the voice of a person being interviewed as well as the natural sound of the environment. Just make sure the subject speaks directly into the mic so audio levels remain crisp. If you are just collecting audio, make sure you mount the mic in a holder so that you don't pick up noise created when you fumble with the mic. If you cannot mount the mic, try to hold it steady, close to the speaker's mouth. Do not change the distance between the mic and the mouth, or your audio levels may vary. If you are also collecting video, a handheld will be noticeable and could be distracting. In this case, a lapel mic is usually better.

Headphones: Headphones can be used during the interviewing and editing stages. While conducting an interview, you may want to wear them to hear how the recording will sound. You may also choose to wear them when you are editing your audio story. They will help cancel out the noise of your surroundings, allow you focus on the story, and help ensure the audio levels are correct.

Editing software: Many students use Audacity to edit audio stories because it is free and easy to use. There are a few other free audio editors that you can search for online. If you have a few bucks and want a higher-end program, consider Adobe Audition, ProTools, or Soundtrack Pro. Audio editing programs are generally pretty intuitive because they display audio files on a timeline. You can easily remove portions of audio from a track, adjust levels, and save to a number of different file formats.

the person to collect or record the sound, it is conceivable that others on the multimedia team will help with that process.

Information graphics driven by dynamic animation can also benefit from audio narrative in the place of traditional text-based explainers. Chapter 10 explores interactive graphics in greater detail. However, one category—narrative graphics—generally makes use of audio in more significant ways than the others. Narratives are similar to video because they allow the viewer to watch an animated explanation of a process or event. For example, a narrative of a space shuttle launch could combine a step-by-step animation with descriptive audio.

There are two key steps to effectively using audio as a means for explaining an animation. First, like video, narrative graphics play through in a linear fashion. Therefore, the audio that is playing must match the visuals as they emerge on the screen.

Second, the animation must be dynamic and constantly moving. If images remain static for more than a couple of seconds, your viewers are likely to get bored and wander away from the screen. So, keep it moving!

Reporter voiceover/narrative. Narratives often are powerful methods for telling stories that may have otherwise appeared in the form of a written piece. The narrator could be the photographer or another reporter in a multimedia team. And most of the time, a good voiceover starts with a good script. In general, be succinct so that listeners can easily take in the narrative. And remember that once the words have been spoken, they evaporate into the air. There is no physical text listeners can revisit if they missed something. Review Chapter 6 to explore writing for various types of multimedia, including scripts for audio or video pieces.

Interviews. Audio produced from an interview with a subject is, on the surface, pretty self-explanatory. However, perhaps a bit more complex than the surface definition is the practical application. Most celebrated photojournalists—even the ones who are only presenting photos with captions—spend as much time listening, watching, and asking questions as they do making pictures. Likewise, a good interviewer goes into an assignment having already researched the story. Get answers to questions of fact from existing sources and use the interview as an opportunity to get answers to questions you cannot find from other sources. For example, names and titles of individuals can be collected ahead of time. Likewise, listen carefully as the subject talks and make note of additional questions that arise during the interview. Avoid going into an interview with blinders on, and don't focus your story so tightly in the beginning that you fail to leave room for the subject to take the story another direction.

Natural, ambient sound. Natural, ambient sound exists in the real world. For example, a photo package that chronicles an Olympic swimmer's quest for a gold medal may include natural sound from swim practice. The sound of water splashing and a coach shouting encouragement may be used at full volume by itself or in the background as the subject talks about how hard she has been working to achieve her goals. Natural sound may be subtler, such as a chicken clucking on the farm your subject owns or the pop of a gun that fires blanks used to start a foot race. Even the low hum of a motor or the din of a classroom full of third-graders can provide depth to your presentation. Regardless, natural sound can help set the scene or support images that illustrate events during which the sound was collected.

COLLECTING AMBIENT SOUND

Although it is not appropriate to use sound effects or ambient sound you did not collect at the actual scene, it is perfectly acceptable to record ambient sound outside the context of an interview. In fact, if you intend to run an ambient soundtrack simultaneously with an interview or narrative track, it is often necessary to record them separately. If you collect them on the same track at the same time, you have little control of the relative volume of each. Collecting them separately allows you to lace them together and create the strongest audio quality and control audio levels to match the storyline. For example, consider a story that occurs outdoors or in a public place with specific, scene-setting sounds. Ambient sound might come in the form of birds chirping, machines whirring, crowds bustling, or music playing. Record a couple minutes of those sounds separately and from a variety of distances so that you can create a full-scale ambient sound bed to run alone or beneath reporter narrative or interview tracks in the final piece.

At the same time, listen for noises that are unplanned and not pertinent to your story, such as airplanes flying overhead or loud traffic noises. If you don't notice these hazards until you are already in the editing phase, you may be stuck with inconsistencies in the pitch and volume of your piece or footage interrupted by unwanted sounds.

Visit the multimedia examples section of www.oup.com/us/palilonis and select audio from the drop down menu for examples of audio-only stories, as well as examples of how audio is combined with other media.

Finding Your Voice

Ever listen to a great audio story and wish you had a better "on air" voice? Ever tried voicing your own audio and cringe at the sound of yourself? Don't worry, you are not alone. Although some people are born with the perfect newscaster voices, others have to work at it. There are two areas of practice that will improve your on air skills. The first has to do with the structure of a recording. Within this category, there are three important considerations for aspiring audio reporters: clarity, tone, and pace. The second category relates to the vocal quality of a recording. And believe it or not, you actually can train and exercise your vocal cords to dramatically improve the quality of your audio stories. Specifically, practice breathing and enunciation, and exercise your vocal cords.

Clarity. Writing for the ear is tricky because you must paint a picture with descriptive words that allow listeners to visualize the story. At the same time, after the words of your script are spoken, they evaporate into thin air, making it easy for listeners to become lost if your story is bogged down by unnecessary words. To better understand this concept, compare the two scripts below. The first is comprised of 38 words and the second is comprised of 28 words. However, notice that none of the meaning or storyline is lost in the edit. In fact, by simply restructuring sentences, eliminating unnecessary words and phrases, and finding clearer ways to state the same point, the script becomes tighter and easer to process. Clarity also refers to the way you enunciate words as you speak them. Dropping consonants (i.e., workin' vs. working), running words together, and mispronouncing words are quick ways to kill your audio piece.

SCRIPT A
THE GUSHING WELL HAS STOPPED. FOR THE FIRST TIME IN NEARLY THREE MONTHS, OIL FROM BRITISH PETROLEUM'S UNDERSEA WELL HAS STOPPED GUSHING INTO THE GULF OF MEXICO. EVEN PRESIDENT OBAMA SAYS HE IS CAUTIOUSLY OPTIMISTIC ABOUT THE FUTURE.

SCRIPT B
THE GUSHER HAS STOPPED. AFTER NEARLY THREE MONTHS, OIL FROM BRITISH PETROLEUM'S UNDERSEA WELL HAS STOPPED GUSHING INTO THE GULF OF MEXICO. EVEN PRESIDENT OBAMA IS CAUTIOUSLY OPTIMISTIC.

Intonation. Be aware of the variations in the tone of your voice and avoid a "sing-song" or repetitive cadence. To prepare, read your narrative script carefully and decide in advance which words you will emphasize. Remember, you are not reading an iambic pentameter poem. You are reading a story that will include some words and phrases that call for decisive emphasis. Other words will deserve less attention. So, avoid repetitive rhythm (e.g., Da-Da, da-da, Da-Da, da-da) and emphasize words with more natural intonation.

BREATHING EXERCISES

Public speakers, actors, and broadcast journalists commonly use breathing exercises to relax their minds and bodies before a lecture or performance. Here are a few of the most common techniques:

Place your hand on your abdomen and take deep, slow breaths. Breathe from your abdomen, not your chest. Focus on pushing your stomach in and out rather then heaving your chest up and down as you breath.

Lie flat on your back and take deep, slow breaths. This will help you get a proper sense of deep breathing. Your stomach should rise slightly upon inhaling and fall upon exhaling.

Begin with slow, deep breaths from your abdomen. Then, as you exhale, make a low humming sound and hold it as long as possible. Pull in your stomach muscles. Then relax.

VOCAL CORD EXERCISES

Your vocal cords are made of muscles, and like other muscles in your body, they tend to get tight if you haven't used them in awhile. There are a couple vocal exercises that are sure to turn your voice from crackly to smooth:

Make a variety of single letter sounds, such as "zzz," "mmm," aaa," "ooo," "uuu," nnn," and "sss." Use different pitches as you speak, and hold each sound for a few seconds. Be deliberate about each sound.

Practice clearly saying hard consonants, such as "b-b-b," "t-t-t," and "k-k-k." Again, be deliberate with each sound and repeat each three to five times.

ENUNCIATION EXERCISES

Before recording audio, make sure you know how to pronounce all of the words in the script. Then, make sure you speak each word clearly and precisely. Although it is not necessary to overemphasize consonants, make sure your listeners can hear the difference between like-sounding letters (like d and t) and that you separate words and phrases with pauses of appropriate length. This will ensure that each word comes across clearly. Although they may seem silly, there are a few exercises that can help you improve your enunciation.

Choose a couple nursery rhymes or tongue twisters, such as "Peter piper picked a peck of pickled peppers," or "Mary had a little lamb whose fleece was white as snow." Say each one slowly and deliberately, overenunciating each word. Then repeat each one using your "on-air voice."

Visit the resources/exercises section of www.oup.com/us/palilonis and select audio resources to watch video examples of the breathing and enunciation exercises discussed here.

Pace. There is a fine line between "too fast" and "too slow" when it comes to narrating an audio story. If you read too quickly, you will likely agitate listeners who may be desperately trying to keep up. If this happens, it will not be long before they tune out. By contrast, if you read too slowly, listeners will likely become bored and lose interest. Of course, there is no perfect speed or pace. But remember that although you may know the story inside and out, your audience is hearing it for the first time. Give them time to process what you are saying by speaking clearly, pausing at the appropriate times, and enunciating every word.

Likewise, make every word count. In other words, read each word of your script with confidence and authority. Be yourself. Don't try to change or transform your voice into something it is not. And think carefully about how your piece will end. Your last words should give your audience something to think about or summarize a story, leaving it with a sense of completeness. In other words, make it memorable.

Professional Perspective

Art Silverman • *Executive Editor*

All Things Considered *National Public Radio*

Art Silverman is a senior producer for National Public Radio's award winning program All Things Considered. *His work has taken him to China, Vietnam, and Nigeria. And he has covered some of the most significant news stories in the past 30 years, including the 2008 Sichuan Earthquake and the twentieth anniversary of the Tet offensive. He was also on one of the first flights from Alaska to Far East Russia in 1994. He began his news career as a reporter for the* Claremont (New Hampshire) Daily Eagle *in 1971 and later became the managing editor. He started at NPR in 1978 as a production assistant.*

Don't think for one minute that the history of radio starts with the contribution of Guglielmo Marconi. In fact, the important ingredients were cooked up in a cave somewhere around 8000 B.C.

That's when a family of hunter-gatherers sat around a dim campfire. Among their number, a storyteller dazzles the others with a recollection of the day's high points.

That was a primitive radio program. It had everything except a transmitter. As the audience listened, this fireside story ignited their imaginations. The pictures were created where good radio pictures always appear: in the minds of the audience.

Radio producers like me have come to realize that sound is far more vivid than any widescreen TV. Or cave painting, for that matter.

Listeners combine what they hear with what they already know about the world. The effective radio producer outsources a lot of the work to the minds of our audience: people form images in their brains.

When I set out to tell a radio story, I go through this informal checklist:

- What do people care about?
- How can we surprise them?
- What sounds can we put on the air to make the show interesting?
- How many ways can a story be told?

The mathematician Paul Erdos once said:

"A mathematician is a machine for converting coffee into theorems."

Public radio producers are machines, too. With or without coffee, we ingest the world and spit out radio. We do that by understanding what makes for a good story. The process, to be fair, is not that difficult to understand. As my colleague Jonathan "Smokey" Baer says: "Throw out the bad and keep the good."

What is bad? It's a wide range of things: starting with the junk that proceeds and follows the information. It's the repetitions—where there are two versions of an idea. It's knowing where a piece of audio should end.

In our business, we tell breaking news stories and create longer form stories about how people live their lives.

To put together a daily newsmagazine called "All Things Considered," we satisfy our own curiosity about the world and find the best people to do that. We create a wide-awake dream for commuters in cars and cooks in kitchens. Our sounds and speech connect to individual assumptions and interests.

To get to that point, we become human vacuum cleaners, surfing newspapers and magazines, sampling what friends are saying, and watching TV and movies. This eternal, continual research results in small ideas that take a few hours to go from conception to air, and with enormous projects that engage us for months.

One of the smallest conceits offered to our listeners was an idea that occurred to me from listening to a phrase in the political air in 2008. All I did was ask in a meeting, "Has anyone ever tried to actually put lipstick on a pig?" Hours later, this went out on the airwaves:

ROBERT SIEGEL, host: *Well, speaking of pork, we now have some thoughts on the phrase that sent the political world buzzing overnight. Yesterday, Barack Obama said this about John McCain.*

Senator BARACK OBAMA: (Democrat, Illinois; Presidential Nominee) *So I guess his whole angle is, watch out, George Bush. Except for economic policy, health care policy, tax policy, education policy, foreign policy, and Karl Rove-style politics, we're really going to shake things up in Washington.*

SOUNDBITE OF APPLAUSE

Sen. OBAMA: *That's not change.*

SIEGEL: *And then he invoked the wisdom of barnyard cosmetology.*

Sen. OBAMA: *You know, you can put lipstick on a pig.*

SOUNDBITE OF LAUGHTER

Sen. OBAMA: *It's still a pig.*

SIEGEL: *And we have found instances of many other politicians—Democrats and Republicans—speaking the truth about pigs and lipstick.*

Now, the real test. Has anyone actually put lipstick on a pig? Well, joining us from Swoope, Virginia, where he's co-owner of Polyface Farms, is Joel Salatin. Welcome to the program, Mr. Salatin.

Mr. JOEL SALATIN: (Co-Owner, Polyface Farms) *Thank you. It's—well, I'm not really with you. I'm out here in the field with the pigs.*

SIEGEL: *I gather you have both a pig and some lipstick?*

Mr. SALATIN: *Yes, sir. I've got some ruby red here in my pocket, and I've got about 50 pigs here that are coming up around me. Here's a black and white one. Come here, pig. Come here, pig. Here. Here. Well, it's kind of like putting lipstick on a hairbrush. You know, they don't have much lip.*

SIEGEL: *Have you done it already?*

Mr. SALATIN: *Yeah, it's mainly nose here.*

SIEGEL: *Aha.*

Mr. SALATIN: *They seem to want to eat it.*

SIEGEL: *Well, have you managed to get any of the lipstick on the pig?*

Mr. SALATIN: *Well, yeah.*

SIEGEL: *Does the pig look any better with the lipstick on him or her?*

Mr. SALATIN: *No, they really don't. Now, you know, if you put a cummerbund around his loins and some Birkenstocks on his hooves, it might improve him a little bit.*

SIEGEL: *Well, Joel Salatin, I just want us to agree here. I can't see what you've done, but I assume that no harm was done to any animal in the making of this story.*

Mr. SALATIN: *No. In fact, they really didn't like it and they've all gone and started lying down. So I think I bored them.*

SOUNDBITE OF LAUGHTER

SIEGEL: *Perhaps they're smart animals. Mr. Salatin. . .*

Mr. SALATIN: *They are, indeed.*

SIEGEL: *. . . thank you very much for talking with us.*

Mr. SALATIN: *Thank you.*

SIEGEL: *That's farmer Joel Salatin of Swoope, Virginia, demonstrating that indeed, you can put lipstick on a pig, probably on its nose, but it is still a pig.*

At the other end of the spectrum, was a 30-minute documentary that took three months in 1985.

I created an hour-by-hour sound portrait of what occurred in Saigon on April 30, 1975, when the United States left Vietnam after the long, bloody war there. We heard the voices of former U.S. military personnel, embassy employees, civilians, and lots of journalists. I even got the last helicopter pilot to tell us about the hurried evacuation of the city. It was a huge audio jigsaw puzzle. Both ends of the spectrum obeyed the rules of being no longer than it had to be to tell the story. And I was very happy with both efforts.

I grew up about the time when radio receivers shrank small enough to allow a kid to listen under the covers at night. My transistor found the voices of broadcast geniuses like Jean Shepherd and Arthur Godfrey. You may not know their names, but they were storytellers who made you want to listen because they let you step into their shoes.

Public radio is the child of those commercial radio pioneers. It is the kind of radio that satisfies the human need for stories. We have to entertain sometimes, inform other times. It's a balance, but not too delicate of one.

A few years back, a media consultant told something unpleasant: "Public radio is like the last open store in a strip mall after all the other businesses have failed."

But is audio storytelling dead? I believe iPods and other portable devices may replace the live transmission of modulated electromagnetic waves. No one can say for sure where the future of audio will be found—but rest assured, there will never be a time when we don't want to rest the eyes and use the imagination.

If the future multimedia journalist respects the ear and understands that it is an awfully clever organ, what we practice today at NPR on programs such as "All Things Considered" will continue. Whatever add-ons the poor content-provider of the next decades will have to carry as tolls, the common denominator will be the ability to be a good listener.

Exercises

1. Roll out of bed one morning and immediately record yourself reading the script provided below. Then, spend five to 10 minutes doing the breathing, vocal, and enunciation exercises offered in this chapter. Then, record yourself reading the script a second time. Play back both recordings to see if the quality of the audio improved. Then post the finished audio clips to your WordPress site.

   SAMLPE AUDIO SCRIPT
   THE GUSHER HAS STOPPED. AFTER NEARLY THREE MONTHS, OIL FROM BRITISH PETROLEUMS UNDERSEA WELL HAS STOPPED GUSHING INTO THE GULF OF MEXICO. EVEN PRESIDENT OBAMA IS CAUTIOUSLY OPTIMISTIC.

   A CAP HAS BEEN PLACED ON THE WELL THAT EXPLODED ON APRIL 20TH. VIDEO FROM TWO UNDERWATER ROBOTIC CAMERAS SHOW

NO OIL LEAKING FROM THE WELL. BP'S SENIOR VICE PRESIDENT KENT WELLS SAYS THE CAP MAY BE HOLDING NOW BUT THE WELL IS FAR FROM FIXED.

FOR NOW BP OFFICIALS WILL CONTINUE TO MONITOR THE PRESSURE INSIDE THE WELL CAP. WORK WILL ALSO CONTINUE ON TWO RELIEF WELLS THAT ARE CONSIDERED A MORE PERMANENT SOLUTION TO THE PROBLEM.

I'M JANE DOE REPORTING.

2. Visit www.oup.com/us/palilonis and find the resources/exercises tab. Select audio resources from the drop down menu and download the audio clip found there called "Audio Editing." Open the file in the editing program of your choice and tighten the clip by editing out unnecessary words, stutters, long pauses, interjections, repetitive statements, and subordinate clauses. When you are finished, save your new file. Consider whether you have preserved the speaker's intended meaning while considerably shortening the clip. Post the finished audio file to your WordPress site.
3. Come up with a story idea that is well suited for audio presentation. Conduct all of the research, collect interviews, and develop the narrative. Then, create a 90-second audio piece that is structured in this manner:
    1. Begin with a few seconds of ambient sound to set the scene.
    2. Lead with a reporter track or compelling interview clip to introduce the story.
    3. Weave in interview clips and reporter-spoken transitions for the body of the story.
    4. Add ambient sound to lend a sense of place.
    5. Conclude with a reporter track or compelling interview clip that sums up the story.

Post your finished audio story to your WordPress site.

Notes

1. Old Time Radio Link Society. "Radio Days: A Radio History," http://www.otr.com/index/shtml.
2. Keith Jenkins, "The Best of Multimedia Photojournalism: The Era of the Ear," http://www.poynter.org, April 3, 2007.

CHAPTER 9

Video

Visual Storytelling and News in Motion

Video is, first and foremost, a visual medium. And strong video stories have a clear narrative arc and a powerful human focus that help audiences connect with issues and individuals. Thus, video stories are best when movement and live action contribute something that could not be conveyed any other way. For example, no other medium can tell the story of a firefighter safely pulling three small children from a burning building better than video. Of course, you may not be there with a camera when that happens. But if you are, video will certainly be more powerful, immersive, and dramatic than a written piece.

Today, viewers can watch local, regional, and national news on a variety of stations, as well as on computers and mobile devices. And in recent years, newspapers have begun to use video on their websites in significant ways. In fact, the majority of multimedia content on news websites comes in the form of video. Likewise, more and more people are accessing video on their mobile devices. According to The Nielsen Company's first quarter 2010 report, the number of people watching video on mobile devices has passed the 20-million-user-mark.[1] Although users are not necessarily watching for long periods of time, the number of people watching

EARLY BEGINNINGS

Network news programming has been prevalent since the early 1950s. And by 1965 television penetration of U.S. households was 92.6 percent. Television news started as short, 10- to 15-minute evening news briefs in the 1930s, but it wasn't until the 1950s that modern television news formats began to emerge. Edward R. Murrow is widely regarded as the pioneer of television news in the United States. In 1951 Murrow created See it Now (CBS), on which he presented live reports with journalists from across the country. See it Now was the first program that transmitted live from coast to coast.

grew more than 50 percent between 2009 and 2010. And statistics like these have media outlets working overtime to deliver more and more video to online.

Numbers like these should also be the first indication to aspiring multimedia journalists that understanding how to craft and edit strong video stories is an important skill. In an 2009 article on digitaljournalist.org, videographer and blogger Ken Kobré writes: "We feel that it's best, for individuals and staffs, to be thoroughly trained in shooting, editing and producing video—so they understand the medium's strengths and weaknesses—but ultimately there will be plenty of room for those who shine solely as shooters, or editors, or producers. Let's face it—in the print world, reporters are trained to write and edit, and yet there are plenty of great writers who can't edit and great editors who can't write. And yet it's important that each comprehends and appreciates the tasks of the other. The same holds true in videojournalism."[2] In other words, regardless of your specialization, understanding the power of video is paramount.

The chapter that follows provides an overview of what constitutes a strong video story. We explore types of video packages, video storytelling techniques, interviewing, camera shots, editing and technical considerations, and equipment. Some of you will go on to specialize in videography and dig much deeper into this topic. However, even those of you who don't will greatly benefit from an introduction to basic video storytelling. It will not only improve your multimedia storytelling skills overall, but it will put you in a position to be a stronger multimedia collaborator.

Video News Packages

Standard video news packages for television or the web are relatively straightforward, and there is a basic process you can use to create one. This process is generally comprised of three segments: preproduction, production, and postproduction. All good stories have a clear beginning, middle, and end with memorable subjects that the audience can connect with and care about. Of course, deadlines, resources, and access to locations and people can affect your ability to develop the most ideal narrative arc. However, commitment to an engaging story will show in your work regardless of those constraints that are out of your control. In other words, if you approach every story with a focused attention to establishing a storyline, the process will become second nature.

Preproduction

Preproduction includes all the steps you should take before you begin shooting, including establishing a solid focus for your story, thoroughly researching your subject, and finding people to interview. A methodical approach to preproduction can go a long way toward getting a solid story off the ground.

Choose a story that is well suited for video. Dynamic visual stories with compelling subjects often make for good video. Good video lets the viewer get inside the story, so to speak. So, search for stories that need that level of connection to resonate with audiences. For example, a story about children orphaned by the 2010 earthquake in Haiti is a deeply human story that will likely give way to emotional interviews and compelling footage. Video would allow audiences to connect and understand the dynamics of the story.

After you have settled on a story, identify your sources. Remember that balanced stories require multiple perspectives. So choose sources that represent different aspects of the story. For example, the story about Haitian orphans should include social workers, government officials, children, foster and adoptive parents, and adoption agencies, to name a few. And once you have established a list of sources, put together a preliminary set of interview questions. Likewise, conduct any research necessary for you to fully understand all of the dynamics of a story before reporting it. A journalist should never go into a story unprepared.

Editing a video story is a complex process. Although the bulk of the editing occurs after all of the footage for a story has been gathered, the process actually begins before you go into the field. In fact, solid editing—and storytelling, for that matter—includes a number of important steps that can be divided into two categories: conceptual approaches and technical functions. The conceptual approaches to editing include establishing the focus for a story, developing a plan for how you will approach the story, and preparing for the interview. The technical approaches to editing include transferring your raw footage to a computer, cropping and trimming, sequencing, adding transitions and titles, and inserting narration and other natural sound when appropriate. All of these steps are of equal importance.

Never underestimate the amount of work that should be done before you begin reporting. Researching and planning your story in advance are important steps to ensuring this information gathering process is smooth.

Focus your story before you go into the field. Of course, in those early stages, you will not be able to anticipate all of the aspects of the story, nor should you. As a journalist, your job is to find the story and then report how it naturally unfolds.

Develop a plan for how you will approach the story. Storyboards are discussed at several points in this book. In Chapter 3, storyboards are described as a way to systematically plan all of the parts of a multimedia story. But, individual pieces of the story—particularly feature or documentary videos—may also benefit from a preliminary storyboard. For a video reporter, the storyboard is a chronological sketch of each scene, with notes regarding corresponding audio, voiceovers, or music. Storyboards will help you work through problems before you shoot the story. And, if more than one person is working on the story, the storyboard becomes a visual road map. Include the script and music with the drawings to make post-production editing go more smoothly.

Shoot to edit when you are in the field. "Show me, don't tell me" is an important mantra in video storytelling. In other words, showing a story unfolding with footage of live action is always preferred over using talking head interview footage to explain what happened. Likewise, the quality of a video is largely determined by the nature of the surroundings. Make thoughtful choices about where to shoot a video by exhausting all possible locations. Set the scene for the viewer, consider how the different segments you shoot will work together, and shoot a variety of angles and types of shots to ensure a dynamic package. Finally, consider how you, the reporter, will fit into the story. Will you record any narrative audio? Will you appear on camera during interviews or through stand-up segments? Or will you be completely invisible and allow your interview subjects tell the story? Regardless, all of these questions should be answered before or during the reporting process. It probably will not be possible to go back and get the footage you need later.

Prepare for a solid interview. We often spend a great deal of time developing questions for the interviews we conduct. The interviewer's job, after all, is to get answers. However, listening is actually one of the more important skills an interviewer can possess. In fact, one of the most deadly mistakes an interviewer can make is to get so wrapped up in the questions she intends to ask that she fails to listen to the answers. If you aren't truly listening to your subject you will likely miss opportunities to flesh out the interview and dig deep into the topic being discussed. Likewise, a good interviewer is prepared, makes the subject comfortable when the camera is rolling, quickly assesses the subject's responses, and asks thoughtful follow up questions.

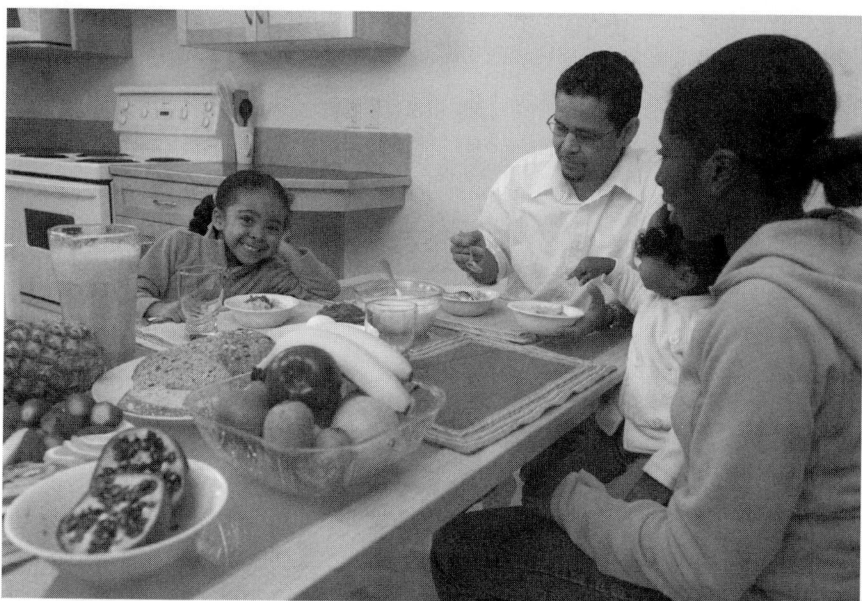

FIGURE 9-1: B-roll

Production

There are three basic kinds of footage you should collect for your package: b-roll, interviews, and on-screen talent (or reporter stand-up). Make sure you have an adequate amount of footage in each category to ensure your edited news package is well rounded and has a variety of storytelling devices. Also, although you will likely have a pretty well established timeline for when you shoot (i.e., scheduled interviews or events), plan on shooting before and after an event, not just during. This will ensure that you don't miss key elements of a story.

B-roll (see Figure 9-1): B-roll is supplemental footage that relates to your subject. For example, a story about a breast cancer survivor could include b-roll of her daily activities, participation in charity events, or interaction with her family. Avoid using weak b-roll as filler. B-roll should be compelling and interesting and add visual context to the story. An ideal video uses interview footage to fill in description where there are holes in the active footage you have collected. The amount of b-roll you need for a single story depends on the length of your piece and the nature of your story. But a good rule of thumb for a 90-second piece is to shoot 20 to 30 minutes of b-roll and try to get a variety of shots to choose from that relate to your topic.

FIGURE 9-2: Interview

FIGURE 9-3: On-screen talent (aka reporter stand up)

Interviews (see Figure 9-2): Conducting a good interview can mean the difference between a great story and one that falls short. Establishing a narrative thread, connecting with the audience, and maintaining focus are all utterly dependent upon how well your sources contribute to storytelling. And although there are lots of people who just don't interview well or whose on-camera presence is weak, a poorly conducted interview means your story won't even get out of the gate. By contrast, video pieces comprised entirely of talking heads and weak b-roll tend to leave viewers feeling less than inspired. So find powerful images that show the story and that correspond with the information provided by your interview subjects.

On-screen talent (see Figure 9-3): Standard news packages often include shots of the reporter introducing, transitioning, or concluding the story. These could be shot live in conjunction with the final edit, but usually are recorded in the field. Limit the amount of reporter stand ups because talking head video becomes boring fast. A reporter track or interview footage combined with engaging b-roll will be more effective.

Visit the multimedia examples section www.oup.com/us/palilonis and select video from the drop down menu for live examples of b-roll, interview footage, and on-screen talent shots.

Finally, do not underestimate the importance of good audio and natural sound. Often the sounds that exist in the natural settings of news events are as valuable to helping tell a story as the more concrete audio forms, such as interviews or reporter narratives. So listen for these sounds and consider how best to incorporate them into your piece.

Additional Video News Formats

Contemporary news video doesn't stop with the traditional approach outlined above. In fact online, news organizations often go beyond the standard news package. And there are a few variations of news video that can be particularly effective on the web.

Edited narratives are similar to long-form documentaries in that they combine compelling subject interviews with engaging live action video that needs little explanation. Online, however, these documentary style pieces are generally much shorter that what you are used to seeing on television. For example, a piece by the *San Jose Mercury News* titled "Basketball Faith" chronicles how one man is making a difference through the sports ministry he helped create. It is very much like a traditional documentary in that in allows the subject to tell his own story and includes dynamic documentary footage. Coming in at only two minutes and 33 seconds, this piece is much shorter than a documentary you might see on television.

Visit the multimedia examples section of www.oup.com/us/palilonis and select video from the drop down menu for more examples of edited narratives, video diaries, moving pictures, and vodcasts.

Video diaries feature a reporter or subject who speaks into the camera, sharing thoughts, opinions, or experiences related to a specific topic. Some news organizations have experimented with using the video diary style for commentary or product reviews, to name a few. For example, the *New York Times'* website features a weekly technology review video by David Pogue. In it, Pogue speaks directly to the audience as he provides commentary about technology trends or new products. But his diary-style clips are far from talking head pieces. Pogue's videos are witty, energetic, and even a bit theatrical, creating fun, intimate vignettes that audiences can easily connect with. Pogue is the *Times'* personal-technology columnist, and in addition to the videos, he contributes a weekly print column, online column, and popular daily blog, "Pogue's Posts." Pogue is also an Emmy Award–winning tech correspondent for CBS News. And in 2009, the *Las Vegas Sun* ran a series on gambling addiction that featured a video diary shot by the subject,

FIGURE 9-4A

In "Basketball Faith," a video narrative published by the *San Jose Mercury News,* Michael Allen, a local sports ministries director, talks about the basketball league he helped cultivate. The video only contains interview footage and b-roll and as Allen narrates. The reporter is completely invisible in this piece.

Source: Image courtesy of the *San Jose Mercury News.*

FIGURE 9-4B

In 2009, the *Las Vegas Sun* ran a series on gambling addiction. The series contained a number of multimedia pieces, including this video diary shot by the subject, Tony McDew, and edited by Sun editors. McDew documented his addiction with his own video camera, hoping that sharing his experience could help others.

Source: Image Courtesy of the *Las Vegas Sun.*

FIGURE 9-5

This *Seattle Times* piece provides shots from around the city during a rainy weekend. The piece is only comprised of b-roll. There is no voice over, no reporter standup, and no interviews. The video is so compelling it speaks for itself.

Source: Image Courtesy of the *Seattle Times.*

Tony McDew, and edited by *Sun* editors. McDew documented his addiction with his own video camera, hoping that sharing his experience could help others.

Moving pictures contain little to no narration and are most often used to illustrate a text-based story much like a still photo does. Moving pictures presentations often supplement more descriptive pieces, such as a text-based story. For example, a piece by

The Seattle Times titled, "Rain City," provides shots from around the city during a rainy week. The piece includes only a brief caption, the video footage, and the natural sound that accompanies it. No other narration is necessary because the piece speaks for itself.

Vodcasts often replicate typical television broadcasts that present multiple short stories in a linear format. Some news organizations have experimented with the vodcast approach to provide collections of short video bulletins or briefs. The *Daily Tele-*

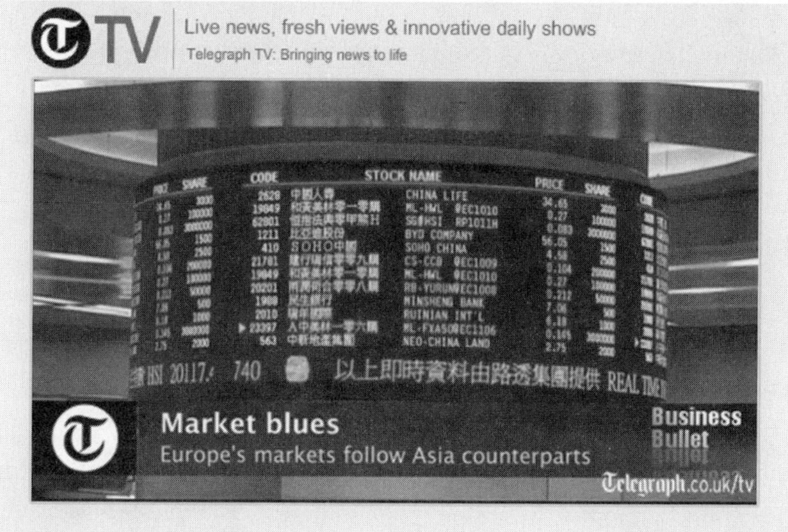

FIGURE 9-6

The Daily Telegraph website includes a Vodcast titled, "Business Bullet." On this program, an anchor discusses the latest city and business news in a program-style format. Clips are short to serve web users more effectively.

Source: Image courtesy of ©Telegraph Media Group Limited 2010.

graph's "Business Bullet," for example, is similar to a television news broadcast in that an anchor discusses the latest city and business news in a program-style format. The clips are shorter (about 60 seconds each) and presented in the form of brief news bulletins.

Camera Shots

Video quality largely depends upon how well the videographer executes camera shots. Likewise, good visual storytelling requires varying shots in a single piece to keep the viewer's attention and create a dynamic presentation. Regardless whether you intend to become a professional videographer or specialize in another area of storytelling, you should be conversant in different shot techniques, as well as understand how to implement them in a story package.

Extreme wide shots (see Figure 9-7) are achieved when so much distance is established between the camera and subject that the subject is not visible. Extreme wide shots are often used as the establishing shots to give the viewer information about where a story takes place. They also help set the scene, provide visual context for a story, and/or show the expanse of a scene before offering tighter detail shots. Establishing shots usually come at the beginning of a sequence.

FIGURE 9-7: Extreme wide shot (EWS)

FIGURE 9-8: Very wide shot (VWS)

Very wide shots (see Figure 9-8) show less background information and more of the subject. However, the emphasis is still on establishing the subject in the surroundings. The subject is barely visible.

FIGURE 9-9: Wide shot (WS)

Wide shots (See Figure 9-9) bring the subject into full frame so the visual emphasis is no longer on the surroundings. However, the shot still includes enough of the scene that the viewer gets a sense of the visual context for the story. Wide shots are also referred to as long shots.

FIGURE 9-10: Mid shot (MS)

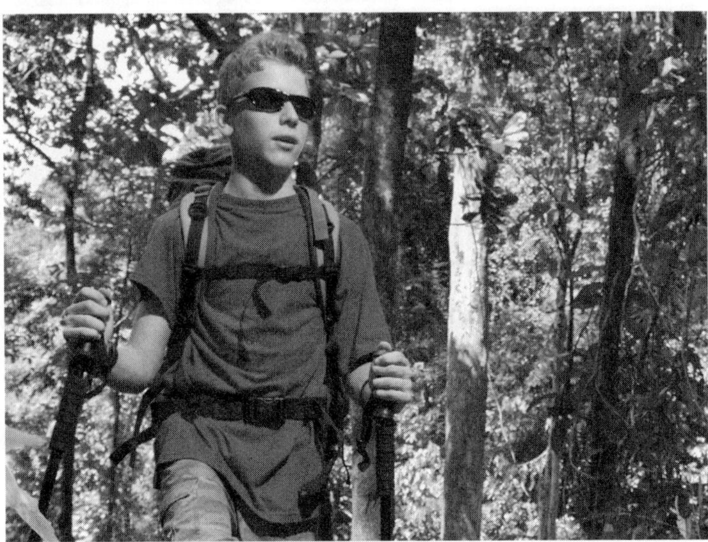

Mid shots (see Figure 9-10) zoom in even closer on the subject, drawing more attention to a particular area, such as a person's face. However, a bit of the scene is still visible in the frame.

FIGURE 9-11: Medium close up shot (MCU)

Medium close up shots (See Figure 9-11) are a little closer than mid shots, causing the surroundings to become less obvious. The focus is clearly on the subject's features and expressions.

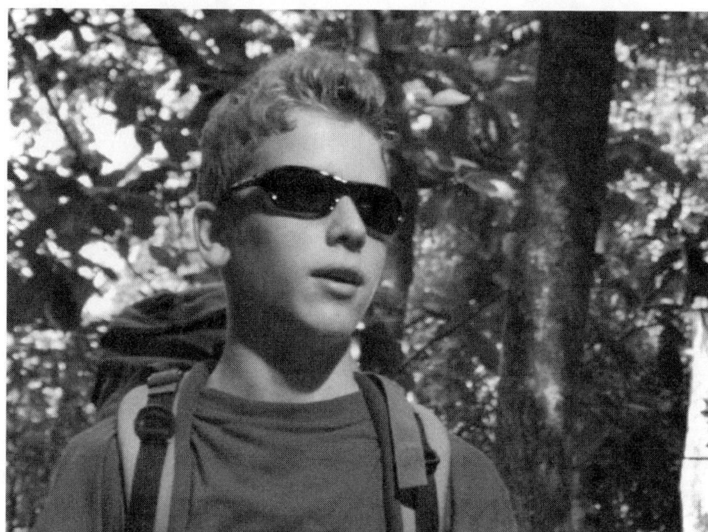

FIGURE 9-12: Close up shot

Close up shots (see Figure 9-12) frame the subject from head to shoulder. Close ups are often the best way to focus on human emotion by offering tight shots on faces, expressions, or body language.

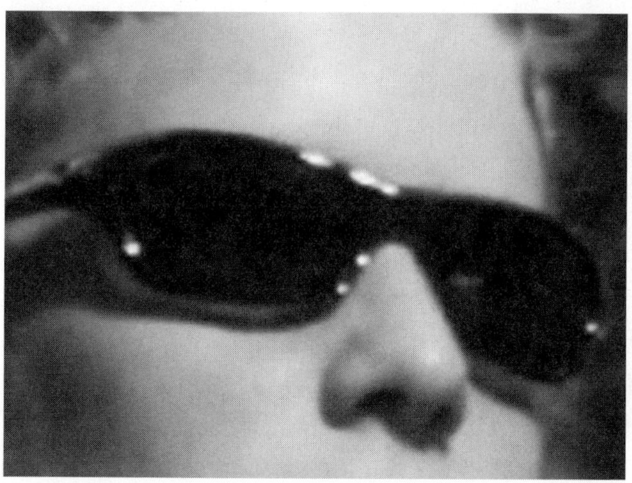

FIGURE 9-13: Extreme close up shot (ECU)

Extreme close up shots (see Figure 9-13) of a person could easily fill the frame, showing the greatest degree of detail.

FIGURE 9-14: Cut in shot (CU)

Cut in shots (see Figure 9-14) are close ups or extreme close ups that show other parts of a subject. These can be used in concert with close ups of the face to combine expressions with body language. This method can help viewers connect with the subject and story.

FIGURE 9-15: Cutaway shot (CA)

Cutaway shots (see Figure 9-15) are comprised of supplemental footage, or b-roll. Cutaways can be used as transitions between shots or to add information not offered by shots of the main subject or scene.

FIGURE 9-16: Point of view shot (POV)

Point of view shots (see Figure 9-16) show a scene from the subject's perspective. These help place the viewer in the subject's shoes and provide a personal perspective.

FIGURE 9-17: Piece to camera

QUICK TIPS

SHOOTING

Avoid camera shake by using a tripod.

Use an external microphone for recording audio. You will get better quality than if you use your camera's mic.

Look for a variety of shots to make your video more visually engaging.

Pay attention to details and when they are visual, capture them on camera.

Charge the batteries for your equipment right before going out on assignment, and carry extras in case your originals fail. And if you are using a camera that requires it, always bring extra tape.

Begin recording for a few seconds before starting an Interview. Then, leave the camera running for a few more seconds at the end. You can edit this "dead air" out later, but it will ensure that you don't have an abrupt start or ending.

Piece to camera (see Figure 9-17) shows the reporter speaking directly to viewers through the camera. Sometimes piece to camera shots comprise the whole report and are often shot at the scene of an event or news story. Other times, they are inserted in between other shots to link together parts of the visual narrative.

Camera Movement Techniques

It is important to evaluate a scene for all of the potential angles of view. And a videographer should shoot from several of points of view to ensure variety. For example, footage taken from both the right and left of or above and below a subject may be combined to offer a more dynamic presentation. Likewise, there are a number of camera movement techniques that can make video presentations more dynamic. However, they should no be overused in news presentations. Often, straightforward, focusing clean shots is best practice. However, when camera movement is appropriate, here are a few options:

Zooming is adjusting the camera lens from telephoto to wide-angle or from wide-angle to telephoto. Zooming-in narrows the point of view. Zooming-out widens the point of view.

Panning is moving the camera horizontally to follow the action. Panning may create a panoramic view or keep a moving object or person from exiting the frame.

Tilts move the camera vertically to capture action or accentuate the height of an object or person. A "tilt up" while zooming-in or a "tilt down" while zooming-out help establish rhythm for many shots.

Depth of field is determined by the distance of the subject to the camcorder and the focal setting of the zoom. The degree of sharpness of the area in front of and behind the subject defines depth of field. A shallow depth of field isolates a subject by blurring the foreground and the background, focusing only on the center of interest.

Tracking is moving the camera so it follows a moving subject. This effect accentuates the subject's movement.

Visit the multimedia examples section of www.oup.com/us/palilonis and select video from the drop down menu for live examples of the camera shots and camera movement techniques described in this chapter.

Composition

There are many ways to frame a shot. And the composition of various shots within a piece can make or break your visual storyline. Again, remember to vary shots within a package and examine every shot to ensure you have an aesthetically pleasing composition. Here are a few important compositional factors to consider:

Headroom refers to the placement of a subject's head in the frame. The subject's eyes should be positioned at the optical center of the frame so that there is not too much headroom at the top or too little at the bottom of the frame. The subject's head should be placed so that there is space on either side of the frame as well.

Distractions are objects that may detract from the focal point. Too many unnecessary details in a frame may ruin the impact of the shot. For example, if a person is standing in front of a pole, it may appear that the pole is sticking out of the person's head. Too much movement in the background of your shot can also be distracting. You can avoid this problem by either moving so that your angle of view is different or by zooming in on the subject to crop out distractions. Consider changing the position of the subject (if possible) so there is less activity behind him or her.

Exiting the frame refers to the way an individual moves from on camera to off camera. If the action is not natural, viewers may find the shot to be jarring. One way to establish a clean entrance and exit is to shoot the subject walking toward the camera and then continue past on either the left or right side of the videographer. If the subject is walking from side to side in the shot, the camera should follow the subject until the subject is midway through the shot. Then, simply stop panning the camera and allow the subject to exit the shot.

Rule of thirds refers to the distribution of space in a shot. The focal point should not reside in the middle of the space. Instead, a 2:3 ratio should be used to create a more interesting visual composition. Divide the viewfinder into vertical and horizontal thirds. The viewers' eyes are drawn to where those lines intersect.

FIGURE 9-18

FIGURE 9-19

FIGURE 9-20

Figure 9-18 is more static because the focus is perfectly centered. However, by changing the composition of the shot the area of interest is emphasized and a rule of thirds is implemented.

Postproduction

After you have established the story angle and all of your footage has been collected, you can begin editing it into a cohesive package. Review all of your interview footage and create a rough outline of the most important parts of your story. It sometimes helps to go back to the core journalistic questions: who, what, when, where, why, and how. As you review your interview footage, search for sound bites that answer those questions. Then find additional sound bites that add color, context, or transitions for your story. Again, a methodical approach to post-production will help ensure that you produce a tight, cohesive story.

Once you have established the narrative path your story will take, stay on it! The biggest disservice you can do to your story is to wander away from the main themes or dilute it with secondary information. Remember, unless you are producing a long-form documentary, most of your video stories will be short. So cut out anything that does not relate directly to the story at hand.

Organize the interview clips to correspond with your outline. Then, go through your footage to determine which portions of the interview you will use b-roll with and which portions you will leave as talking head footage. If necessary, record voiceovers for key points in the story, important descriptions, or necessary transitions. Remember to guide your audience through the story. Finally, add on-screen talent shots and be sure to identify talking heads with on-screen text.

Of course, the postproduction process is also dependent upon your knowledge of a video-editing program. There are a number of great editing programs out there like Final Cut Pro and Avid. But when you are just starting out, you might want to get your feet wet by using the free software that came with your computer. If you are on a Mac, that would be iMovie, and if you are on a PC, you will use Windows Movie Maker. After a few quick tutorials, these easy-to-use programs will have you editing video in no time at all.

The technical aspects of editing are concerned with ensuring each scene flows smoothly into the next and the storyline is clear and well developed. To achieve these goals, you must take special care with both the audio and visual components of your story. The visual portions of your story will be broken into a series of sequential scenes or events. In contrast, the audio portions will be more continuous. During the editing process, it is sometimes easier to cut the visuals to match the audio or vice versa. This decision is generally based on what type of video is being produced. For example, when filming an interview, the visual component may contain stills or action video related to what the subject is saying, shots of the interviewer and the interviewee, and other pieces of visual information. All of these shots are then organized and linked together by the verbal components of the interview. Likewise, many scenes are linked together through the narrator whose commentary enables the viewer to make sense of how individual scenes are related and relevant.

From camera to computer: Regardless of what computer platform or editing software you use, you will likely attach your camera to the computer through a Firewire or USB connection. Once connected, follow your editing program's directions for transferring the video from your camera to the computer.

Trimming your footage: If you have done a good job collecting footage in the field, then you'll likely have extraneous footage you don't need. Trimming is the act of editing down your raw footage into tightly focused video clips.

Sequencing: The order and pacing of your video clips are really the keys to establishing a coherent storyline. Start by getting rid of any raw video that is difficult to see, contains distractions, or that isn't steady. Next, monitor the pace of the video and be sure to vary the sequence of shots. For example, if you begin with a wide establishing shot, move in closer in the next segment to achieve variety. If it seems too slow or too fast in places, change the sequence of shots accordingly.

Adding transitions and titles: Transitions appear between key scenes in a story and are used to tie segments together. Many hard news veterans will tell you that visual transitions aren't necessary at all. Instead, rely on reporter narrative, meaningful b-roll, and interview clips to transition from one major scene to another. In fact, for news, quick cuts from one scene to another are often preferred because they are more straightforward and clean. If you decide to use transitions, avoid anything more than simple fade in and fade out transitions. Your editing software program will offer a number of options for transitions, from ripple to page curl effects. However, these are rarely appropriate for news packages. Fades may be used to transition from one image to another or gradually bring an image in or out of view.

Titles are often used to introduce a video story but are not always necessary for news video. However, always include text that identifies the subject of an interview just below the person's face. These titles are often referred to as "lower thirds" and ensure that the viewer knows who is talking and why. Applying titles and lower thirds to videos is an easy process. In fact, most video editing programs offer templates for titles that can be easily inserted over your video footage.

Adding narration and/or other sound: Matching video with audio takes a great deal of patience and care. Narration and other sound clips must be timed and paced to fit the clips they accompany.

Technical Considerations for Online Video

Video may well be one of the most complicated forms of media to effectively produce and display for online formats. In the very least, all videographers and photographers should be well versed in streaming video concepts. But, even those less likely to shoot and edit video should have a basic understanding of the concepts of bandwidth, data rates, video resolution, compression issues, and delivery modes.

Streaming video is sent in compressed form over the Internet and displayed to the viewer as it arrives. This way, only a small amount of video comes across at a time, which is not as taxing on the Internet stream. This progressive download allows producers to transmit high quality video without having to pay for and/or maintain a streaming server. As servers and Internet connections become faster, an increas-

VIDEO FILE FORMATS

There are many different video file formats—too many to keep track of. And of course, the higher the resolution, the bigger the file size. Video that will be broadcast on television can be saved at higher file sizes. But video that will be played on the web must be compressed, resulting in a smaller file that will load and play more quickly. However, the result is a lower quality video.

Thus, video files can be compressed in a variety of ways with different software programs. And choosing the right compression is a careful balance between quality and speed. The format each program renders is indicated by a three-letter file extension at the end of the file name. Some of the more common file types used by multimedia journalists are:

.flv: Flash Video Format is the most common format used for online video because it offers a small file size while maintaining image quality. Flash Video Format is compatible with most computers and browsers and is used by some of the most popular video sharing sites, including You Tube and Hulu. One drawback to Flash Video Format is that it is not supported by Apple's iPad and iPhone.

.wmv: Windows Media Video is a highly compressed Microsoft format. Although Windows Media Video is one of the smallest compression formats, the resulting quality is generally pretty low. Windows Media Video files are sufficient for e-mail distribution but can be problematic online. In addition to being low quality, they will also not play on Macs without first converting them to a different format, a task most users won't be willing to do.

.mov: Quicktime Movie files are creating using Apple's movie editing software, iMovie. Quicktime files are common, produce relatively low file sizes, and maintain good image quality.

MPEG4: MPEG4 is a sharing format that produces small file sizes with relatively good image quality. MPEG4 files are generally smaller than .mov files, resulting in lower image quality. However, the trade off is generally worth the gains in load time.

Which file format is best depends on how it will be used and where it will appear. You might also consider the magnitude of the news story. For example, a number of low-quality videos appeared on news sites across the country after the 2011 Tsunami in Japan or the devastating tornadoes that wiped out Joplin, Missouri, in the spring of that same year. In these cases, the image quality took a backseat to storytelling. In the wake of such vast devastation, it's more important to get the story out, and users are generally more forgiving when content is compelling.

ing number of news organizations stream live events online. For example, in May 2011, just moments before President Barack Obama announced to the world that U.S. forces had killed Osama bin Laden in Pakistan, the *Washington Post* prepared to stream the president's announcement live on washingtonpost.com. And in 2008, more than 27 million people watched Obama's inauguration on CNN.com, generating more than 140 million page views.

THE VIDEOGRAPHER'S TOOLBOX

For updated links to some of the latest and best devices and software programs, visit the video resource section of the website that accompanies this book.

Video cameras come in many varieties. So rather than focus on a specific brand or model, we will address general camera concerns. First, know your delivery system. There's no need to buy more camera than you need. Video developed for broadcast television requires a much more powerful camera than video shot for the web.

There are three basic types of cameras: consumer, prosumer, and professional. The biggest differences among them are related to how much control the videographer has over various settings. Consumer cameras generally range from $400 to $700. These do not have interchangeable lenses but are sufficient for projects that involve shooting b-roll and simple interviews for the web. And this category includes pocket-sized cameras. Prosumer cameras range from about $700 to $1,500. These generally have interchangeable lenses and focus faster than consumer lenses. Professional cameras start at about $2,500 and go up from there. If your videos will be broadcast on TV, consider a prosumer or professional camera. Understand that the more control you have over the camera, the more expensive it will be. Likewise, you won't likely use the features you aren't familiar with. So be realistic about what you need and can afford. And don't break the bank with your first camera. The more advanced you become, the more likely you'll want to upgrade.

Also when it is time to buy a camera, make sure it's comfortable in your hands and you can easily work the controls. Make sure the file type generated by you're the camera is compatible with the editing software you are going to use. Likewise, purchase a camera that stores an SD card or something similar. Digital storage is more convenient than mini-dv tapes, for example. Finally, make sure the camera can be connected to a tripod and has an external mic jack.

Tripods ensure that the camera doesn't shake or move around while shooting. Tripods have three legs and attach to the bottom of the camera. Hand-held video cameras generally produce images that are jerky and unpredictable. If you don't have a tripod, try resting your video camera on your shoulder or another sturdy foundation, such as a fence or a car.

Microphones and headphones should be used to ensure the best audio quality possible. Microphones that are built into video cameras are not very effective because they often leave the sound muffled or difficult to hear. External microphones, such as lavalier or hand-held mics, produce a better quality soundtrack. Those types of mics are outlined in greater detail in Chapter 8. Also, when recording sound, wear headphones to effectively monitor audio quality. Any headphones will do, but if you can afford them, noise-cancelling headphones are best.

Secure digital (SD) cards are standard memory cards used in portable devices. SD technology is used by more than 400 brands and more than 8,000 models. Standard SD cards run from two to four GB. SDHC (high capacity) cards run from four to 32 GB.

Bandwidth refers to the user's connection speed to the Internet and can have a dramatic effect on usability. Higher bandwidths, such as those provided by cable and DSL connections, give users faster access and the ability to smoothly view higher quality video. And in recent years, the number of households connecting to the Internet through high-speed networks has increased exponentially. By 2011, the U.S. broadband penetration among active Internet users was 95 percent. So most video producers try to find a balance between user experience and their own bandwidth expenses, and as a result, the maximum video resolution offered by most sites is 640 x 480, and the maximum data rate is 600–700 kbps.

Data rate (aka, bit rate) refers to the amount of data per second transmitted by a compressed video file and is expressed in kilobits/second or megabits/second. Data rate is the most significant factor to consider when streaming video because lowering the data rate is the same as compressing your video. Thus, the lower the data rate, the lower the quality.

Frame rate refers to the number of video frames played per second. A good rule of thumb is to shoot and deliver video for the web at a rate of 24 frames per second. This is a standard frame rate, and you generally won't have to decrease the frame rate to save bandwidth. When you decrease frame rates, you may slow down the motion of a video so much that it becomes noticeable and unnatural to the viewer. Be especially careful with high-motion video because it won't take much to make it appear choppy. Likewise, it is not a good idea to degrade frame rates for tight shots in which someone is talking because the syncing could become noticeably off.

Resolution refers to the number of pixels per inch of an image or video file. Most video begins at 720 × 480 (345,600 total pixels) or 1,920 × 1,080 (2,073,600 total pixels). The greater number of total pixels in a video, the higher the data rate must be to maintain quality. Thus, streaming video is usually displayed at 640 × 480 (307,200 total pixels) or smaller. The most common video resolutions for 4:3 video are 640 × 480, 440 × 330, 400 × 300, 320 × 240, 240 × 180, and 160 × 120. The most common resolutions for widescreen 16:9 videos are 640 × 360, 480 × 270, and 320 × 180.

Video and Screen Size

Nowadays, screen size and viewing experience are key considerations for how video is shot. Watching television is a 10-foot viewing experience on a relatively large screen. By contrast, watching video on a computer is more of a three-foot viewing experience with a much smaller video frame. And watching video on a mobile device, such as a tablet or cell phone, is a one-foot experience with an even smaller viewing screen. Thus, when shooting news video, try to consider the types of platforms on which your audience will view your piece. Tighter shots are generally preferred if you know your audience will be viewing your piece on a smaller screen.

Professional Perspective

Suzy Smith • *Assistant Professor of Telecommunications*

Ball State University

Suzy Smith is an Assistant Professor of Telecommunications at Ball State University where she teaches courses in news reporting and writing and multimedia storytelling. Before joining the faculty at Ball State, Smith spent 24 years in news and sports broadcasting working as a senior producer at CNN.com, The Weather Channel, CNN/Sports Illustrated, and as a producer at CNN Sports.

I sat at my desk and watched as the images passed by on the television screen. The storm surge pushed water beyond its banks, breaching levees all around New Orleans. The water filled every nook and cranny, forcing open a path where there once wasn't one. The water stood as high as 12 feet in some places and stretched to what seemed like infinity.

I kept watching as the images of Hurricane Katrina continued to stream in front of me. There were endless shots of people pleading for help. They lined any street not covered by water. Buildings looked as if they had been through what I could only imagine a nuclear war might be like: glass shattered, pieces of metal bent like paper clips, light and power poles knocked over like rows of toothpicks, and trees completely uprooted and resting on top of cars, on homes, and across streets.

The video continued to stream into the network, shots of people on their roofs waiting for someone to help and signs scrawled on buildings asking for assistance.

We had been covering the storm's buildup for several days, following the usual protocol for an approaching hurricane. We had covered it well with live shots, video of people preparing, information on how to evacuate, and guidelines for those who decided to stay. CNN's resources were either already on the ground or were on their way to Louisiana.

It was August 2005, and earlier that month I had just started working at CNN.com after nearly three years with the Weather Channel. I was working on a start-up product called *Pipeline* (later called CNN.com/Live). It was a subscription-based service offering live streaming video online. *Pipeline* was not quite ready to be rolled out to the public, but our team was going through rehearsals and providing video and stories for the video-on-demand service.

My entire career to that point had been in broadcast television, working either in sports or weather. I had seen the power of video—or so I thought. In the world of sports, the power of video was seen in broadcasted events like Joe Theismann's career-ending broken leg, or Clint Malarchuk's slit throat while in goal for the Buffalo Sabres. These were visuals that made an impact.

Katrina produced the kind of video that jolts you; the kind that stays with you; the kind that makes you cringe or cry or laugh. It's the stuff you remember. The video from Hurricane Katrina had that "where-were-you when it happened?" quality. The 1986 space shuttle Challenger disaster had the same affect. A whole generation can tell you where they were in 1963 when President John F. Kennedy was assassinated. For many today, the events of 9/11 stand out in that way too. Who can forget the video of the World Trade Center on fire, or the video of the second plane hitting the south tower, or those gut-wrenching moments when many of us watched live as the towers came crashing down to the earth?

It is difficult to call something so devastating amazing, but moments like these *are* amazing. In the days after Katrina made landfall, the endless video that came into the CNN newsroom of the widespread destruction across such a huge expanse of the Gulf Coast kept me and my colleagues mesmerized.

In broadcast we crave those moments and that video. Good or bad, it is what makes the audience take notice, understand, and most important, remember. But what is it that makes such video so memorable, so incredible, and so mesmerizing? It's not just the images themselves; it's the *emotion* that those images express. As storytellers, we are taught that telling a good story involves good writing and using descriptive words to convey a message. But what we sometimes forget is that compelling video can often tell a story better than any words could. As a journalist, when you are lucky enough to come across video with that kind of impact—the wow factor—you have to let the video write the story.

Sometimes, knowing when *not* to say something is harder and more important than knowing *what* to say. To use an old cliché, a picture is worth a thousand words. In the case of Katrina, moving images were worth so much more. They offered profound accounts of horror and human emotion.

And when you look back at the video of 9/11 or the *Challenger* disaster or Hurricane Katrina, it's not just the images that you remember. You recall how those images made you *feel*. Anger, excitement, sadness, pain, even empathy are all emotions that make those images more than just moving pictures, they make it amazing video.

Hurricane Katrina will stay with me for a long time, not only because it was one of the big stories of the early part of the twenty-first century, or because so many friends and colleagues spent weeks in the field covering its aftermath, or even because it was such a visual story. Hurricane Katrina will stay with me because it made me feel.

Exercises

1. Visit www.oup.com/us/palilonis and find the resources/exercises tab. Choose video resources from the drop down menu, and download the package of video clips called "Video Editing". Open the files in the video-editing program of your choice and edit them into a 30- to 45-second story. You are free to trim clips and determine how they should be sequenced. When you are finished, save your completed video story. Post the finished video story to your WordPress site.
2. Using a digital video camera, shoot 10 30-second clips that illustrate the following concepts:
   1. Extreme wide shot
   2. Very wide shot
   3. Wide shot
   4. Mid shot
   5. Medium close up shot
   6. Close up shot
   7. Extreme close up shot
   8. Cut in shot

   Post the finished video clips to your WordPress site.
3. Identify a story or multiple stories that would make for good video packages. Then, develop the following types of video stories:
   1. Standard video news package that includes b-roll, interview footage, narrative audio, and on-screen talent footage.
   2. Edited narrative.
   3. Video diary

4. Moving pictures
5. Vodcast (or video briefs)

Post your finished video stories to your WordPress site.

4. Identify a story that would make for a good moving pictures presentation. Then, create a 60-second clip with ambient sound. Post your finished clip to your WordPress site.

Notes

1. Nielsen Company, "Three Screen Report" (Volume 8, First Quarter 2010).
2. Ken Kobré, "The Future of Videojournalism: Stay Ahead of the Curve by Following These Trends." Digitaljournalist.org, April 2009.

CHAPTER 10

Information Graphics

Visualizing the News

In communications design, the visualization of data and complex processes combines the best of art and information architecture. Data visualizations are not only useful for simplifying complex information, but they can be beautiful, engaging, and creative. Illustrative graphics have the power to take you places not readily accessible to photographers. Ultimately, information graphics are capable of explaining some events and processes in ways that words alone cannot touch. Information graphics can stand alone or supplement other story forms. And in the multimedia world, there are a significant number of possibilities for how journalistic visual information is presented. Thus, all multimedia journalists should be well versed in the types of information graphics available and how they can be used to enhance storytelling.

Online, maps, charts, and diagrams are dramatically enhanced by the web's multimedia potential. Now, the ability to animate adds a level of realism to graphics that show step-by-step processes or how things work. Users have more control over navigation, allowing for a nonlinear presentation of information. And the potential for interactivity allows us to experiment with new storytelling strategies that draw on gaming and other digital formats. Online we can also combine other media, such as audio and video, with our graphics. Thus, multimedia graphics are quickly becoming a popular method of storytelling because they offer a truer depiction of events or processes.

A number of news sites are considered leaders in multimedia graphics reporting. The South Florida Sun-Sentinel in Fort Lauderdale (http://www. sun-sentinel.com) is widely considered a pioneer in the multimedia graphics effort. Its multimedia gallery "The Edge" features hundreds of interactive graphics, data visualizations, and games.

A number of other sites, including msnbc.com, washingtonpost.com, and discovery.com consistently produce award-winning multimedia graphics. And nytimes .com has begun to perfect the interdisciplinary collaborative process that is often necessary to produce effective multimedia graphics. In addition to some very talented reporters, editors, and illustrators, the online staff of the New York Times also includes statisticians who regularly help create data-rich visualizations and interactive, searchable statistical displays.

This chapter explores information graphics from two perspectives. Regardless of publication format, print or digital, information graphics are generally broken into three categories: charts, maps, and diagrams. So, we will first define and explore their key characteristics. Second, as charts, maps, and diagrams migrate to the web, the potential for animation, nonlinear navigation, enhanced interactivity, and multimedia combinations has created new classifications: instructives, simulations, narratives, journalistic games, and data visualizations. So, we will expand the concept of information graphics beyond the simple, print-centric definitions to more complex multimedia forms.

Mapping the News

Maps are the most common types of information graphics. They serve a variety of purposes in communication design, such as forecasting the weather, locating an event, or geographically plotting statistical information. Maps are also routinely used by government, private and public companies, and community organizations.

Cartography, the act of making maps, mixes geography with many other fields, including mathematics and meteorology. A cartographer's job often includes research, data analysis, and illustration. Newspapers, magazines, online publications, and broadcast media frequently use maps to apply news and information to cartographic illustration. Thus, multimedia journalists should know what types of maps are available to advance storytelling when "where?" is one of the central questions a story must answer. There are different kinds of maps available to graphics reporters.

GRAPHICS HISTORY AND RESEARCH

Graphics appeared in publications throughout the late 1800s and beyond. But it wasn't until the early 1980s that sophisticated maps, charts, and diagrams became regular story forms in print. The evolution of desktop publishing and graphics programs like Adobe Illustrator made it easier to create information graphics. And as a field, information graphics reporting has evolved rapidly during the past 25 years. Publications such as USA Today and Time magazine were early adopters of information graphics. And in recent years, information graphics have migrated to the web, offering journalists even more methods for telling visual stories.

The combination of words and visuals that occurs in information graphics has also been the subject of notable studies in cognitive psychology. For example, in 1971, psychologist Allan Paivio proposed that recall and recognition are enhanced when information is presented in both visual and verbal forms because it stimulates a "dual coding" of information. In other words, because both the literal and visual regions of the brain are simultaneously activated, information graphics can stimulate more brainpower than stories comprised of visuals or text alone. Other studies have examined how this verbal/visual equation affects the processing, recall, and understanding of information. And more recently, multimedia experts have begun to explore how animation and interactivity affect recall.

The most common are locator, geological, and statistical; and each serves a different purpose.

Locator maps offer an x-marks-the-spot depiction of a location and can be either passive or active. They provide recognition and general reference for stories and are usually relatively small. Passive maps are intended for at-a-glance consumption. Active maps, by contrast, are a bit more complex. In addition to offering an x-marks-the-spot location, they also may show how a specific event unfolded in relation to the location. For example, when a plane crashes, it is often necessary to show its point of departure, where it was going, and where it crashed. Active maps may use visual cues such as arrows or sequential numbering to help a viewer understand the sequence of events in relation to place and time. All locator maps may also include insets that show either zoomed out or zoomed in views of the area of interest to provide greater context or more detail.

FIGURE 10-1

Passive maps like this one offer an "x-marks-the-spot" approach to storytelling. Statistical maps, discussed later in the chapter, are also considered passive.

Geological maps show the Earth's formations, such as fault lines, surface characteristics of a land mass or mountains, valleys, and bodies of water. The two most common types of geological maps are land use and topographic. Land use maps show how communities and individuals use land, as well as how chunks of land are zoned. For example, counties use land use maps to show what portions of a city are designated for schools, residential areas, industrial areas, parks and playgrounds, cemeteries, or other public, private, or institutional areas. Topographic maps show the physical features and surface characteristics of a landmass, or the "lay of the land." Topographic maps may show mountains, valleys, or ocean floors, and can be helpful in displaying important geological information in a news presentation. Sometimes, topographic maps are illustrated to appear three-dimensional. When this is the case, a topographic map is also called a "relief" map.

Statistical maps correlate numerical data with geographic locations. For example, dots and other symbols can be used to represent numbers of people in a given

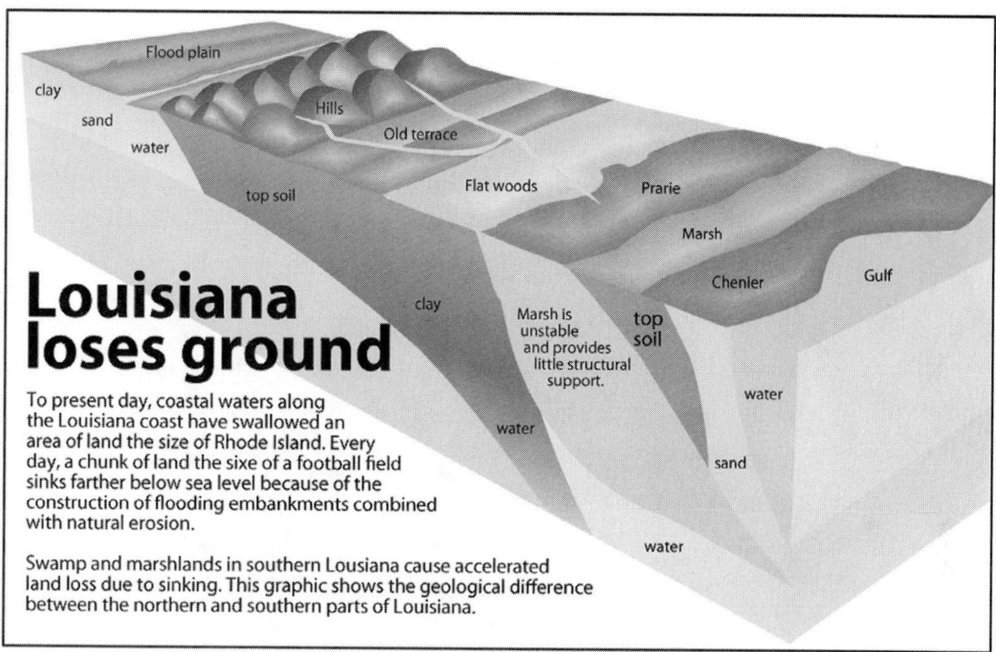

Flood plain
clay
sand
water
Hills
Old terrace
top soil
Flat woods
Prarie
Marsh
Chenier
Gulf
Louisiana loses ground
clay
Marsh is unstable and provides little structural support.
top soil
water
water
sand
water
To present day, coastal waters along the Louisiana coast have swallowed an area of land the size of Rhode Island. Every day, a chunk of land the sixe of a football field sinks farther below sea level because of the construction of flooding embankments combined with natural erosion.
Swamp and marshlands in southern Lousiana cause accelerated land loss due to sinking. This graphic shows the geological difference between the northern and southern parts of Louisiana.
BSU NEWS 485: Josh Engleman, Yardley Younhans, Christy Dollar

FIGURE 10-2

Topographic maps often show the lay of the land. This cutaway shows the physical features and surface characteristics of a landmass. *Source:* Josh Engleman, Ball State University.

area. And color-coding is used to denote numerical values or weather patterns. Three common types of statistical maps are choropleth, isoline, and dot distribution.

Choropleth maps are created by first categorizing numerical data according to value sets. For example, a choropleth map could be used to offer an at-a-glance depiction of the number of Hispanic Americans living in the United States based on census data. For this story, the data should be broken down into a number of numerical ranges, such as 0–10,000, 10,001–20,000, and so on. The value ranges in each category should be equal amounts. After categories have been established, different colors are assigned to each value set. Finally, each state is colored accordingly.

Isoline maps show similarities in bands or blocks of value, which, like choropleths, are colored to match specific value sets. While choropleth maps link numerical information to specific units of land (like states), isoline maps use color to represent patterns of data. For example, temperatures gradually increase or decrease as you travel across land. Thus, weather maps use bands of color to

U.S. unemployment rates by state

At the end of December when states reported their monthly and yearly unemployments rates all reported a increase in unemployment in both monthly and yearly periods. According to The United States Department of Labor unemployment rose from 6.8% to 7.2% in December and rose 2.3% from 2007 to 2008. The Midwest and west reportedly had the highest average. These are the unemployment rates per state as reported in January 2009 by the United States Department of Labor.

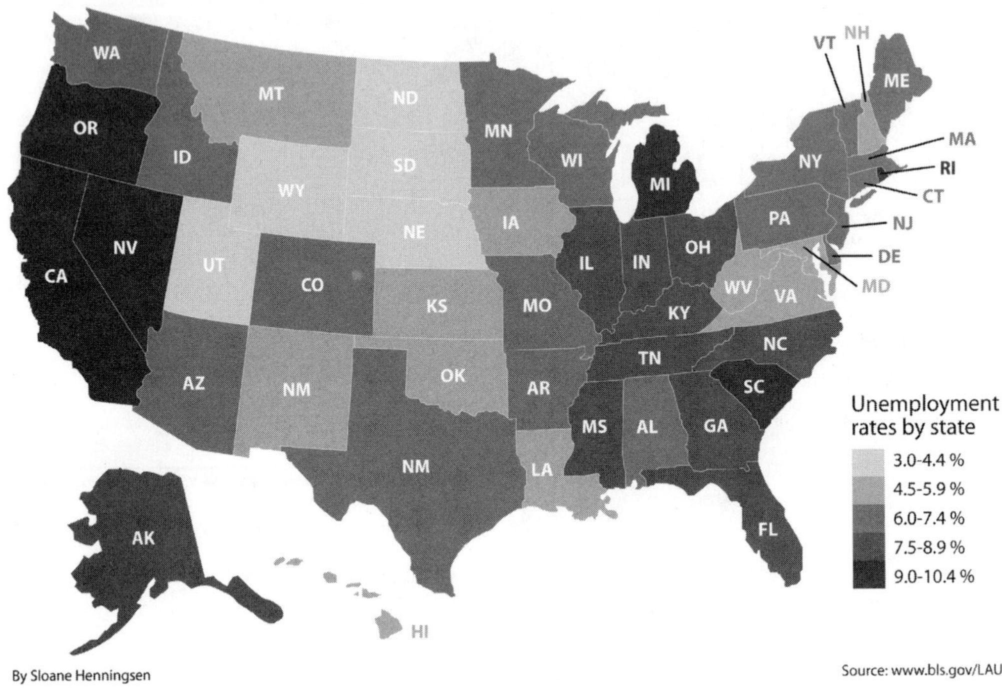

FIGURE 10-3

Choropleth maps apply color-coding to ranges of data. This map shows the number of unemployed Americans by state. Data is broken down into equal ranges, each range is given a color, and states are color-coded according to the data range into which they fall.

Source: Sloane Henningsen, Ball State University.

represent temperatures, amounts of precipitation, and other pressure systems sweeping across the land. Color bands connect similar temperature patterns from region to region with lines and shapes. The shapes are then filled with gradient colors to represent the gradual nature of weather.

Dot distribution maps use dots to represent value sets. Dots are most often related to a ratio, with one dot equaling a larger number of items. For example, you could use a dot distribution map to show annual potato production in Idaho. For

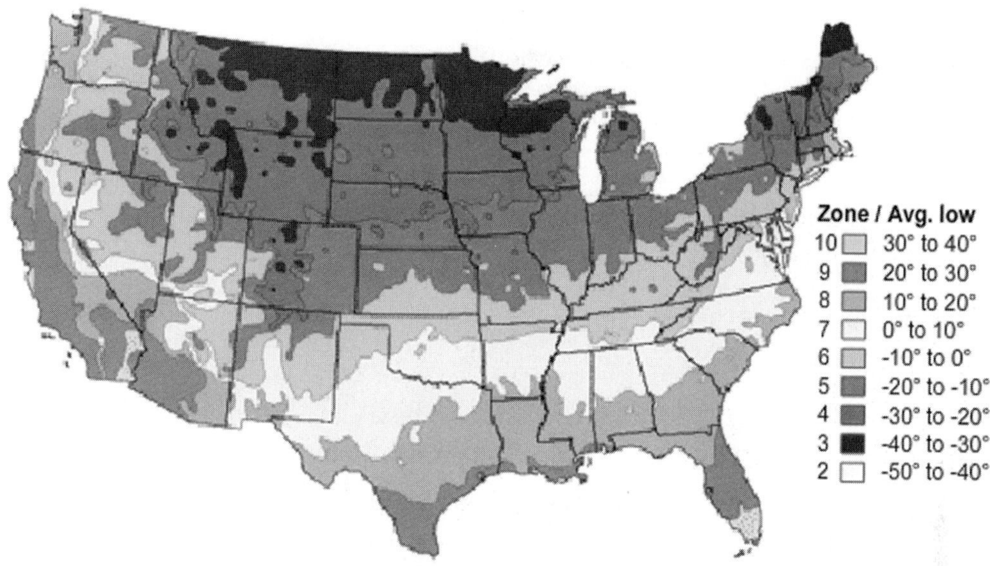

FIGURE 10-4

Isoline maps are most commonly used for weather maps. Isoline maps correlate color-coding with weather so viewers can see significant patterns at a glance.

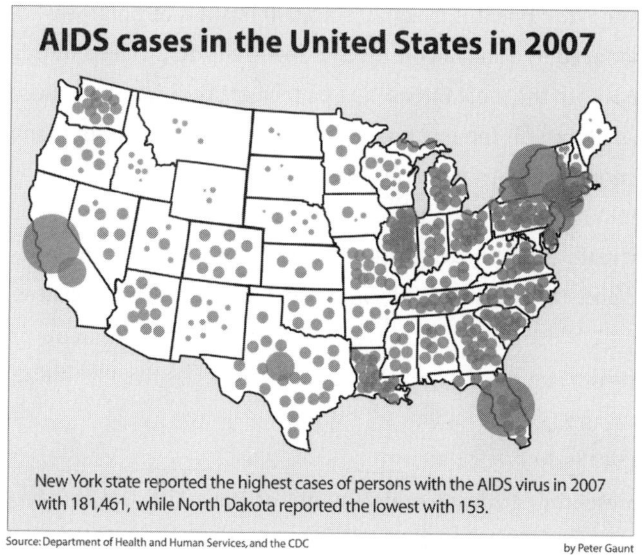

AIDS cases in the United States in 2007
New York state reported the highest cases of persons with the AIDS virus in 2007 with 181,461, while North Dakota reported the lowest with 153.
Source: Department of Health and Human Services, and the CDC
by Peter Gaunt

FIGURE 10-5

Dot distribution maps show how a data set is distributed on a map. Population and other census data are commonly presented in this form.

Source: Peter Gaunt, Ball State University.

QUICK TIPS

MAPS

Find a good reference. A strong base map will ensure that your reproduction is accurate. Keep a list of map references, including a world atlas and a detailed map of the city in which you work.

Edit the fat. Pinpoint the area of interest on your base map. Then determine which surrounding streets, cities, boundaries, landmarks, bodies of water, and so on provide important context and which ones are unnecessary to understanding the news event. Get rid of those that are less important.

Determine what type of map should be used. Is it active? If so, make sure you show that action. Is it passive? If so, make sure the focal point is placed in a central position on the map. Is it statistical or geographic? Make sure you understand the data and its relationship to the map.

Adhere to type and color palettes. Most publications will have previously established color and type palettes for information graphics. You should strictly follow those guidelines to maintain hierarchy, order, and consistency.

this story, you might assert that one dot is equal to 10,000 bushels of potatoes. So, if 50,000 bushels are produced in a single county, five dots should be placed in this area of the state. The areas with the most intense dot pattern are the highest producers. Note that if the dot-data ratio is too low, sparse areas will be covered with many dots, making it appear more concentrated than it really is.

Likewise, a ratio that is too high will make a more densely populated area appear to be much more sparse than it really is. Because this type of map is meant to convey information at a glance, your audience may be misled if the ratios aren't closely proportionate to actual numbers.

Speaking to the Eyes

Charts are capable of presenting a considerable amount of statistical data in a relatively small amount of space. The concept of charting data emerged during the eighteenth century. Invented in the late 1700s by William Playfair, a Scottish architect, pie charts and bar charts suddenly allowed data to "speak to the eyes." But don't underestimate a chart's power or complexity. The nature of the information at hand will dictate which type of graphic should be used. And what attracts the eye may not engage the brain. So to be effective, charts must be clear and precise, accurate and consistent. Although there are many different approaches to charting data, the three most common in communications design are pie, fever, and bar charts.

Pie charts, or circle graphs, represent parts of a whole. Data displayed in pie charts must always be represented in percentages. Because the circle metaphor is associated with a complete amount, the sections of a pie chart should always equal 100 percent. It is also important to define the total number that is being broken down into percentages. Ten percent of 10 is one. Ten percent of 100,000 is 10,000. If the audience is not given a clear indication of what the whole amount is, it is left with no context for the percentages you have offered.

Bar charts compare data using bars to represent whole amounts. Because the bars are sized relative to the amounts they represent, bar charts make comparisons

QUICK TIPS

Pie Charts

Always represent a whole
Percentages must equal 100 percent
More than two wedges, less than seven
Wedges should have % displayed
State the total of the breakdown

Bar Charts

Show comparisons
Vertical bars = time along *x*-axis
Horizontal bars = time is not a factor
No grid necessary; use common baseline
Display totals with bars

Fever Charts

Demonstrate a trend
Best for showing dynamic ups and downs
Need background grids
x-axis = time; *y*-axis = amounts
Display beginning and/or ending totals

among different categories easy to see. If time is a factor, use a vertical bar chart so that time can be along the x-axis. If time is not a factor, make your bar chart horizontal because it is easier to discern differences when lines read left to right.

Finally, bar charts are easier to read when each bar is accompanied by the total amount it represents. Do not make the audience guess what the exact figure is. Bars make differences clear at a glance and the numbers reinforce the actual numerical differences.

Fever Charts are also called "line graphs" and compare two related variables. The concept of the fever chart originated in 1637 when René Descartes outlined the "Cartesian grid," a system of plotting points on a graph made of intersecting lines. Fever charts require that each variable is plotted along the *x*- or *y*-axis, and they are most commonly used to show change over time. The *x*-axis should represent equal time intervals (i.e., days of the week, months of the year, consecutive years, etc.), and the *y*-axis should represent related amounts.

Illustrating the News

Diagrams show how something happened, the process by which something occurs, or the inner workings of both animate and inanimate objects. Diagrams combine substantial text with detailed illustrations to dissect the important parts of objects or chronicle a chain of events. Thus, diagrams require strong textual and visual reference materials, and graphics reporters may spend a good deal of time away from their desks conducting research. Because they are generally illustration-driven, diagrams often require a bit more artistic ability than other types of graphics. So finding a good illustrator with whom to collaborate is often necessary.

Like maps, diagrams can be both passive and active. Passive diagrams generally dissect an object and accurately label its parts. Although a passive diagram may explain how something works or happens in text, it will not actually illustrate that action. Active diagrams, by contrast, both dissect an object and illustrate actual or implied movement. So, although a passive diagram of the human heart would just label and perhaps explain the chambers and arteries of the heart, an active diagram might actually illustrate blood flow. In print, arrows would be used to show movement and online the graphic can be animated. Regardless, all diagrams have passive qualities, but not all are active.

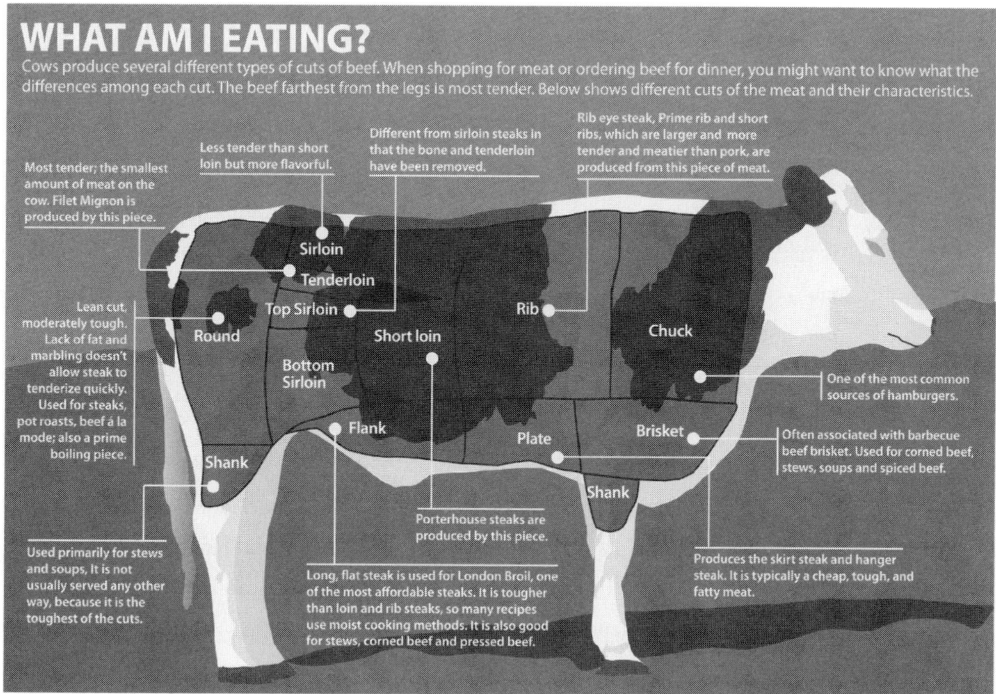

FIGURE 10-6

Passive diagrams label the parts of an object. They can include additional descriptive information along with labels.

Source: Danielle Aber, Ball State University.

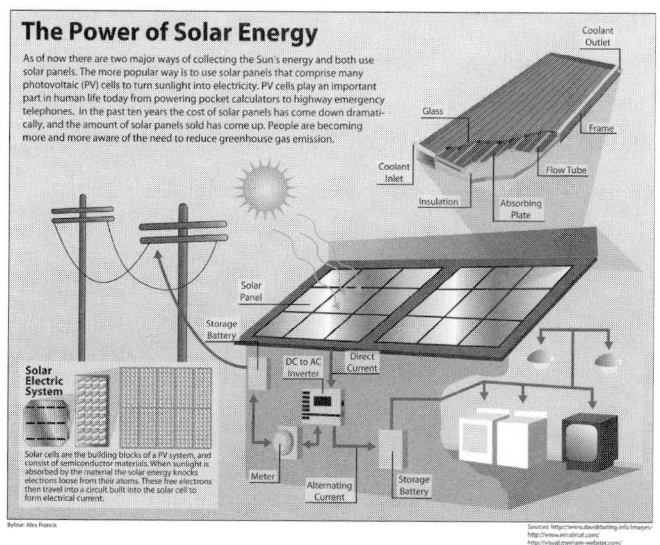

FIGURE 10-7

Active diagrams use arrows or other visual cues to imply motion. Often, active diagrams are used to explain complex processes like how solar energy can be used to power homes.

Source: Alex Francis, Ball State University.

DIAGRAMMING A DIAGRAM

Headline: One of the five essential components of an information graphic, the headline helps establish the basic focus.

Illustration: If your graphic is composed of multiple illustrations, make sure that one is visually dominant to establish a sense of hierarchy and visual rhythm. Although many illustration styles exist and are appropriate, a graphics reporter should consider the nature and tone of the story before establishing a specific visual texture, color palette, and general style.

Inset: An inset is often used to show a view that is zoomed in or out. They can also be used to present secondary graphic information that supports the main illustration.

Introductory Explainer: Also called "chatter," the introductory text is essential. Two- to five-sentences in length, the chatter provides context for the package, giving the audience a general explanation of what is presented and why. The length of introductory chatter depends on the amount of detail and the available space. Chatter should be written in present tense, active voice. It should be clear and direct, providing an overview for the diagram.

Labels/Callouts: In addition to the introductory chatter, most information graphics also include additional labels and callouts (secondary explainers) that better define and explain various portions of a diagram. Labels are often two- to three-word headers. Callouts are usually one- to two-sentences (or sentence fragments) in length.

Byline: Just as a written story needs a byline for the sake of credibility and identification of the reporter, so does a graphic.

Source Line: Diagrams should include a source line that lists the specific references used to develop the graphic. Remember, you will have both textual and visual reference materials to cite here. It is generally acceptable to cite only the major references consulted.

Graphics in Motion

As a graphic migrates to the web, the potential for animation and interactivity fundamentally change structure and navigation. Web graphics go a step further than print graphics by providing a more immersive user experience. Online graphics can

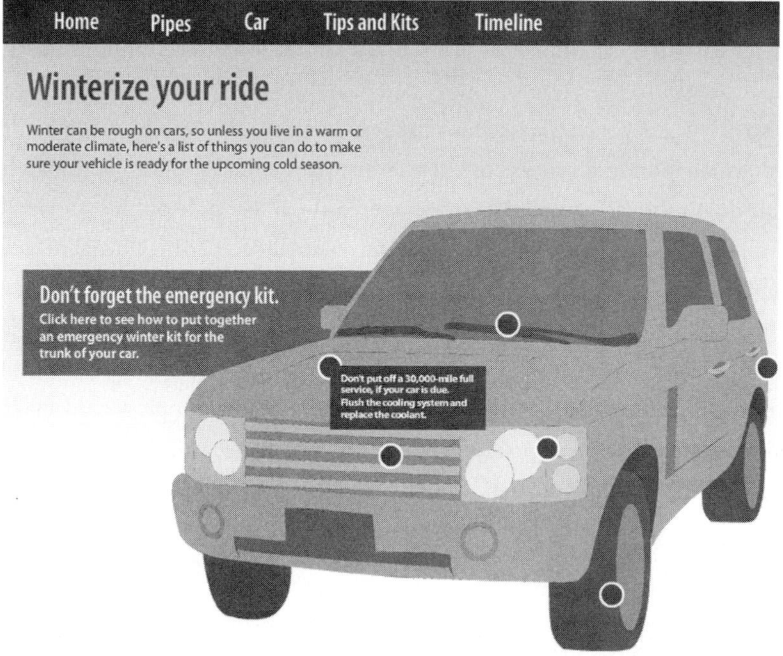

FIGURE 10-8

This simple instructive graphic provides links to several diagrams that show techniques for winterizing your car and home. Individual illustrations include rollovers that offer informative tips when activated. *Source:* Kyle Lewis, Ball State University.

be presented in a nonlinear fashion. They can simulate real world experiences and employ game strategies. And they can implement sound and animation to enrich understanding and better reflect reality. Interactive graphics can be divided into five main categories: instructives, narratives, simulations, journalistic games, and data visualizations.

Instructives explain how something happens or how something works by enabling the user to sequentially step through the visual and textual content of the graphic. Instructives are good for showing processes, such as how a tornado forms, how to winterize your car, or how a specific news event unfolded. They are immersive because they allow the user to control the pace at which the graphic is consumed. However the sequence of events is generally predetermined. Often, instructive graphics are divided into discreet "scenes" and the user can click a "next" or "back" button to navigate from scene to scene. Virtually any topic that has a visual component can be presented in instructive form. And because they are relatively easy to create, intructives provide a logical route when time is short and resources are slim.

Narratives are much like videos in that they allow the viewer to watch an animated explanation of a process or event. Narratives combine audio voiceover with graphic depth and rich animation. For example, in 2011, Circle of Blue (circleofblue.org) ran a narrative that explains how water is desalinated. This format allows for a simple and accurate depiction of a complex process. Because narratives involve very little interactivity, the animation must be dynamic and relatively constant. If too much time passes with little or no animation, the user is likely to become bored and lose interest in the graphic. Thus, when deciding whether a topic would make for a good narrative graphic, consider whether the illustrative portions of the graphic have enough animation potential. Good narrative topics include how a space shuttle

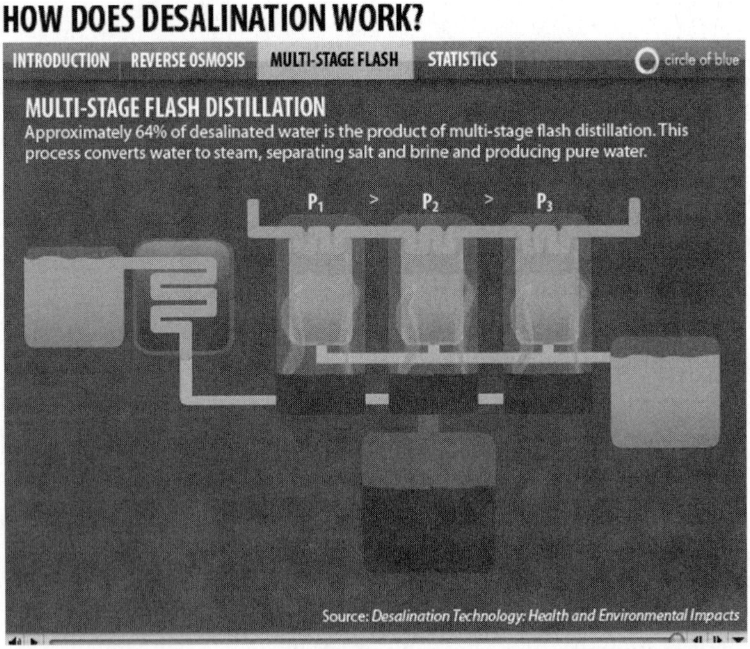

FIGURE 10-9

This narrative graphic explains the process of desalination through animation combined with audio voiceover. *Source:* Greg Hudson, Ball State University & Circle of Blue.

launches or the phases of the moon. Audio voice over should be also concise, active, and match the animation as it unfolds.

Simulations represent real-word phenomena. Highly immersive, simulations allow the user to experience an activity that resembles its real-world equivalent. In 2001, for example, the *Sun-Sentinel* created a simulation that allowed users to try out the new electronic voting machines that would soon be implemented in Dade and Broward counties. To create this sim, graphics reporters replicated the visual appearance of the voting machine right down to the typefaces, offering users a very realistic opportunity to learn how to properly cast their votes in the coming election. Generally, only topics that are effectively simulated using a computer interface are suitable for simulations. For example, if you want to show users how to plant a garden, you should probably go with an instructive because it will be difficult to replicate that experience on a computer. However, if you want to offer users a virtual piano lesson,

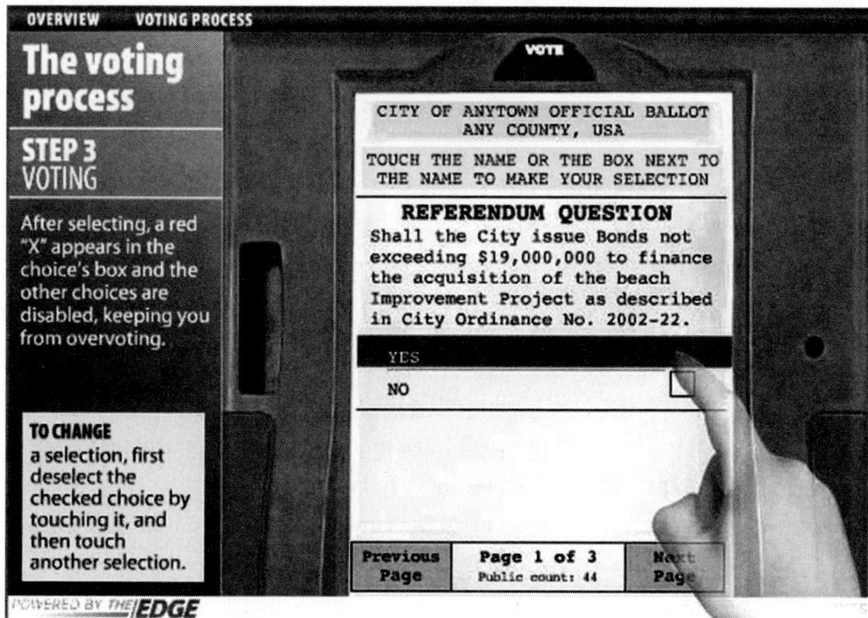

FIGURE 10-10

Simulations create immersive experiences that help users better understand a complex topic, event, or issue. This *Sun-Sentinel* simulation allowed users to practice using new electronic voting machines before Election Day. *Source:* Image courtesy of the South Florida *Sun-Sentinel*.

THE RELATIONSHIP BETWEEN DESIGN AND PROGRAMMING

If you intend to be a graphics reporter, one of the best things you can do is consider a double major or at least a minor in computer science. Individuals who are both good storytellers and who have the programming skills necessary to develop the types of interactive graphics discussed here are in high demand. Among some of the more valuable programming languages for visual journalists are HTML5, CSS, JavaScript, and ActionScript for Flash. Likewise, the ability to build databases and knowledge of PHP code is a tremendous asset. However, it's just as likely that you will be on a multimedia team that includes a programmer.

go for it! Using computer keys and clicking a mouse can be adequate actions for this topic.

Visit the multimedia examples section of www.oup.com/us/palilonis and find the resources/examples tab. Select graphics resources from the drop down menu to see examples of the different types of interactive graphics discussed in this chapter.

Journalistic Games are like simulations because they offer highly immersive, interactive experiences. However, they go a step further by actually applying traditional gaming strategies to serious storytelling. The idea is that the more you can immerse users in the graphic, the more they will learn and stay engaged. Journalistic games are very difficult to pull off because they have to be both accurate and appropriately serious in tone, illustration, and content. At the same time, they must be fun, engaging, and worth playing. Likewise, they must have a storyline that pulls the user through the game. They must also make room for winning and losing or offer some "payoff" in the end. Journalistic games must explain the rules of play, as well as employ tasks that are reasonably achieved using a computer interface. In 2010, a group of students and professors at the University of North Carolina developed a game that challenges users to address the future energy demands by keeping consumer costs and carbon emissions down. Users make decisions about how resources for nonrenewable and renewable energy sources should be allocated. When they are finished, they can receive a report that helps them understand the benefits and consequences of their decisions. These kinds of games help news audiences understand the complexities of some stories by allowing them to experience an event or grapple with an issue firsthand. Journalistic games are commonly combined with other multimedia story packages. For example, the graphics package about a day in the life of an American

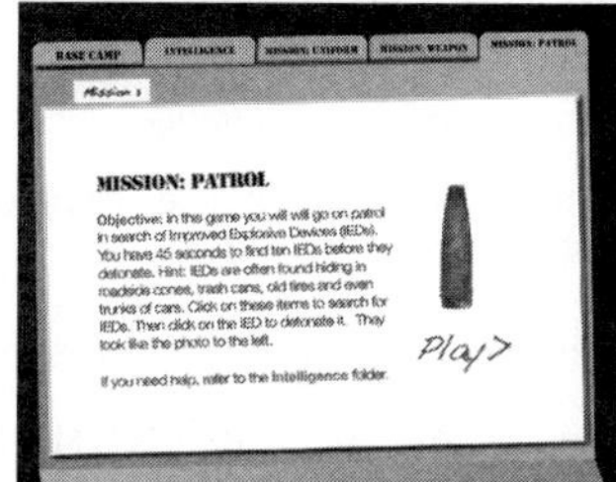

FIGURE 10-11

In this journalistic game, users are challenged to search for improvised explosive devices (IEDs) in a warzone scene. The scene resembles one described in a related news story about the types of operations U.S. soldiers in Afghanistan commonly execute.

Source: Amy Buck, Marina Heflin, and Ben Green, Ball State University

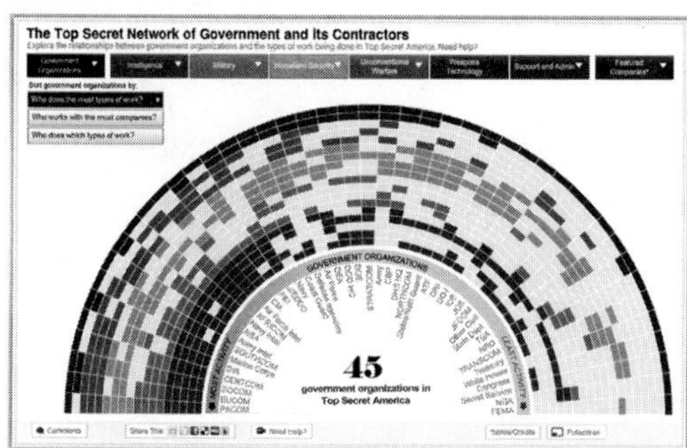

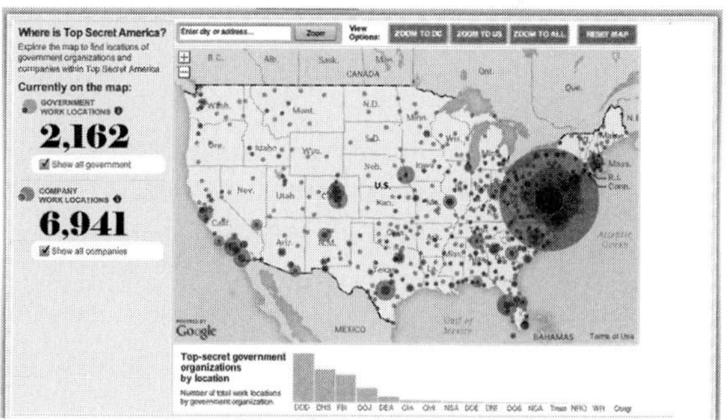

FIGURES 10-12 & 10-13

More than a dozen *Washington Post* journalists spent two years developing "Top Secret America," an investigative story that describes the national security buildup in the United States after the September 11, 2001, attacks. The project included a number of data-driven interactive graphics that are highly immersive, visually descriptive, and elegant. *Source:* Images courtesy of the *Washington Post*

soldier shown here combines simple games with updated news stories and other content about ongoing wars in the Middle East. The game allows the user to complete daily tasks, such as assembling a riffle or searching for IEDs.

Data Visualization is a term that can be used to refer to any type of information graphic that turns complex data into visual presentations. So maps, charts, and diagrams as they have been defined here are, in fact, data visualizations. However, contemporary data visualizations go way beyond these traditional approaches. In fact, one of the most remarkable things about modern data visualization is its application of unique, creative design ideas that in some cases turn data into beautiful, elegant, descriptive art. Likewise, journalistic storytelling combined with motion and often-stunning artistic displays engage audiences on a number of levels.

Journalistic data visualizations most commonly come in the form of maps or charts. And even more important than the visual display of data is the ability to understand and effectively synthesize the data. According to statistician, designer, and data visualization specialist Nathan Yau, "While having interesting data can really make a visualization intriguing, so can what you actually do with the data. When you design a visualization, it's always best to consider the purpose and audi-

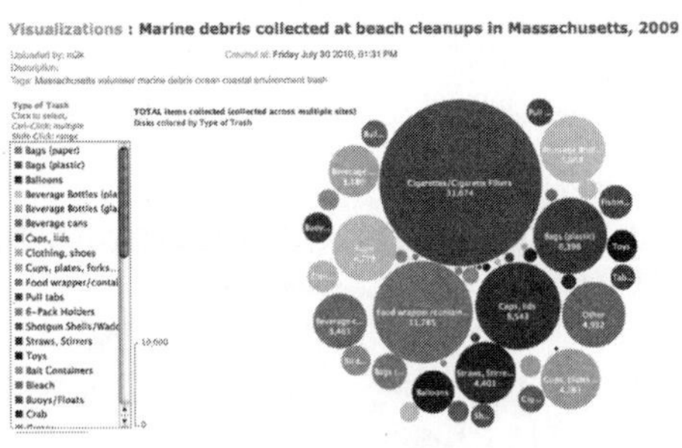

FIGURE 10-14

This Many Eyes visualization shows the how much and what kind of debris is most commonly collected at beach cleanups in Massachusetts. Users can isolate different categories by clicking on the menu to the left.

Source: Image courtesy of International Business Machines Corporation, copyright © International Business Machines Corporation

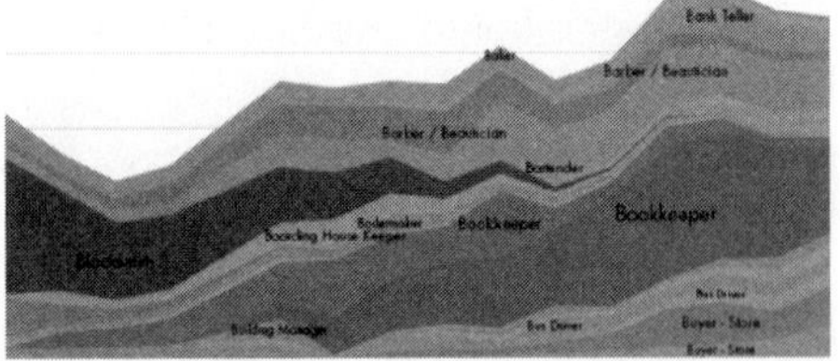

FIGURE 10-15

This Flare visualization uses a stacked time series to visualize 150 years of changes in the U.S. labor force. Data appears dynamically when users roll over different parts of the chart.

Source: University of California, Berkeley Visualization Lab

ence. If the visualization is for the early stages of analysis, you're going to design much differently than if the visualization is for a publication."[1] Likewise, you must carefully consider how colors, contrasts, organization, and structure affect storytelling.

In spite of the highly artistic nature of most data visualizations, creating them is not as difficult as you may first think. In fact, there are a number of open source solutions online that allow even the least artistic journalists to create rich, animated graphics. Open source programs are generally available for download from the web and can be used free of charge. Google mapmaker and Google chart tools, for example, provide several tools for making data more comprehensible. And special URLs can be used to embed graph and chart images in users' own web pages.

And, IBM's Many Eyes (http://manyeyes.alphaworks.ibm.com/manyeyes/) offers a number of open source visualization tools in an effort to "democratize visualization and to enable a new social kind of data analysis."[2] Users can upload data sets, choose from a library of innovative visualization patterns, and with the press of a button transform data into images. Likewise, the University of California, Berkeley's Visualization Lab offers Flare (http://flare.prefuse.org/), an open source ActionScript library for creating visualizations that run in the Adobe Flash Player. "From basic charts and graphs to complex interactive graphics, the toolkit supports data management, visual encoding, animation, and interaction techniques."[3] The emergence of these tools proves that now, more than ever, all journalists should be thinking visually and analytically when reporting complex data.

Planning Multimedia Graphics

There are two important concepts related to planning online graphics: effectively choosing which type of graphic is most appropriate for a particular story and developing a clear understanding of the user experience. For example, the technical ability to implement a visual effect should not be equated with free license to use it. In fact, an effective graphics reporter knows when to show restraint where animation is concerned. The decision to animate must be preceded by a carefully scripted plan that includes a storyboard representing a fluid and concise play-by-play of the action. A well-directed storyboard can lead to a clear and tightly edited information graphic. Review Chapter 3 for more on how to create storyboards.

Animation also introduces a complex technological challenge. Illustration software programs, such as Adobe Illustrator, while extremely rich and complex, have relatively shallow learning curves compared to animation programs such as Adobe Flash. Of course, the more illustratively complicated the print graphic, the more time and technical savvy it will take to develop. And online readers have a greater amount of control over the pace and order in which they receive information. Thus, a graphics reporter cannot assume that the audience will engage with various parts of a graphic in any particular order. Of course, a graphic that provides a step-by step progression of information or a narrative animation will often require a linear presentation. However, simulations, serious games, and data visualizations often allow the audience to choose, click and navigate in a random fashion. Thus, the graphics reporter must assume that all portions of graphic are encountered independent of one another. The most effective online graphics promote interactivity and observe a clear and logical organization.

Professional Perspective

Len De Groot • *Trainer*

Knight Foundation Digital Media Center

Len De Groot is the interactive design and data instructor at the Knight Digital Media Center, teaching mid-career journalists skills to tell stories on the web. He has nearly 20 years of newsroom experience and was graphics director for WSFL-TV and the Sun-Sentinel *newspaper in South Florida. While there, he created and directed news graphics for print, interactive graphics for the web, and animated news graphics for a morning television news show and television station promotions.*

It is an exciting time to be a multimedia journalist. Walls between departments are crumbling as newsrooms adapt to rapid changes in the media landscape. Newsrooms are employing multiple storytelling techniques and choosing the best format based on story content. They are willing to experiment and try fresh approaches. Interactive content is no longer hidden away in multimedia ghettos. It frequently rises to the home page where it is high profile, high impact, and pulls in high numbers of page views. And while some managers may not completely "get it," most understand that investing in multimedia is a competitive necessity.

The reason for multimedia's success is simple. People want to make sense of data and information that affects their lives. Readers and viewers have become users. More correctly, they are platform-agnostic consumers of information. In their eyes, no type of story is better. They don't hold antiquated prejudices for text and photos that journalists developed over decades in newsrooms. They want content in the best form for consumption, be it text, photos, video, or graphics.

For these reasons and others, jobs are less traditional. Some multimedia skills are expected in young journalists. They may report, write, illustrate, design, and program story pages. Ambitious and creative young individuals with these skills are in high demand. Their flexibility makes them attractive hires and often tips the scales in their favor when being considered for a job.

Storytelling

Interactive multimedia makes sense of complicated issues, connects with readers emotionally, and gives users the opportunity to discover relevant information through their own exploration. Put simply, they tell stories. But beautiful graphics or data visualizations without journalistic skills are often facile and lack relevance and meaning for consumers. Knowing when an interesting story is relevant is important to its success. It sets journalists apart from programmers and translates across media.

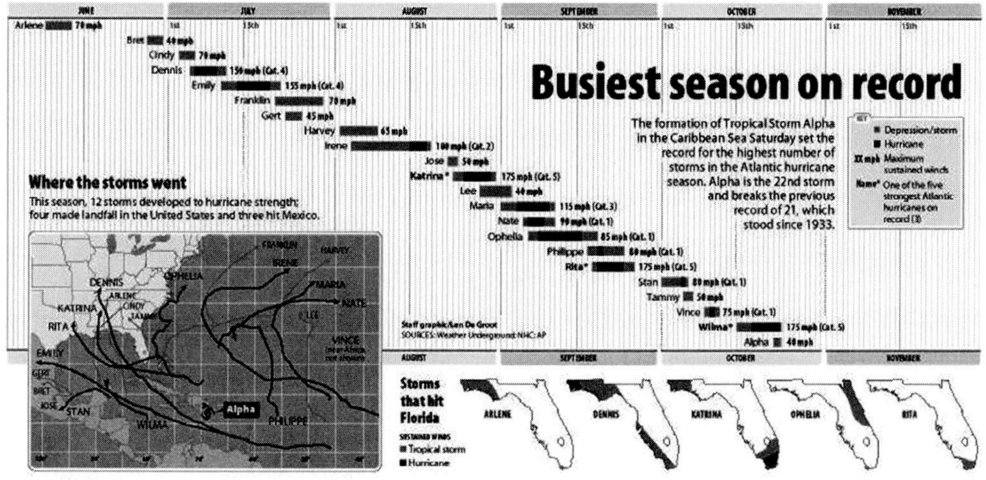

FIGURE 10-17

Source: Image courtesy of the South Florida Sun-Sentinel.

The Busiest Season

I produced the graphic seen in Figure 10-17 in 2005 at the *Sun-Sentinel*, when more hurricanes and tropical storms formed in the Atlantic than ever before recorded. It illustrates the frequency of concurrent storms in the Atlantic and the scarcity of days without any storms. The graphic is about hurricanes, but it resonated with readers because it quantifies fatigue. It's hard to explain the stress associated with being under a storm watch for five months straight. The constant state of readiness—not knowing if you need to hunker down or flee—takes a physical and psychological toll. Reactions to the graphic reflected that. "Oh! That's why I'm so tired!" and "Good, I'm not crazy," were common responses.

The Power of Interactivity

The static image is good but became more powerful when we handed over control of the content. Scott Horner and Karsten Ivey used the graphic as a timeline and paired it with a NASA video of the storms so that people could explore the season in ways that interested them. There's more detail in the path of every storm than we could ever hope to write about. This makes available information that would have gone unreported in the past. And it does so without sacrificing the emotional resonance.

The information breaks free of the limits of a traditional narrative. A linear story with a beginning and end transforms to a funnel shape with consumers entering the small end. The narrative expands as they explore. They can play the graphic through to see the whole season—or not. They can stop at something that interests them and replay, moving back and forth.

Whatever the consumer does, the goal of the interactive graphic is achieved. Some might consider this a technical achievement, but it's really journalistic. Most programmers, brilliant as they are, would not think to build this. It's not their fault. They are problems solvers, creating technical solutions and tools without a concern for storytelling. The brilliant programmers who created the amazing Flare visualization tools (http://flare.prefuse.org/) admit they need journalists to put them to larger use.

Journalists are comfortable working in shades of gray. We look for stories that affect peoples' lives. Then we figure out how to best tell them. As an example, the *Sun-Sentinel's* 2008 presidential election coverage included a series of maps (see

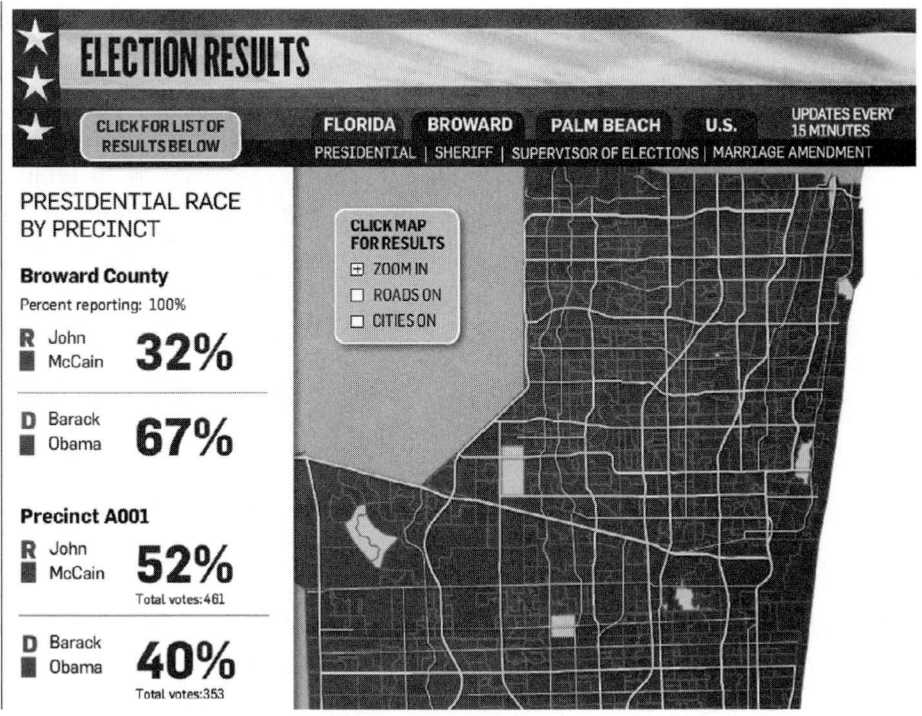

FIGURE 10-18

Source: Image courtesy of the South Florida *Sun-Sentinel*.

Figure 10-18) on key races that updated every 15 minutes on election night. The collection of maps included nationwide and precinct level data and were an important tool to understanding how people voted. They served as a vehicle for breaking news and later, as an archive of a historic election. But an important component to the storytelling was a list of results below the map. Lists make results easy to consume and searchable. Both are important considerations when designing for users.

Data Visualization

The sheer amount of data that becomes publicly available every day is staggering. Federal, state, and local governments share results from studies, surveys, elections, and more. The data isn't even low-hanging fruit. It lies rotting on the ground.

All this data has potential for telling important stories. The trick is knowing the difference between technical and journalistic sophistication. Finding a balance helps visualizations connect with consumers outside the data nerd community. An interactive, searchable database is an easy and effective way to offer large collections of information to consumers. The example below (Figure 10-19) lists people sentenced to death in Florida, an issue that many people care deeply about. It's easy to use and informative. Maps are also an effective way of explaining data. The graphic shown in Figure 10-20, created by students at Berkeley Graduate School of Journalism, explores food availability in the city of Oakland. The red dots are liquor stores, the green boxes are grocery stores and the dark areas on the map are the poorest. The data speaks for itself. It was created with publicly available data reported by the students. Additional layers that are available but not shown are race, ethnicity, farmers markets, and so on.

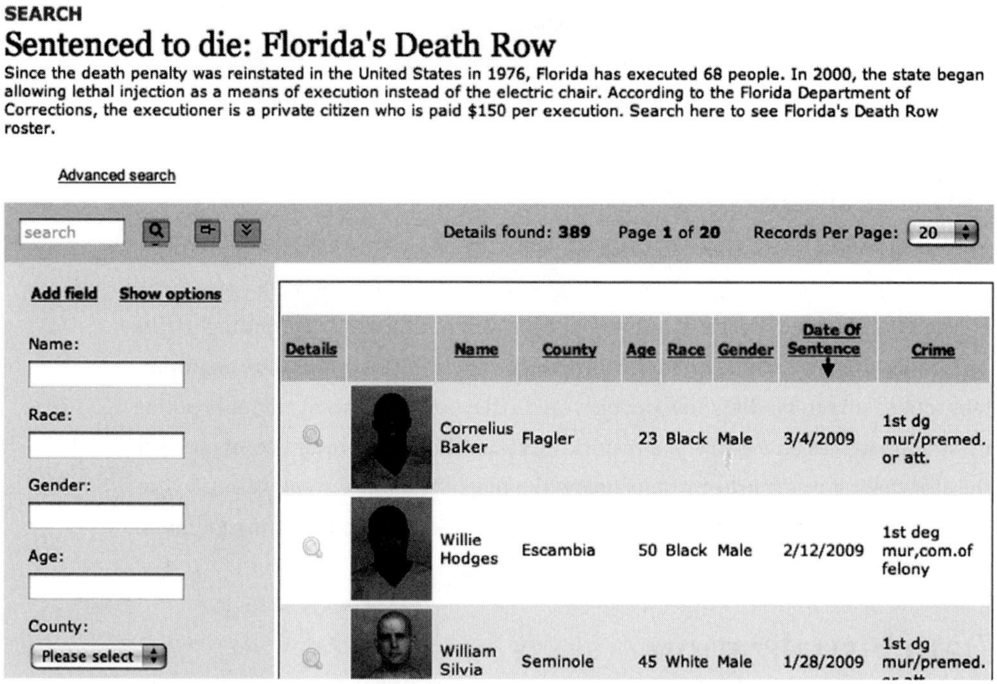

SEARCH

Sentenced to die: Florida's Death Row

Since the death penalty was reinstated in the United States in 1976, Florida has executed 68 people. In 2000, the state began allowing lethal injection as a means of execution instead of the electric chair. According to the Florida Department of Corrections, the executioner is a private citizen who is paid $150 per execution. Search here to see Florida's Death Row roster.

Advanced search

search Details found: **389** Page **1** of **20** Records Per Page: 20

Add field Show options

Name:

Race:

Gender:

Age:

County: Please select

Details		Name	County	Age	Race	Gender	Date Of Sentence	Crime
		Cornelius Baker	Flagler	23	Black	Male	3/4/2009	1st dg mur/premed. or att.
		Willie Hodges	Escambia	50	Black	Male	2/12/2009	1st deg mur,com.of felony
		William Silvia	Seminole	45	White	Male	1/28/2009	1st dg mur/premed.

FIGURE 10-19

Source: Image courtesy of the South Florida *Sun-Sentinel.*

In Oakland, it's easier to buy booze than bananas

FIGURE 10-20

Source: Image courtesy of oaklandnorth.net

Where We Are Going

Interactive visual storytelling tools are maturing very quickly. They make it easier to create sophisticated graphics with minimum of effort and programming. And increasingly, they are open source and free. They remove bottlenecks in graphics departments. Interactive graphics can be produced quickly (and cheaply), increasing their value. Let's look at some examples:

GeoCommons: Frequently shapes, like those seen in a shaded map, are needed to tell a story. The Oakland map was created with the free GeoCommons web service. It allows users to upload data and merge it with several types of polygon map files. In English, that means that an interactive zip code map that once required specialized skills to produce, can be created and shared on a website in minutes.

Protovis: A descendant of Flare, Protovis is a simplified version of JavaScript. It allows a journalist to create charts with the same amount of programming skill needed for HTML. Because it is JavaScript, it's viewable in any modern browser, including iPhone and iPad. It is open source, so if you like someone else's visualization, find the code on his web page and alter it for your needs. There are several samples on the Protovis site that can be altered and reused.

MaPublisher: This plugin turns Adobe Illustrator into a GIS mapping program. It allows you to create one map that you can export for both print and web. It exports an interactive Flash map without ever having to open Flash. Several media companies use it, including *The New York Times* and *Forbes*. Student versions (no upgrades) are available for as little as $249. Professional version (free upgrades for a year) can cost as much as $1,400.

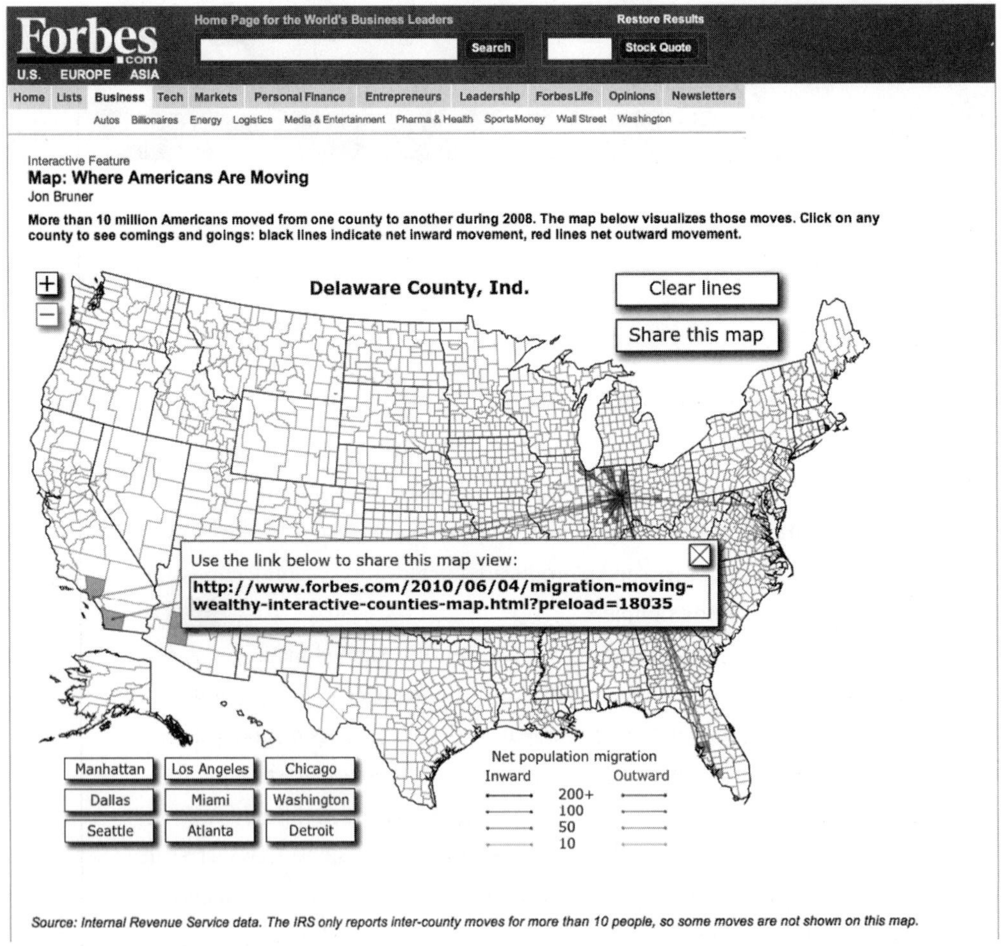

FIGURE 10-21

Source: Reprinted by permission of Forbes Media LLC ©20107

Making interactive graphics social: In the past few years, a multitude of web tools have allowed journalists to create interactive graphics that they could embed and share. Most notably, Many Eyes, Google Docs, and Swivel let users upload data, create a graphic and embed it on a web page just like a YouTube video. But that's really the tip of the iceberg. We're starting to see the power of storytelling put in the hands of consumers.

The *Forbes* emigration map seen in figure 10-21 was created using MaPublisher and allows consumers to explore the data to find the story that interests them and email a link to their custom version to a friend. Sense.us (http://Sense.us) takes it a step further. Created by the same people who made Flare, Sense.us allows users to alter a visualization and comment about what they found. A thumbnail of their discovery and a link are automatically included. Users log in using Facebook so their posts are automatically added to feeds for their friends to see. This example looks at the return on investment for college educations by school.

Final Thoughts

Of course, this is a lot to learn so don't try to do it all at once. It's better to become a good journalist and learn proficiency in one new skill per year. A steady approach will help you excel in just a few years. It will establish a pattern that will equip you to evolve with technology. And don't forget to have fun. It's rewarding work that can make a difference in peoples' lives. And it should enrich yours.

Exercises

1. Visit www.oup.com/us/palilonis and find the resources/exercises tab. Select graphics resources from the drop down menu. Click on the "Graphics Potential" link. There you will find two written stories. Read each story and brainstorm graphics potential. Consider a graphics strategy for both print and online presentations. Write a brief description of your strategy, and include sketched storyboards where appropriate. Post your finished graphics strategy to your WordPress site.
2. Search the web for examples of each of the following types of graphics: instructive, narrative, simulation, journalistic game, and data visualization. Analyze each graphic and write a review that includes a brief description of the graphic

and its parts, an assessment of the navigational structure, and a critique of the overall visual storytelling. How well does the graphic explain its subject matter? Is it easy to understand? Is it will illustrated? What are the overall strengths and weaknesses of the graphic? Post your finished analysis to your WordPress site.

3. Visit http://manyeyes.alphaworks.ibm.com/manyeyes/. Click the "Create Visualization" link and use one of the existing data sets on the site. Examine the data and then click the "visualize" button. You will be offered a number of possibilities for how to visualize the data. Explore different visualization structures until you land on one that you feel best represents the data set you chose. Post your finished visualization to your WordPress site.

Notes

1. Renee Martin-Kratzer, "Design + numbers = more meaningful data." Viewpoints newsletter. Winter 2009, Volume 9, Issue 1.
2. Many Eyes website, http://manyeyes.alphaworks.ibm.com/manyeyes/page/About.html.
3. Flare website, http://flare.prefuse.org/.

UNIT 3

ONWARD & UPWARD

IN THE CURRENT MEDIA LANDSCAPE, HAVING SKILLS AND UNDERSTANDING the nature of multimedia storytelling will go a long way toward making you marketable. But believe it or not, it doesn't stop there. Today's multimedia journalists must also understand how to produce complete story packages and manage large amounts and different kinds of multimedia content. And, perhaps most important, contemporary journalists must be more enterprising than ever before. At the moment, whether you realize it or not, you are preparing for your first job out of college and perhaps a number of subsequent jobs as well. And those future positions may look very different than the one you will land right after graduation.

Successful multimedia journalists will know how to apply their storytelling and story production skills in both traditional and less traditional environments. And they will likely find venues for their work in journalistic and nonjournalistic settings. In fact, being a journalist in the twenty-first century is an extremely exciting proposition because multimedia storytelling skills have a wide variety of applications. The possibilities for your future are endless.

This final unit explores how multimedia stories come together, and how to manage content, as well as how to be entrepreneurial in a multimedia world. Likewise, it will briefly explore the role of social media in journalistic storytelling and offer tips on how to harness its power as both a storytelling tool and promotional aid. Finally, the chapters that follow offer a collection of some of the best and most inspiring multimedia resources in the world. These will help you effectively stay on top of the evolution of journalism long after finishing this book.

CHAPTER 11

Story Packaging

Multimedia Design and Content Management

For the majority of this book, individual story forms have been isolated so that you could explore them according to their individual strengths and weaknesses. At the same time, it has alluded to ways in which they naturally combine. For example, interactive graphics may combine explanatory text and audio with rich illustration. And photo slideshows combine compelling images with narrative audio. However, we have yet to explore one of the most important concepts: developing a complete multimedia package.

An effective multimedia story allows the audience to focus on the whole story. In fact, when multimedia content is packaged well, the whole is greater than the sum of its parts. Packaging multimedia content is a complex process for a number of reasons. First, it is easy to assume that multimedia design is merely an exercise in web design. However, an increasing number of people use other devices, such as mobile phones, tablet devices, and other touch-screen interfaces to consume information. Second, all too often both journalists and their audiences define "multimedia" storytelling as only a digital media endeavor. However, a true multimedia approach to storytelling is not limited to web-based formats but also includes other platforms, such as print and broadcast.

Newspapers and magazines have contained multiple story forms for decades in their packaging of text, photos, and information graphics. Television news has, too, with video, audio, photos, and graphic animations. Additionally, most print and broadcast organizations also publish websites. More and more, they are also publishing mobile media sites and tablet-based applications. Thus, we should not leave any platform out of the multimedia story packaging and design equation. Now, for the purposes of keeping this textbook on point, we cannot digress into a lengthy discussion of newspaper design, magazine design, interactive television design, mobile applications design, tablet design... well, you get the idea. In fact, each subject is worthy of an entire book. However, in the very least, we must address how multi-platform publishing affects how we package a story for more than one delivery mechanism as well as strategies for ensuring we capitalize on each platform's strengths. And there are a few basic design principles that apply to all platforms.

We must also address how a single story composed of multiple story forms is best designed. Of course, the already established content management and web design styles of a particular publication will largely determine how stories will be presented and formatted. However, there are a number of possibilities for how digital multimedia content can come together, and each results in a different user experience. Budding multimedia journalists should be exposed to those different styles so they can make informed choices to best accommodate the stories and audiences they serve.

This chapter will address multimedia story packaging and design from two important perspectives: (1) the platform(s) on which content will be encountered and (2) how the pieces of a story come together in a physical, designed space. And although it is relatively easy to separate these two concepts in theory, it is much more difficult to do so in a practical analysis. So, you will see the two concepts wind around one another as we proceed.

Information Architecture

Information architecture relates to the interpretation and expression of information for complex delivery systems. There are many different fields that apply information architecture, including both traditional and contemporary library systems, such as card catalogs and digital databases; content management systems through which content can be easily modified and updated; and software programs that allow users to execute complex tasks using built-in tools. Richard Saul Wurman first operationalized the term "information architect." Wurman was an architect and graphic designer and was lauded as a pioneer in making information understandable. He writes: "I mean architect as in the creating of systemic, structural, and orderly principles to make something work—the thoughtful making of either artifact, or idea, or policy that informs because it is clear."[1]

Journalists have served as information architects since the dawn of their respective fields. For example, newspaper journalists make many decisions in a day's work that directly affect the expression of content. Writers decide which stories are worthy of coverage, what aspects of a story are most important, and how language will be used to best convey the story. Photographers decide how to frame photos and which scenes to capture. And editors and page designers decide which stories go on the front page; how stories are ordered on a page; how big and bold headlines for each story will be; and which stories will be accompanied by photos, illustrations, or graphics. Likewise, television reporters, videographers, and producers make similar decisions. Hours of video are often edited into a short, 90-second piece. Certain sources are considered to be more important than others, and stories are aired in order of importance—a value judgment made by producers, not audiences. And as technology evolves, our methods for organizing and disseminating information evolve as well.

Of course, not all journalists are good information architects, and many journalists have erred in not taking these responsibilities seriously enough. But, to assume that these decisions do not dramatically affect how a story is consumed, interpreted, or understood is irresponsible, to say the least. For journalists, "architectural" decisions are paramount to good stories and ease of use.

It is also worth noting that the term "design" has come to mean many things to many people. There is graphic design, environmental design, architectural design, instructional design, interior design–the list goes on and on. In the multimedia framework, many of these types of design are relevant. We must determine whether video or still photos will be used for the visual narrative. If a story has graphics potential, we must determine which type of graphic best suits our data. Graphics reporters and designers are often responsible for creating the visual style and illustrations for interactive graphics, establishing type and color palettes, and considering the structural aspects of a package. We also engage in user experience (UX) design when we make decisions about the location and function of navigational elements in a package, as well as the platforms on which our work will appear. Thus, design is both an important and multifarious concept where multimedia storytelling is concerned.

Bringing It All Together

It is easy for multimedia editors and designers to become overwhelmed when fieldwork is completed and the time comes to edit content generated for a single story package. You may have hours of video and audio footage, hundreds of photos, more than a few written words, and/or data that indicate interactive graphics potential. Now what?

First, talk yourself down from the ledge and go back to your project plan. You started this project with a vision. So instead of losing sight of it by becoming overwhelmed by content, revisit your original outline and/or storyboards and bring your mission back into focus. Evaluate your information, figure out what has changed from your original vision for the story, and map out what you have and what should appear in each interactive section.

As you plan your story package, there will be two main concerns regarding content. First, the presentation format and overall design of a multimedia package affect how a story flows and how it will be consumed. So a fair amount of time should be devoted to developing a visual style and navigational structure. This is a good time to get a graphic designer and/or multimedia developer in on the project. Second, although you may intend to provide a complete story package with multiple parts, you cannot guarantee your audience will engage with all of those parts or that they will navigate them in a predetermined order. So when planning a presentation, consider whether the individual parts of a story make sense independent of the other parts of the package. Because most multimedia presentations are nonlinear, each user may take a different path through the stories we construct. Thus, individual story forms, such as a photo slideshow that appears as part of a larger package, must hold value on its own.

To ensure this is the case, each piece in a multimedia story package must contain some redundancy. For example, you may choose to develop a multimedia package with four parts, each of which will be told using a different story form (i.e., part one: text, part two: photo slideshow, part three: video, and part four: information graphic). If your story package is nonlinear, your audience may choose to watch/

view/read those pieces in any order. Thus, it is necessary to have some overlap among the story's four parts so that the basic storyline and focus are clear in each part. The key to avoiding unnecessary redundancy is to make sure you don't use the same words or narrative techniques in all four pieces to establish this foundation. Rather, find interesting ways to address the story's main focus differently in each piece. Likewise if the same person or people are featured in more than one piece, you must identify them by first and last name at least once in each piece.

Although all four pieces may work together to form a complete multimedia story package, the package must gracefully degrade into its individual parts. In other words, each story form must be developed to stand alone and each piece must leave the audience with a sense of completeness. One way to achieve this is to break the story down into major themes and then try to cover each theme in its entirety in one of the four parts of the story. By way of example, let's use the story of the breast cancer patient. In this case, the text piece could offer a narrative that explores her daily life in treatment. The photo slideshow could be a story about her family life. An information graphic could explain how breast cancer is detected or how treatment affects the body. And finally, the video could be a piece on her involvement with the Susan G. Komen for the Cure foundation. In this case, each piece works together to tell a complete, well-rounded story. But each piece also stands alone as a story-within-a-story. If users decide to view only one of the parts, they will still come away with a sense that a complete story has been told, even though they did not engage with the entire multimedia package. Of course there are many options for how a collection of content can be designed into a story package. And there are a number of software programs, programming languages, and platforms on which a multimedia story can appear. But when it comes to presentation, one concept should rise to the top: let content drive design.

Designing Multimedia Packages for the Desktop Experience

Packaging multimedia content for a single story is, by nature, an exercise in designing for web-based or application-oriented platforms. On the web, we can combine all forms of media—text, video, audio, still images, and graphics—in one place and create rich interactive experiences. The following few entries offer some common story design formats for online presentations.

Embedded Links

Until recently, the evolution of news websites has been relatively predictable. Online, newspaper and magazine websites center stories on what their traditional print predecessors do best: text. Likewise, most broadcast websites offer video and very short text-based stories that read more like TV news scripts than in-depth narratives. Although most would argue these approaches do not always make the most of the web's potential, it is no surprise that websites for print publications would, in many ways, parallel their print siblings. Thus, one of the most common types of multimedia packages starts with a single story form, like a text-based story, and then adds other forms as sidebars. In this case, links to other media are generally embedded in or near the base story. For example, a text-based story could be combined with a small inset box with links to video, photo slide shows, or information graphics related to that story. Or words in the text-based story could be highlighted as hyperlinks that open pop-ups containing other story forms. Embedded links can be useful when additional media is meant to supplement a text-based story. However, embedded links are less effective when your goal is to give equal weight to all of the story forms in a package.

Nonlinear Story Tree

The nonlinear story tree divides content types into smaller interrelated chunks of information. Chunks can be written stories, information graphics, photos, audio, or video. And unlike embedded links, these are not treated as sidebars to a main story, but rather as discreet parts of a story that work together and complement one another. "Ultimately, this concept helps harness the self-navigating, interactive power of the web so many users find appealing by allowing readers to view or read the chunks in whatever order they want."[2] Navigation of a nonlinear story tree is also varied. In one option, all chunks appear on a single screen that scrolls through anchored categories. This approach provides the user access to the entire story package by either clicking a button or by scrolling down a longer collection of content. In another option, chunks appear on separate pages, allowing users to engage with each chunk separately without having to scroll down long pages of content. The story tree format does a great job of presenting content in a nonlinear fashion to offer users greater choice and interactivity.

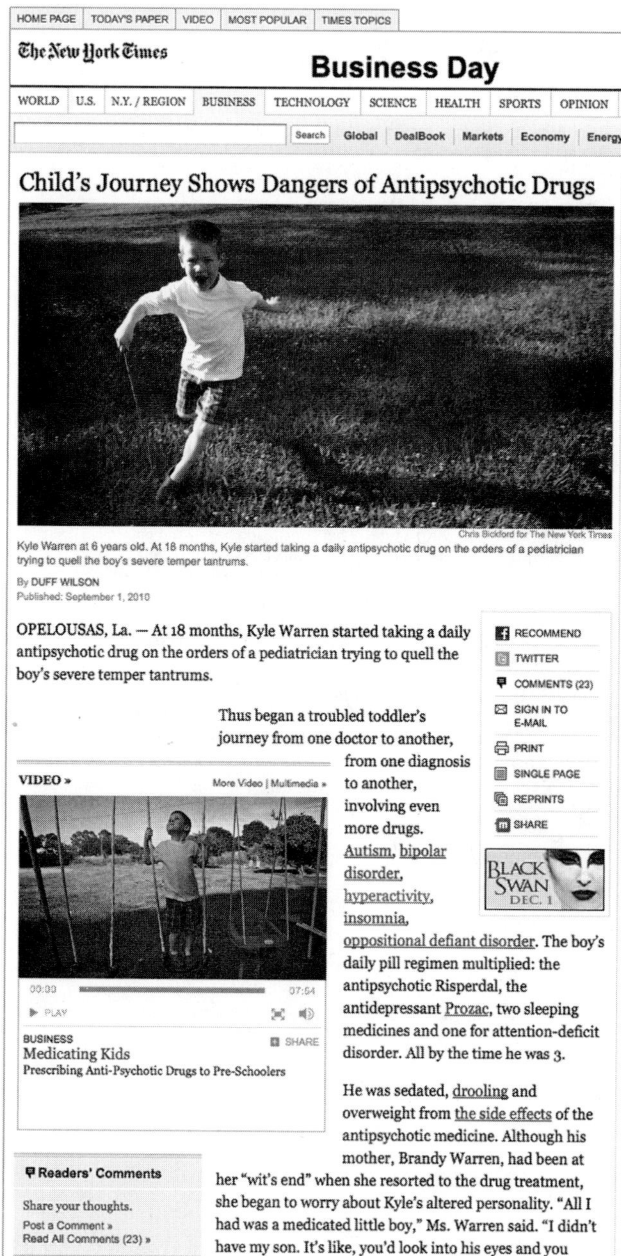

HOME PAGE | TODAY'S PAPER | VIDEO | MOST POPULAR | TIMES TOPICS

The New York Times

Business Day

WORLD | U.S. | N.Y. / REGION | BUSINESS | TECHNOLOGY | SCIENCE | HEALTH | SPORTS | OPINION

Search | Global | DealBook | Markets | Economy | Energy

Child's Journey Shows Dangers of Antipsychotic Drugs

Chris Bickford for The New York Times

Kyle Warren at 6 years old. At 18 months, Kyle started taking a daily antipsychotic drug on the orders of a pediatrician trying to quell the boy's severe temper tantrums.

By DUFF WILSON
Published: September 1, 2010

OPELOUSAS, La. — At 18 months, Kyle Warren started taking a daily antipsychotic drug on the orders of a pediatrician trying to quell the boy's severe temper tantrums.

RECOMMEND
TWITTER
COMMENTS (23)
SIGN IN TO E-MAIL
PRINT
SINGLE PAGE
REPRINTS
SHARE

Thus began a troubled toddler's journey from one doctor to another, from one diagnosis to another, involving even more drugs. Autism, bipolar disorder, hyperactivity, insomnia, oppositional defiant disorder. The boy's daily pill regimen multiplied: the antipsychotic Risperdal, the antidepressant Prozac, two sleeping medicines and one for attention-deficit disorder. All by the time he was 3.

VIDEO » More Video | Multimedia »

00:00 07:54
PLAY
BUSINESS SHARE
Medicating Kids
Prescribing Anti-Psychotic Drugs to Pre-Schoolers

He was sedated, drooling and overweight from the side effects of the antipsychotic medicine. Although his mother, Brandy Warren, had been at her "wit's end" when she resorted to the drug treatment, she began to worry about Kyle's altered personality. "All I had was a medicated little boy," Ms. Warren said. "I didn't have my son. It's like, you'd look into his eyes and you would just see just blankness."

Readers' Comments
Share your thoughts.
Post a Comment »
Read All Comments (23) »

FIGURE 11-1

The New York Times commonly embeds text links in stories that take readers to pages with additional information about a topic. Likewise, they embed other types of sidebar content, like the video seen in this example. When clicked, the video can be played in its place without leaving the rest of the story, or the video can be enlarged to fit the whole viewing screen.

Source: Image courtesy of *The New York Times.*

Rosa Parks

INTRO | IN THE LIFE OF ROSA PARKS | EARLY LIFE | BUS BOYCOTT | ACTIVISM & AWARDS

Introduction

Rosa Parks, the woman known as the "mother of the civil rights movement," has died.

It was nearly 50 years ago, Dec. 1, 1955, when Parks challenged the South's Jim Crow laws–and Montgomery's segregated bus seating policy–by refusing to get up and give her seat to a white passenger.

Her arrest triggered a 381-day boycott of the bus system by blacks that was organized by a 26-year-old Baptist minister, the Rev. Martin Luther King, Jr. The boycott led to a court ruling desegregating public transportation in Montgomery, but it wasn't until the 1964 Civil Rights Act that all public accommodations nationwide were desegregated.

Parks died Oct. 24, 2005, in her Detroit home of natural causes. She was 92.

Rosa Parks

INTRO | IN THE LIFE OF ROSA PARKS | EARLY LIFE | BUS BOYCOTT | ACTIVISM & AWARDS

Bus Boycott

At the time of her arrest, Parks was 42 and on her way home from work as a seamstress. She took a seat in the front of the black section of the city bus in Montgomery. The bus filled up and the bus driver demanded that she move so a white male passenger could have her seat.

"The driver wanted us to stand up, the four of us. We didn't move at the beginning, but he says, 'Let me have these seats.' And the other three people moved, but I didn't," she once said.

When Parks refused to give up her seat, a police officer arrested her.

FIGURE 11-2

The nonlinear story tree is a versatile way to present stories that have been divided into chunks. The chunks can either be text-based like the example above or a mix of story forms, like the one shown on the next page.

Explorative Story Packages

Like nonlinear story trees, explorative packages present multimedia content in nonlinear formats. However, they are often more design-intensive, packaging multiple parts of a story in highly stylized presentations. Exploratives can divide content by story forms or chunks like nonlinear story trees. Or content can be divided by sub-

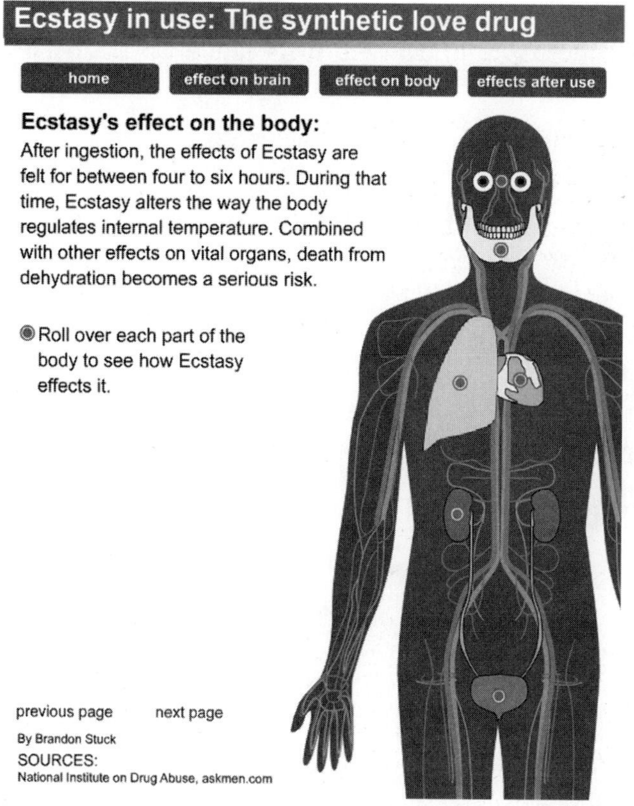

FIGURE 11-3

This nonlinear tree allows users to explore a number of story chunks developed in several formats, including text, interactive graphics, and animation. *Source:* Brandon Stuck, Ball State University.

ject matter. When the latter is the case, a single category may contain several related story forms. For example, a student project about the price of milk as an economic indicator divided the story into three topics: (1) milk as a staple for most families, (2) who profits when the cost of milk goes up, and (3) life on a typical dairy farm. Then, each main category contains a number of story forms. For example, the section about life on a dairy farm includes a written story that profiles a particular farm, a photo gallery that follows the pasteurizing process from the farm to the grocery

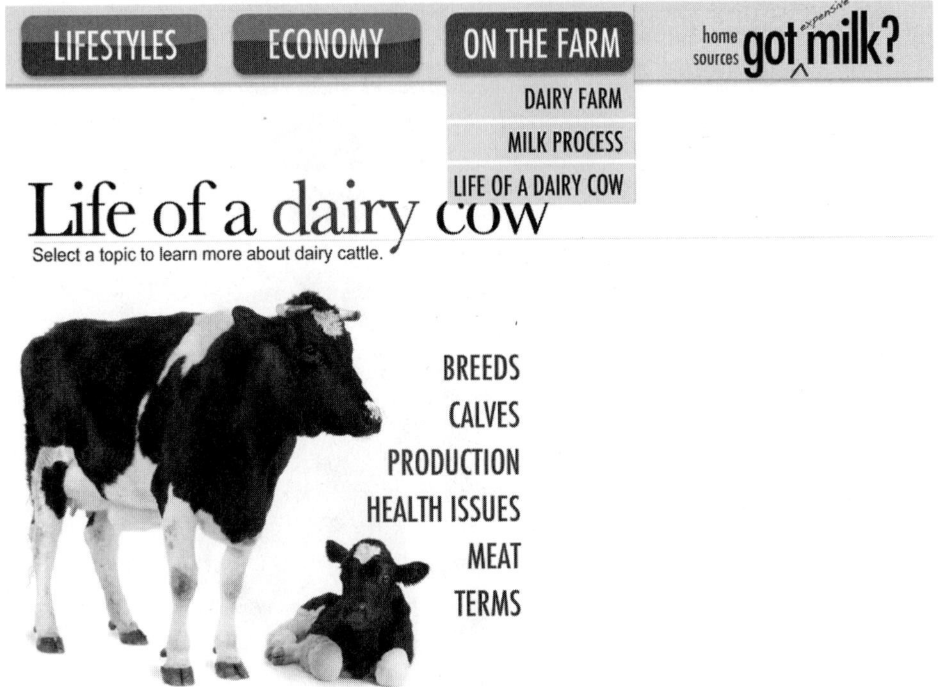

FIGURE 11-4

This explorative package divides the story topically. Each top-level navigation tab includes a dropdown menu that lists the categories for each main section of the story.

Source: Kristen Gibson, Tom Demeropolis, Mike Groder, and Sean O'Key, Ball State University.

store, and an interactive graphic that explains the life of a dairy cow. Exploratives can be developed in number of programs, from HTML to Adobe Flash. Regardless of which program you choose, exploratives generally require that a graphic designer or programmer be involved.

In the same way, entire websites can focus on a single story in an explorative fashion. One such site is the Webby Award–winning BecommingHuman.org. The site is used primarily by sixth- through ninth-grade students and teachers for the investigation of human evolution and research on the human career. Its reach also extends to the general public. The website blends an interactive timeline, scientific but readable essays, and video into a multilayered presentation of human origins. The site was created through funding and support of the Board of Directors of

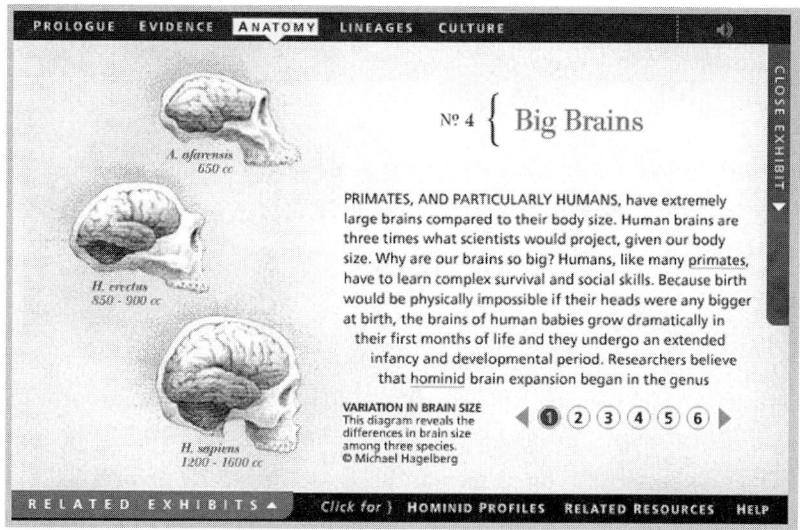

FIGURE 11-5

BecommingHuman.org is a rich explorative website that allows users to dig deep into the topic of human evolution. Content presentations include interactive timelines and graphics, animations, video, and photos. Content is broken into categories and subcategories that provide hours of exploring for the in-depth viewer. IHO's transdisciplinary strategy for field and analytical paleoanthropological research is central to its mission of integrating social, earth, and life science approaches to the most important questions concerning the course, timing, and causes of human evolutionary change over deep time. IHO blends cutting-edge, high-profile field and analytical research on the early human fossil record with public outreach programs promoting scientists as the best interpreters of their research for the public.

Source: Image courtesy of the Institute of Human Origins.

Illustrations by Mike Hagelberg.

the Institute of Human Origins (IHO), which is a research center at Arizona State University.

Although not exhaustive, these concepts are important and effective because they recognize that web-savvy users will not tolerate static online environments that emulate print design and navigation. Rather, they want to be able to interact with and control online content. Notice that all of the examples offered here allow each user's interests to drive content consumption. And as new platforms emerge for consuming digital content, computers are not the only devices on which users will access multimedia stories. Thus, as you make use of the techniques outlined above, remember that your stories may be consumed on a number of devices with a number of different screen sizes. Likewise, the web is not the only venue for multimedia content. Application-based platforms have quickly become a viable option as well.

Designing Multimedia Packages for the Mobile Experience

According to the 2011 Pew Research Center State of the News Media report, 47 percent of the U.S. adult population reports that they get at least some local news and information on their cell phones or tablet computers. Consequently, the desktop Internet experience switches to "on the go" when users leave the house and "the handheld becomes a complementary access point to connect with people and digital content wherever a wireless network reaches."[3] At the same time, news organizations across the country have begun to develop mobile media sites. And as the number of touch screen models such as the Apple iPhone, Blackberry Storm, and Palm Pre increases, content producers and publishers continue to look for ways to take full advantage of the touch screen experience. Thus, "as a large portion of the online population gravitates to wireless and mobile access to supplement their home high-speed wired connections, the supply of and demand for online content increases."[4]

But mobile users are typically less interested in lengthy presentations. Smaller bandwidth connections, limitations brought by small keyboards, poor graphic representation because of small screen displays, and the fact that interactivity on most mobile phones is currently limited to basic tasks, necessitate a different usability model for cell phones than desktops. However, the proliferation of touch screen phones has increased smart phone use, causing some to predict that mobile devices will become the primary content delivery method of the future. By 2011 there were more than 5.3 billion mobile phone subscribers around the world, roughly three-quarters of the global population. Nonetheless, mobile news and information consumption also occurs in small spurts in between other activities, such as waiting for a train or in between meetings or classes. In other words, although people are becoming more and more attached to their mobile devices, they generally don't want to read long documents or watch hours of news video on them. Rather, users tend to engage in "information snacking," or brief periods of intense interaction. Thus, some have suggested that multimedia content intended for mobile applications should be optimized for smaller screen sizes and the shorter attention spans of mobile users. For example, video should include more tight, close-up shots so that images are clearer and easier to discern on small screens. And video pieces should be even shorter (20 to 30 seconds) to better serve snacking audiences.

At the same time, another mobile platform—the tablet reader—has quickly gained popularity among contemporary audiences. Perhaps no new platform has generated more excitement and expectation than the Apple iPad, released in the United States in April 2010. By March 2011 Apple reported that sales had topped 19 million, leaving many communications professionals salivating at the possibilities for a print industry that has been struggling for several years. At a June 2010 tablet seminar hosted by the Poynter Institute for Media Studies, design guru Mario Garcia said: "As I started to study the iPad, and to conduct workshops for media organizations planning to develop apps to tabletize, it became even more obvious that the tablet was, indeed, a landmark moment for the industry. We are, indeed, at that point

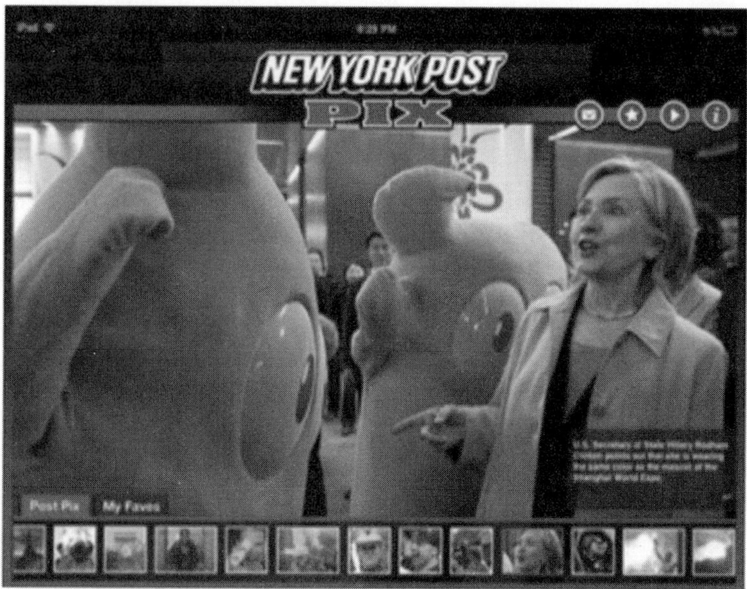

FIGURE 11-6

A number of newspapers and magazines offer interactive applications for the iPad. The *New York Post* Pix app offers twice-daily photo galleries.

when what we do with and about the tablet will determine the fate of our media. It is that important. It is that decisive a player in how information is disseminated, consumed, and how revenue will be derived from its use."[5] This enthusiasm has been shared by many editors and designers, with *Time* and *Wired* magazines diving headfirst into the tablet craze with interactive versions of their complete publications. Mashable.com reported that 24,000 people purchased the *Wired* app on the first day it appeared in the app store; and sales reached 80,000 in the first month.[6]

Larger screens that are similar in size to traditional magazines provide designers and editors with a format that is closer in look and feel to a print experience. Thus, many of the early tablet applications have looked a lot like traditional magazines or books. However, the tablet platform offers one major difference: now video, animations, audio, and other interactive features not possible in print could suddenly be embedded right into a magazine or newspaper page.

Several early models emerged for packaging content for tablet applications. Some publications like the *New York Times* developed iPad-optimized websites. In other words, to access a complete edition of the *NYT* on an iPad, users visit a web page that has been designed for the iPad screen through the web browser. This allows daily publications like newspapers to quickly update content in a format that is tablet-friendly. Other publications, such as *Time,* offered full issues in custom tablet applications. So rather than visit a website, users purchase unique apps for each issue. These combine touch screen navigation with content-driven design and information architecture built with the iPad in mind. Other publications chose to tabletize parts of their products, offering mini-apps that focus on some of the more popular content they offer. For example, the first *New York Post* iPad app, titled "*New York Post* Pix," offered a twice-daily dose of celebrity, sports, and news pictures in a gallery format. Likewise, *Entertainment Weekly's* first app, "The Must List" contained editors' picks of the 10 movies, TV shows, books, music, viral videos, games, or apps of the week. Users could read brief overviews, listen to audio tracks, watch video trailers, and read reviews from *Entertainment Weekly*, all without leaving the app. Users could also add items to their personal Must Lists or even tap a button to purchase content on the spot.

Of course, new phones, tablets, and media devices will continue to emerge. So, it is less important that you focus on understanding everything there is to know about the latest device. Rather, the twenty-first-century journalist must be willing to cross platforms, develop content with a number of different users in mind, and understand that as soon as you begin to feel comfortable with one device, a new one will emerge. Learn to embrace change, and you just might have a fighting chance!

Digital Asset Management

Digital asset management refers to the annotation, tagging, cataloguing, storage, retrieval and distribution of digital content. For multimedia journalists, this task is primarily focused on photos, animations, videos, and audio files. Such assets are generally tagged with metadata, which includes the description of the asset or keywords associated with the file.

Effectively managing digital assets is a complex process. But there are a few simple techniques that many successful sites use to ensure digital content is organized and accessible.

Think like a user. Digital assets should be easy to find both internally, by your colleagues, when it's time to go live with the content and externally, by your users, when they seek out that content through a search engine. Therefore, choose keywords that are clear and concise. If you are tagging a photo from the opening of a new museum of modern art, make sure the exact name of the museum, the date of the opening, and a brief description of the subject of the photo are included in the metadata.

Enlist good writing skills when authoring metadata. Avoid jargon, write for a general audience, be thorough in your descriptions, and avoid unnecessary words.

Apply consistent naming conventions. When naming photos, videos, or other file types, make sure the same structure is used. For example, most digital cameras enlist standard naming conventions such as DSC01358.jpg. You may want your naming system to be more meaningful so that files can be identified more quickly. That's fine. But remember to keep them relatively concise and to be consistent. So, all photos should employ the same naming convention. Videos should employ the same convention, and so on.

Enlist a solid content management system to organize content. Most news organizations—large and small—have a content management system in place to make organizing and distributing online content easy on deadline for a number of producers. A good CMS meets the needs of the organization using it. Thus, a news operation should employ a CMS that facilitates publishing on a 24/7 news cycle.

Content Management Systems

If you are designing a package using an existing content management system (CMS), you will likely have a number of guidelines for how your files should be sized, saved, and uploaded. If you take a job as a multimedia producer/editor, you will quickly be trained on a CMS. Ultimately, a content management system is based on a collection of procedures that help manage collaborative workflow. And in the multimedia arena, these procedures are generally computer-based. A good CMS for journalists allows a group of people within the organization (sometimes, hundreds) to contribute and share content, from video files and written pieces, to photos and graphics. In this context, a CMS is used to store, control, revise, edit, and publish.

There are a number of different content management systems in use. Some are custom-made for the organization at hand, and others are based on open-source software freely available online. WordPress, for example, is a basic content management system. More than 25 million websites worldwide are powered by WordPress, most of which are blogs, but some of which are rich, multimedia venues. Other open-source tools in include Joomla!, Drupal, and DotNetNuke. Some systems are more complex than others. Some offer more features than others. And most are customizable, making it easy to change site design, play Flash video and graphics, and embed photo slideshows. And although a knowledge of programming language is not necessary to operate these systems, the more you know about HTML and CSS, the more you can do with a content management system. However, the general mission of a CMS is the same: provide content producers with an easy-to-use, remote publishing platform that helps manage both content and collaborative workflow.

Likewise, all journalists should understand the importance of "tagging" online content. Tagging is the practice of attaching keywords to articles, visual content, or whole websites so that they are searchable. A collection of keywords is also called "metadata" or, data that provides information about a piece of data. Metadata can include the means of creation of the data, its purpose, time and date of creation, the name of the author, where the data was created, or the standards used to create the data. For example, a digital image may include metadata that describes the contents of the picture, when and where it was taken, and who took it. Likewise, the metadata of a text document may contain information about how long the story is, who the author is, when the story was written, and a short summary. And a number of online services (such as Taggle or Technorati) have emerged that allow users to type in a keyword and get back all the hits that have that word as a tag.

Exercises

1. Make a list of three multimedia stories you will cover over the next two weeks. It is up to you to determine the types of story forms that will be included in your story (i.e., text, photos, video, audio, graphics). Once you have a plan in place, collect the content for your stories and post them to your WordPress site. Remember other open source tools such as Many Eyes and Google Charts if your story has graphics potential. You may do this exercise collaboratively by yourself.
2. If you have mastered WordPress and want to explore content management systems that have more features, try setting up a Joomla! site. The learning curve for Joomla! is a bit steeper than WordPress, but it is still relatively simple. Unlike WordPress that is managed online, Joomla! includes files that you will need to download and install on your computer. Start by visiting http://docs.joomla.org/Quick_Start_Guide and follow the tutorial provided there for setting up a basic Joomla! site. This will allow you to explore the backend of the Joomla! structure and see how it works. (Note: If this link ever becomes broken, visit joomla.org and type "quick start guide" in the search box.)
3. Put together an interdisciplinary team that includes a graphic designer and Flash or HTML developer (perhaps you are one of these individuals). Then, turn one of the stories you created in exercise two into an explorative package. Work with the designer to create a visual style and navigational structure for the package. Then, post the presentation to your WordPress site.

Notes

1. Richard Saul Wurman, *Information Architects* (Graphics Inc., 1997).
2. Lori Demo and Jennifer George-Palilonis, "WebFirst: How Small Newspapers Can Harness the Power of the Web," paper presented at the Newspapers and Community-Building Symposium XIII, 2007.
3. John B. Horrigan, "Wireless Connectivity Has Drawn Many Users More Deeply into Digital Life," Pew Research Center Publications.

4. John B. Horrigan, "Wireless Connectivity Has Drawn Many Users More Deeply into Digital Life," Pew Research Center Publications.

5. Mario Garcia, "The Power of the Tablet" seminar, June 14–15, 2010. Live blog transcript.

6. Jolie O'Dell, "Wired Sells 24,000 iPad Apps in One Day," mashable.com.

CHAPTER 12

Looking Forward

The Future of News . . . and Your Place In It

By the time this book is published, new software programs will have been released, thousands of multimedia stories published, and hundreds of new ideas will have begun to percolate in the multimedia sphere. In fact, one might question the wisdom of even including a chapter on the future of news. After all, if there is one thing the digital age has shown us, it is that things change so rapidly that the "future" rushes upon us at breakneck speeds, and "new" becomes "old" with the blink of an eye. However, this chapter will not attempt to predict where news and journalism will be 10 years from now. It will not advocate hardware or software programs that will certainly be updated frequently and replaced with new programs. Rather, this chapter attempts to summarize practical things you can do to help prepare for a career in multimedia journalism.

It is safe to say that there are still a number of unknowns when it comes to how the print, broadcast, and online news industries will evolve in the coming years. It's also unclear how new devices and wireless technologies will change the ways we consume and connect with audiences. According to a Pew Project for Excellence in Journalism State of the News Media report, the past couple of years have been a time of experimentation for all kinds of revenue models, "but many have yet to materialize and others have little yet to show in terms of real dollars." In 2009, "the most established revenue source, online advertising, saw declines for the first time since 2002. The declines were partly due to recession, but it is not clear to what extent the declines may also be structural and permanent. And the most talked about new revenue stream—getting users to pay for content—will depend, economists argue, on news organizations offering content that is unique, and this may require specialization and investment by news organizations."[1]

And although the question of how to monetize the growing online audience has yet to be resolved, progress has been made toward defining new business models for digital journalism. Among the economic models that have received the most attention are: charging users subscription fees to access content, targeted and interest-based ad placement, charging Internet service providers (ISPs) and aggregators licensing fees, and seeking donations and grants to fund journalistic efforts.

Subscription fees: Perhaps one of the most talked about revenue models of the last decade is charging subscription fees to users. And, by 2011, the number of people who reported they would be willing to pay for local news had increased. Overall, however, this concept has been a pretty major flop among most online news sites. Several news organizations have experimented with this model, including the *Wall Street Journal* and the *New York Times.* But there the prevailing opinion among most online users is that news and information should be free. And because in the early days of online news, it started out that way, three-quarters of online news audiences report that they aren't willing to pay now.[2]

Targeted ad placement and interest-based ads: Selling ads to support production has been the primary bread and butter for print publications for decades. And in the early days of online news, many newspaper and magazine publishers assumed this model would simply translate to the online environment. However, because web traffic is based on page views and the number of "clicks" a user executed on a single site, it has been much more difficult for online publishers to convince advertisers their money is well spent on online news sites. However, a few organizations have seen some success with targeted ad placement. In this model, ads are combined with specific news stories to improve the chances that a user will be motivated by the ad. For example, a story about the benefits of exercise may be accompanied by an ad for a local fitness club. The idea being that if a person is interested in the story, they may also find the ad to be valuable. Interest-based ads are similar but based on a user's previous online activity. So, if an online news site requires that users register before accessing their sites, they can track their activities on the site through cookies (text that records and saves a user's browsing history). The more the user visits the site, the more their profile develops, allowing publishers to present individualized ads to each unique user.

Charging ISPs and aggregators for content: An aggregator is a site that compiles news and information from other sources. Some examples of popular aggregators are My Yahoo!, Google Reader, and Digg.com. Some aggregators list news stories based on an individual user's interests, and others appeal to a general audience. But the unifying characteristic is that content almost always comes from other sources. A few aggregators, such as drudgereport.com and huffingtonpost.com, combine original and aggregated content. Some publishers have suggested that aggregators and ISPs should be charged a licensing fee to link to someone else's content. Although this idea hasn't fully taken off, there has been some recent momentum around the idea.

Donations and grant funding: One of the more radical ideas that has surfaced in recent years is that journalism, as a public service, should be a nonprofit endeavor. According to a Knight Foundation report, "the challenge is not saving traditional news organizations or traditional forms of journalism. The challenge is creating, strengthening and protecting informed communities and local information ecosystems, of which journalism is a necessary component."[3] The nonprofit model allows journalists to practice their craft without the demands of a for-profit business. Furthermore, "nonprofit news startups have been created in communities across the country, most with funding from major donors or foundations." The Knight Foundation alone has funded more than 200 nonprofit experiments. One example of a nonprofit effort is Circle of Blue (http://circleofblue.org), a group of leading journalists, scientists, and communications designers that reports on the global freshwater crisis. They cover stories related to water and sustainability, the role of freshwater resources on renewable energy efforts, how climate change affects water, and other issues related to water, including health, agriculture, and pollution, to name a few. Circle of Blue has received funding from a number of supporters, including the Ford Foundation, AIGA, and China Environment Forum. Circle of Blue readers can also make donations on circleofblue.org to support the organization's reporting efforts. But according to Circle of Blue founding editor J. Carl Ganter, going the nonprofit route can be an uphill battle. "Non-profit journalism faces a difficult, almost Sysiphean test," he says. "In an era of rapid change, thinning knowledge and what seems to be a declining interest in in-depth research and reporting, successful funding models are few and far between. Some success stories are held high for good reason. The Texas Tribune and Pro Publica are two, but they also rely heavily on outside funding that may be unsustainable. Non-profit news and science organizations have to be nimble while holding tight to standards and mission. Is it more or less tempting to become beholden to funders and advertisers than for-profit media? The key words are trust and integrity."

Ganter also notes that if nonprofit is to be a viable model of the future, more innovation and risk taking is necessary. "The true cost of news is undervalued," he says. "In-depth reporting is expensive, time intensive and risky, and very few for-profit news organizations are willing to break new ground with innovative reporting projects or new ways of delivering news. Is non-profit journalism viable? I have my doubts in the current iteration. Most funders are seeking bricks and mortar outcomes. And journalism seems soft to many foundations that confuse front-line knowledge, data and context with public relations."

How to be Enterprising and Entrepreneurial

A generation ago, journalism was a clearly defined field. Different types of journalists were expected to possess specific skills sets. And there were a few key types of organizations—newspapers, magazines, radio stations, and television stations—that produced journalistic content. If you wanted to be a journalist, you learned those skills and joined one of those organizations. And although all of those organizations still exist, and the foundations of good journalism are still relevant, lines have blurred, roles have evolved, and technologies have advanced. Or, to put it simply: Times have changed.

The majority of this book offers advice and instruction for developing journalistic skills that will be relevant in the twenty-first century. But one of the most important journalistic skills that has emerged with the multimedia movement is much more subtle. Journalists must now be entrepreneurial. Of course, the rather tumultuous state of the news business in recent years has left many traditional journalists jobless or fearing for their futures. By the middle of 2010, nearly 2,000 newspaper jobs had been cut.[3] Some individuals have left the business entirely. And some of the more tenacious have started new careers as entrepreneurial journalists. According to Jeremy Caplan, a recent fellow at the Poynter Institute for Media Studies, "Entrepreneurial journalists spot the seeds of start-ups where others see remnants of the news industry's retreat."[4]

In other words, the likelihood of you graduating from college, easily falling into a career in journalism, and staying in the same job for the rest of your life is pretty slim. However journalism is still a viable career path. In fact, now might be one of the most exciting times for budding journalists because along with the uncertainty comes a million possibilities. But clearly this business is not for the faint of heart. Truth be told, it never has been.

Being entrepreneurial can mean a number of things. And you are only limited by your own skills and imagination when it comes to finding ways to be enterprising. Of course, many of you will take jobs at one of these more traditional outlets. But even traditional newsrooms are experimenting with new ways of doing things. So, working in those environments requires an ability to innovate and find new ways to apply your existing skills. Likewise, some will take less traditional paths, opting instead to work for smaller start-ups or even themselves. Caplan writes, "Journalists have started hundreds of small and large news operations over the past three years. A flourishing ecosystem of news start-ups has yielded a wide range of new solutions for generating stable revenue streams." And this ecosystem has allowed a number of innovators to cultivate some interesting new ideas.

A Practical Discussion of Social Media

According to a 2011 survey of nearly 500 journalists from 15 countries revealed that a growing number of journalists are using Twitter and Facebook to research and verify stories. In fact, 47 percent of respondents said they use Twitter and 35 percent reported they use Facebook to source new story angles. Shortly after the study was released, media blogger Don Irvine wrote, "It won't be much longer before Twitter and Facebook become the major news sources for journalists. For some they have already become the *only* news source they use, thanks to the real-time aspect of these platforms."[4] In fact, some of the biggest news stories from recent years broke on social media sites. In 2009, news of U.S. Airways flight 1549 ditching in New York's Hudson River broke on Twitter. Within 15 minutes of the crash, users broke the news of the incident before the mainstream media. And just a couple weeks before the aforementioned study was released, the first reports that Osama bin Laden had been killed by U.S. forces appeared on Twitter. Just before President Barack Obama addressed the nation with the official news, a message posted by Keith Urbahn, the chief of staff of former defense secretary Donald

In 2010, Adam Westbrook—multimedia journalist, blogger, lecturer, and trainer—released "Next Generation Journalist." In it, his take on contemporary journalism is both optimistic and adventurous, urging us to ignore traditional constructs and dive headfirst into an entrepreneurial mindset. Below is Westbrook's summary of 10 new ways to make money in journalism.

1. **Develop a portfolio career.** A portfolio career allows journalists with multimedia skills to create small web-based businesses to develop a diverse income. For example, many journalists supplement their income by designing websites for clients, shooting photos or video for companies, or writing freelance pieces for a variety of organizations.
2. **Make multimedia for non-profits.** Apply your research, storytelling, video, and photojournalism skills to produce powerful and informative multimedia presentations for charities and the third sector. Compelling stories call people to action, and charities need people to act.
3. **Aggregate content.** Create a web service that aggregates the billions of bytes of data targeted for a particular niche audience. Next-generation journalists don't just look at ways to make money from content; they look for how they can collate, curate, and organize that information in ways that makes their audiences' lives easier.
4. **Make apps for smartphones.** Design, produce, and sell news apps for smartphones that provide journalism or other public service information to make peoples' lives easier.
5. **Set up a hyperlocal website use your story finding, writing, web, and multimedia skills** to set up a hyper local news alternative in your city, providing news, features, or listings of a town or village. Use advertising and a range of other methods to generate revenue.
6. **Specialize in a journalism skill hone in on one particular part of the online news production** process and set up a company that specializes in it, producing it for other outlets in a way that saves them time or money.
7. **Exploit the potential for storytelling use your skills as a storyteller across a range of disciplines** to offer high quality multimedia content to businesses that brings them more customers. In other words, you can become a digital storyteller for non-news businesses too.

8. **Set up a multimedia collaborative create a small, cheap, and flexible journalism company,** bootstrapping on things like office space. Hire everyone as freelancers on a project-by-project basis, allowing you to choose the best collaborators for each project.
9. **Crowdfund projects leverage social media** to solicit donations for individual projects, tasters, or even whole businesses. Crowdfunding your journalism uses the power of your audience to generate capital for vital journalistic initiatives.
10. **Become an "infopreneur" use your research skills** to become an expert in a profitable niche. Use social media and free products to leverage this into a recognizable expertise. And then use your writing and production skills to produce high value products that people will pay for.
    http://www.nextgenerationjournalist.com

Rumsfeld, read: "So I'm told by a reputable person they have killed Osama Bin Laden. Hot damn."

Stories like these confirm that "the news no longer waits for the evening news programs or the morning paper. Instead, it moves at a high speed thanks to improvements in technology that have spawned social media platforms like Twitter and Facebook."[5] Thus, it's no surprise that the demand for social media skills has been on a rapid incline. And as the number of tools like Facebook, Twitter, and mobile apps that encourage connectivity and community increase, so too will the need for journalists who know how to use them. A Los Angeles broadcast station recently posted an opening for someone who, among other things, has "experience working with social networks such as Facebook and Twitter as well as Movable Type blogs." A similar newspaper job posting was seeking a "social media coordinator" who would help "develop strategies for our online interaction with readers via Twitter, Facebook and other social media tools." However, the relative newness of these concepts in journalism and the vast array of tools and skills that could be referred to when we say "social media" may leave you wondering what these ads actually mean. So, in an effort to help you beef up your knowledge and skills of all social media has to offer, here are a few concrete tips:

SOCIAL MEDIA MONITORING TOOLS

There are now more than 100 social media monitoring tools available, some free and some at a cost. Below is a list of some of the most popular free tools that journalists can use to gauge what people are talking about online.

BoardTracker (boardtracker.com) allows you to search forums and discussion boards for specific search terms. Through BoardTracker, you can set up instant alerts that let you know when your search terms appear in a new post.

Google Alerts (http://www.google.com/alerts) allows you to enter a specific name, word, or phrase. You will then receive email each your search term is mentioned online. You can do a "comprehensive" search of the term or ask only for an alert when the term is mentioned in news, blogs, online videos, online groups, or on the web in general.

Google Video (http://video.google.com/) allows you to monitor when certain keywords or names are mentioned as taglines in video posts.

Lexicon (http://www.facebook.com/lexicon/) is a Facebook tool that allows you to see how certain words or phrases are trending on users' walls.

Technorati (http://technorati.com/) allows you to search and track blog topics across the web.

Twendz (http://twendz.waggeneredstrom.com/) is a Twitter app that allows you to track what topics are trending on Twitter at any given moment.

Always put the emphasis on the content rather than on tools. Hopefully, this message resonates throughout this book. Of course, it is easy to get excited about and consequently carried away with every new piece of software, hardware, device, or tool that rushes onto the mass media scene. However, having access to a tool and knowing how to use it are two entirely different concepts. Likewise, weak content is weak content no matter how many bells and whistles or cool new techniques you use to present it. So, start by making your core content good. Collect good data; record good audio; take good pictures; tell good stories. Only then can you use social media as a tool for enhancing and promoting that content.

Understand there is a difference between social media in your social life and social media in your professional life. For example, in your personal life, you may spend most of your time tweeting with your friends. They may care what you had for dinner, where you are going to be in an hour, or how you are feeling right now. However, trivial information is of no use to a community who follows you, the journalist. Share expertise or insights. Share links to other good content. Share links to thoughtful, authoritative information with your community in mind. And don't forget that Twitter is a two-way medium. Use search tools to check out what (and where) conversations are happening.

Take some time to find out what is possible. Half the battle to understanding how to use social media to your advantage is actually knowing what you can do. For example, there are a number of tools out there that will let you search, aggregate, and monitor what millions of people around the world are saying about a given topic at an exact moment in time. This is a pretty powerful concept that has a number of important implications for journalistic efforts. Knowing this is possible suddenly allows you to tap into conversations; sift through them for relevance, importance, and credibility; and filter that information through your stories and to your followers.

Once you know what is possible, make sure you understand how to do it effectively. Seem like an obvious statement? Well, believe it our not, there are a lot of people out there, journalists included, who are not using social media effectively. For example, moderating and managing a community using social media tools is a complex skill set. And there are a number of methods you can employ to manage communities effectively. For instance, implementing reputation systems within communities allows members of the community to rate one another in terms of their credibility or the usefulness of their posts, to name a few. Thus, the community manager (you) can look for individuals who consistently receive low ratings and filter their worthless drivel out of the group. This technique is just one among many, and if you intend to engage in social media activities as a working journalist, it is in your best interests to learn them. Start following some of the best social media practitioners to get more tips and see how the pros are doing it.

Use social media to direct traffic to and promote your content. The larger your following, the more potential there is for you to drive traffic to your journalistic endeavors. You can use social media to drive audiences to your work, as well as cross-promote content you are doing for multiple outlets. But social media isn't just marketing. It's a conversation. You can't simply push out links to your stories and expect to generate a following. You must actively and regularly engage with people and provide a value beyond simply what you write.

Pay attention to the conversations taking place on twitter and facebook. By doing so, you may be turned on to story ideas and sources, find out what people are saying about a topic you are already covering, or follow conversations over time. Social media can be an excellent tool for keeping you on your toes. At the same time, your ability to verify the credibility of these entities is of the utmost importance. Of course, using only the most reliable sources has always been a key tenet of good journalism. However, the potential for fraud has been exponentially magnified in the cybersphere. Anyone can claim anything. Charlatans can falsely claim expertise. And more than ever, there exists a sea of information, not all of which is correct. The twenty-first-century journalist must be ever vigilant against inaccuracy and fraudulent claims.

Preparing for Your First Multimedia Job Interview

Each organization will have different requirements for their multimedia hires. So, of course, whenever applying for a new position, pay close attention to the language used in the job posting and make sure you meet all of the basic requirements. Beyond that, there are a few things every multimedia journalist should keep in mind when preparing for that first interview.

Create a digital portfolio. Regardless of your area of expertise, you should have a digital portfolio that reflects your knowledge of multimedia storytelling. Of course, you should also have hard copies of your work in case a potential employer requests them. However, it's more common to submit a link to an online portfolio. After all, a multimedia candidate who doesn't have a digital portfolio might raise eyebrows. If you are a designer or developer, you may choose to build your digital portfolio from scratch in HTML or Flash. However, there are a number of great portfolio development tools for nondevelopers. Sites such as carbonmade.com allow you to easily manage your online portfolio. And sites such as squarespace.com allow you to integrate social widgets to aggregate data from across your various social networks and track visitors to your portfolio site.

Make sure your portfolio reflects your multimedia skills and work. But show restraint in the number of pieces you include. This little tightrope act can mean the difference between an average portfolio and one that really sings. By way of example, let's revisit one of the job postings we discussed in Chapter 1. Recall the ad for a Phoenix broadcast station that was seeking "... a reporter/photojournalist/video editor who will produce content for multiple platforms as assigned. Successful candidates will have a demonstrated ability to deliver compelling TV and digital media packages, have strong on-camera presentation skills including live presentations, and the time management skills to produce content for multiple platforms on deadline." There are some clear clues in this posting that indicate the types of pieces that should appear in a candidate's portfolio. In fact, the strongest candidate might have some written pieces, photo slideshows, video news packages, and clips of the candidate reporting on camera. Examples should demonstrate both storytelling *and* editing skills and an ability to work across platforms. At the same time, make sure you only showcase your *best* pieces. Like many other things, a portfolio is only as strong as its weakest piece. So, scrutinize your choices carefully. A good rule of thumb is to include eight to 12 pieces in a multimedia portfolio with "additional pieces available upon request."

Practice articulating what it means to be a multimedia journalist. If you make it to the face-to-face interview stage, you'll need to be confident and on top of your game. This is sometimes the scariest part of a job interview for a young journalist. But hopefully, one important lesson you have gained from this book is an understanding of how every story form plays into the multimedia equation. For example, you don't have to be an ace photographer to be able to recognize and articulate what makes for a great photo story. So show up to the interview equipped to discuss the nature of multimedia storytelling, how story forms can be combined to enhance the audience's experience, and how you feel you fit in.

Know your craft. While it's important to let your potential employer know that you have a well-rounded knowledge base, you must illuminate what makes you special. If your passion is photography, then highlight what you know about photojournalism. If you are a graphics reporter, emphasize that this type of visual storytelling is where your strongest skills lie. And make sure your potential employer is aware of your software, hardware, and/or computer systems and programming skills.

Express your passion. Potential employers want to know that you care, that you are eager to work hard, and that you have ideas that will help move their organization forward. A good way to show this is to familiarize yourself with the organization with which you are interviewing. There's nothing worse than a job candidate who knows nothing about the company or job to which he's applying. Be able to articulate what they do well, why you want to work there, and what unique skills and ideas you bring to the table.

Create an Experience

Although there are a number of uncertainties surrounding the future of news, we are living in one of the most exciting times in history when it comes to storytelling. We have more tools than ever for connecting with audiences and each other. Our stories have the potential to be rich and textured. And new business models are surfacing that show promise for journalists with multimedia skills. Of course, good journalism is and always will be rooted in truth, accuracy, balance, and objectivity. And regardless of the kinds of stories you are writing or the tools you are using, these standards should always form the foundation for your work.

However, traditional news models were largely defined as a one-way stream of information from journalist to audience, with little interaction and relatively simple consumption processes, such as newspaper reading and television watching. And now, a number of news organizations are beginning to harness the potential of multimedia by creating rich user experiences that come in many forms. In this sense, they are dramatically transforming how news and information is presented and consumed to create multimedia, multiplatform experiences. Combinations of rich audio and compelling photos offered by NPR are evidence of how organizations are capitalizing on a variety of tools for enhancing stories. The *New York Times* engages audiences regularly with data-driven graphics that offer vast amounts of information in immersive, interactive formats. And nearly every news organization across the country is considering how to recapture news audiences through the web and mobile media.

In a 2009 article for *Online Journalism Review* Cindy Royal wrote, "... News organizations need to understand that an active user is a desirable user and can create significant value for the organization.... Create an experience that people are passionate about and sell that to advertisers by emphasizing the association with the good feelings of the interaction, like Coca-Cola's presence on American Idol. The

WHERE DO WE GO FROM HERE?

A good journalist is forever building a list of trusted sources for the stories she writes. And there is a ton of activity on the web related to multimedia journalism theory and practice. Many of those sources served as inspiration for this book, and most will continue to evolve long after this text lands in bookstores. So, it's important to share the most useful multimedia journalism resources. Thus the following list will hopefully be useful as you continue your journey on becoming a multimedia journalist.

10000words.net
10,000 Words is a resource for journalists and web and technology enthusiasts to learn the tools that are shaping digital journalism. The site offers examples, resources, and tutorials of both new and established technologies.

Designreviver.com
DesignReviver provides web designers with useful tutorials, free downloads, sources of inspiration, and articles covering a wide range of web design topics.

duckrabbit.info/blog/
DuckRabbit is a journalism/production company that works exclusively with still images and audio. They also produce radio documentaries and train journalists in multimedia production.

fuelyourcreativity.com
This site contains articles and links to various sites that will keep you informed on how other creatives get things done. The site includes examples, interviews, and tips.

innovativeinteractivity.com
Described as "a digital watering hole for multimedia enthusiasts," innovativeinter activity.com is an open forum for multimedia producers, interactive web developers, and new media professionals. Content focuses on the dynamics and theory of how people receive and react to different forms of information on the web through visual, multimedia storytelling, and interactive information design.

(*continued*)

WHERE DO WE GO FROM HERE? (*continued*)

interactivenarratives.org

Sponsored by the Online News Association, InteractiveNarratives presents the best of online visual storytelling from around the country and the world. The site highlights rich-media content, engaging storytelling, and eye-popping design in an environment that fosters interaction, discussion, and learning.

Kobreguide.com

Run by Ken Kobré, head of the photojournalism program at San Francisco State University, KobreGuide is an online guide to the web's best video and multimedia journalism. The site features handpicked, high-quality documentary-style journalism produced by major media outlets.

manyeyes.alphaworks.ibm.com/manyeyes

ManyEyes is an open source tool that facilitates data analysis and helps users create data visualizations with easy-to-use tools.

mashable.com

Mashable is a great source for news in social and digital media, technology, and web culture. Mashable reports breaking web news, provides analysis of trends, reviews new websites and services, and offers social media resources and guides.

masteringmultimedia.wordpress.com

MasteringMultimedia is authored by Colin Mulvany, a multimedia producer at *The Spokesman-Review* (Spokane, Wash.) A still photographer for the first 18 years of his career, Mulvany transitioned to shooting video and audio slide shows for his newspaper's online site in 2005. His blog provides commentary, useful tips and advice, and a forum for ideas about contemporary journalism.

mediastorm.com

MediaStorm is an award-winning multimedia production studio that works with top visual storytellers, interactive designers, and global organizations to create cinematic narratives that speak to the heart of the human condition. MediaStorm collaborates with a diverse range of clients and offers training for the next generation of journalists.

mindymcadams.com

Mindy McAdams teaches online journalism in the College of Journalism and Communications at the University of Florida. Her site addresses the changing ways we use technologies for communication, providing tips for journalism educators and working journalists.

multimedia.journalism.berkeley.edu

Sponsored by Knight Digital Media Center, this site promotes workshops for mid-career journalists to enhance their expertise and multimedia skills. The center is a partnership of the UC Berkeley Graduate School of Journalism and the USC Annenberg School for Communication. The site includes a blog, presentations, tutorials, webcasts, and examples of projects produced by the fellows during weeklong training workshops.

multimediashooter.com

This site offers tips, news, and commentary about digital storytelling, with a focus on photojournalism. MultimediaShooter includes examples of multimedia storytelling, recognizes those who do outstanding work, and helps those who want to. The site features a gallery of great examples, tutorials, podcasts, and a comprehensive multimedia archive.

multimediamuse.org

Run by three anonymous photographers who believe in creating a greater corporate news demand for online photojournalism, multimediamuse.org was created in an attempt "to help give our industry's Final Cut creations the display, and their web hosts the clicks, they deserve."

niemanlab.org

A project of the Nieman Foundation at Harvard University, The Nieman Journalism Lab provides news and information related to the future of media in the Internet age.

ojr.org

The Online Journalism Review is sponsored by the Knight Digital Media Center and the USC Annenberg School for Communication and Journalism and provides articles, tips, and resources about the future of digital journalism.

(*continued*)

WHERE DO WE GO FROM HERE? (*continued*)

smashingmagazine

Smashing delivers useful and innovative information to web designers and developers. The site informs readers about the latest trends and techniques in web development.

sun-sentinel.com/broadband/theedge

One of the pioneers in interactive graphics reporting, the South Florida *Sun-Sentinel* (Fort Lauderdale, Fla.) has been producing multimedia stories since 1996. The Edge is their online encyclopedia of games, interactive graphics, databases, interactive maps, and widgits. The gallery contains hundreds of illustrative graphics on a variety of topics.

vis.stanford.edu/protovis

Protovis is an open-source tool for data visualization. Protovis composes custom views of data with simple marks such as bars and dots. Unlike low-level graphics libraries that quickly become tedious for visualization, Protovis allows for a simplified construction of visualizations. Although programming experience is helpful, Protovis is designed to be learned by example.

value is more than just exposure. It is in the way that a user feels about a community in which he actively participates and how that feeling can be transferred to a sponsor."[6] In other words, find a way to give people what they want. Find ways to enhance, educate, and engage. And understand that although content should always drive design, presentation is as much a part of the telling of a story as the words and pictures that comprise it.

And in spite of the uncertainties that surround the future of news, there is no denying that the need and desire for news and information is as strong as ever. And, if pressed to give budding journalists one piece of advice moving forward, it would be this: In order to thrive in this incredibly dynamic media landscape, you must have vision. Vision allows you to prepare not just for your first job after graduation, but the second and third jobs as well. Vision helps you see how your multimedia storytelling skills apply to other fields, providing you with more outlets for your talents. Vision ensures that you find your niche in an evolving field.

Notes

1. The State of the News Media 2009 report, Pew Center for Excellence in Journalism.
2. The State of the News Media 2011 report, Pew Center for Excellence in Journalism.
3. Christopher Sopher, "Seeking Sustainability: A Nonprofit News Roundtable." John S. and James L. Knight Foundation report, June 11, 2010.
4. Jeremy Caplan, "Debunking 5 Myths of Entrepreneurial Journalism." www.poynter.org, July 29, 2010.
5. Don Irvine, "Social Media's Influence on Journalism Continues to Grow." Accuracy in Media, May 22, 2011.
6. Cindy Royal, "Making Media Social: News as User Experience." *Online Journalism Review*, May 13, 2009.

INDEX